DEMOCRACY IN DIVIDED SOCIETIES

Electoral Engineering for
Conflict Management

BENJAMIN REILLY

CAMBRIDGE
UNIVERSITY PRESS

PUBLISHED BY THE PRESS SYNDICATE OF THE UNIVERSITY OF CAMBRIDGE
The Pitt Building, Trumpington Street, Cambridge, United Kingdom

CAMBRIDGE UNIVERSITY PRESS
The Edinburgh Building, Cambridge, CB2 2RU, UK
40 West 20th Street, New York, NY 10011–4211, USA
10 Stamford Road, Oakleigh, VIC 3166, Australia
Ruiz de Alarcón 13, 28014 Madrid, Spain
Dock House, The Waterfront, Cape Town 8001, South Africa

http://www.cambridge.org

First published 2001

Printed in the United Kingdom at the University Press, Cambridge

Typeface Minion 10.5/12pt   *System* 3b2   [CE]

A catalogue record for this book is available from the British Library

Library of Congress cataloguing in publication data

Reilly, Ben.
Democracy in divided societies: electoral engineering for conflict management /
Benjamin Reilly.
    p.   cm. – (Theories of institutional design)
Originally presented as the author's thesis (doctoral – Australian National University).
Includes bibliographical references and index.
ISBN 0 521 79323 8 (hardback) – ISBN 0 521 79730 6 (paperback)
1. Elections – Case studies.   2. Conflict management – Case studies
3. Case studies.   I. Title.   II. Series.
JF1001 .R39 2001   324.6′3 – dc 21   2001025238

ISBN 0 521 79323 8 hardback
ISBN 0 521 79730 6 paperback

For Andrea

Contents

Illustrations

Figure

Tables

Acknowledgements

Many people have contributed to this book, which has its genesis in the doctoral thesis I began at the Australian National University almost a decade ago. My primary thanks must therefore go to my doctoral supervisor, Ron May, who has been a constant source of good humour and wise counsel over a number of years. Other scholars at the Australian National University whose contributions I wish to acknowledge include John Ballard, Clive Bean, Scott Bennett, Hank Nelson, Yaw Saffu, Bill Standish, Tony Regan, and the series editor of Cambridge's Theories of Institutional Design series, Bob Goodin.

Many of the arguments in this book were improved by virtue of my four years at the International Institute for Democracy and Electoral Assistance (IDEA) in Stockholm, Sweden. IDEA is a wonderful meeting point between the policy and scholarly worlds, and I benefited enormously from my time there. I was also fortunate to enjoy, in the course of writing this book, a visiting studentship at Nuffield College, Oxford University, and fellowships at the Macmillan Brown Centre for Pacific Studies at the University of Canterbury and the National Centre for Development Studies at the Australian National University. The support of these institutions, and the generous financial assistance of the United States Institute of Peace, is gratefully acknowledged here.

I would also like to thank some of my fellow political scientists for discussing, responding to and making suggestions on my work at various times: these include Arend Lijphart, Iain McMenamin, Alistair McMillan, Michael Maley, Andrew Reynolds, Nigel Roberts, Robert Richie, Timothy Sisk and particularly Larry Diamond, Donald Horowitz and Colin

Hughes, who read and gave extensive comments on an earlier draft of this book.

A number of people assisted me in Papua New Guinea, Sri Lanka and Fiji in the course of writing this book, and gave generously of their time to be interviewed or share their thoughts. In Papua New Guinea, these include Reuben Kaiulo, Anthony Siaguru and Warren Dutton. In Sri Lanka, I was extremely grateful for the warm hospitality of Dominic Trindade and Alex Reiger, with whom I stayed in Colombo for several weeks, and for the assistance of Kingsley de Silva and of the former electoral commissioner, R. K. Chanandara de Silva. In relation to Fiji, my primary thanks go to Walter Rigamoto of the Electoral Office, and to Brij Lal and Peter Larmour of the Australian National University.

My greatest debt of gratitude, however, is to my wife Andrea, who has been an unshakeable source of love, encouragement and support. In addition to enduring long periods of separation during my doctoral studies, Andrea's attention has improved this work in countless small ways. I dedicate this book to her.

Abbreviations

ALP	Australian Labor Party (Australia)
AV	Alternative Vote
CRC	Constitution Review Commission (Fiji)
DLP	Democratic Labor Party (Australia)
ECIEP	Electoral Commission of Inquiry into Electoral Procedures (Papua New Guinea)
FAP	Fijian Association Party (Fiji)
FLP	Fiji Labour Party (Fiji)
FPTP	First Past the Post
LTTE	Liberation Tigers of Tamil Eelam (Sri Lanka)
MMP	Mixed Member Proportional
MP	Member of Parliament
NFP	National Federation Party (Fiji)
PA	People's Alliance (Sri Lanka)
PANU	Party of National Unity (Fiji)
PNG	Papua New Guinea
PR	Proportional Representation
PUP	Progressive Unionist Party (Northern Ireland)
SDLP	Social Democratic and Labour Party (Northern Ireland)
SLFP	Sri Lankan Freedom Party (Sri Lanka)
STV	Single Transferable Vote
SV	Supplementary Vote
SVT	Soqosoqo ni Vakavulewa ni Taukei (Fiji)
UGP	United General Party (Fiji)
UNP	United National Party (Sri Lanka)
UUP	Ulster Unionist Party (Northern Ireland)
VLV	Veitokani Ni Lewenivanua Vakaristo (Fiji)

1

Introduction: democracy in divided societies

The question of whether, and how, democracy can survive in divided societies has long been a source of controversy in political science. Some of the greatest political thinkers have argued that stable democracy is possible only in relatively homogeneous societies. John Stuart Mill, for example, believed that democracy was incompatible with the structure of a multi-ethnic society, as 'free institutions are next to impossible in a country made up of different nationalities' (1958 [1861], 230). This was a view prevalent amongst many scholars and policy-makers until at least the 1960s, with the perils of 'tribalism' and ethnic division frequently cited as causing the failure of democracy in the newly independent states of Africa and Asia in the post-war period (see, e.g., Low 1991, 272–3). Much of this conventional wisdom regarded ethnic conflicts as primordial and irrational manifestations of traditional rivalries and passions, leaving little room for explanations based on the objectives and interests of those involved in such conflicts. When scholars did turn their attention towards such interests, many saw more reasons for the failure of democracy in divided societies than for its persistence. A classic example is the rational-actor arguments against the likelihood of stable democracy in divided societies put by Rabushka and Shepsle (1972), who argue that would-be political leaders typically find the rewards of 'outbidding' on ethnic issues – moving towards increasingly extremist rhetoric and policies – greater than those of moderation. Because ethnic identities tend to be invested with a great deal of symbolic and emotional meaning in such circumstances, aspiring politicians hungry for electoral success have strong incentives to harness these identities as a political force, and to use communal demands as the base instigator of constituency mobilisation.

Because strategies based on outbidding are often easier to instigate and maintain than those based on cooperation, politics can quickly come to be characterised by *centrifugal* forces, in which the moderate political centre is overwhelmed by extremist forces. The failure of democratic politics is often the result (see Sisk 1995, 23).

How is it possible to design political systems which avoid such conflicts and instead promote inter-ethnic accommodation, multi-ethnic political parties and centripetal, centre-based politics? In this book, I argue that divisive, zero-sum outcomes are not an inevitable characteristic of politics in divided societies, but often a reaction to the institutional 'rules of the game' under which the democratic competition of the electoral process takes place. Changes to these institutional rules – for example, by the introduction of electoral systems which facilitate cross-communal communication, bargaining and interdependence between rival politicians and the groups they represent – can have a major impact on the promotion of moderate politics, and thus on prospects for democracy, in divided societies.

The question of the relationship between democracy and ethnic conflict has been thrown into particular prominence by two countervailing themes that have dominated world politics over the past decade: the 'third wave' of democratisation, and the explosion of inter-communal ethnic violence around the globe. Beginning with the collapse of authoritarian regimes in Spain and Portugal in 1974 and working its way through Eastern Europe, Latin America, Africa and Asia, the 'third wave' of democratisation has seen a threefold increase in the number of democratic governments around the world (Huntington 1991).[1] At the same time as this massive transformation, however, the world has witnessed a great upsurge in intra-state violence and ethnic conflict. Transitions from authoritarian rule to democracy have been accompanied, in many cases, by rising levels of internal conflict, particularly ethnic conflict (de Nevers 1993). Most of today's violent conflicts are not, as in former years, wars between contending states, but take place within existing states. According to one count, of the 110 major armed conflicts in the ten-year period between 1989–99, only 7 were traditional inter-state conflicts. The remaining 103 took place within existing states, mostly focussed around identity issues (Wallensteen and Sollenberg 2000). Between them, these parallel processes of democratisation and ethnic conflict have defined the

[1] This process has naturally encouraged a considerable literature dealing with democratic transitions and their consequences, and the relationship between institutional choices and the consolidation of democracy. See, for example, Huntington 1991; Diamond and Plattner 1996; Diamond, Linz and Lipset 1988, 1989 and 1995; O'Donnell and Schmitter 1986; Linz and Stepan 1996; Diamond 1998.

international agenda in the post-Cold War period. They have also focussed both scholarly and policy attention directly on the question of the relationship between democracy and ethnic conflict in divided societies. But what do I mean by 'democracy', how do we define 'ethnicity' and 'ethnic conflict', and what is a 'divided society'?

Democracy, ethnicity and ethnic conflict

In keeping with an increased focus on institutions across the social sciences, scholarly discussion of democracy and democratisation increasingly emphasise normative and procedural concerns. Perhaps the most influential definition of democracy along these utilitarian lines was first formulated by Joseph Schumpeter, who defined the democratic method as 'that institutional arrangement for arriving at political decisions in which individuals acquire the power to decide by means of a competitive struggle for the people's vote' (1947, 269). By the 1970s, Huntington argued, this 'modest meaning of democracy' was widely accepted:

> theorists increasingly drew distinctions between rationalistic, utopian, idealistic definitions of democracy, on the one hand, and empirical, descriptive, institutional, and procedural definitions on the other, and concluded that only the latter type of definition provided the analytical precision and empirical referents that make the concept a useful one. (1989, 6–7)

Successive generations of political scientists have attempted to refine or restate Schumpeter's basic definition. Thus Riker (1986, 25), for example, argues that 'the essential democratic institution is the ballot box and all that goes with it'; while Huntington himself defines a twentieth-century political system as democratic 'to the extent that its most powerful collective decision-makers are selected through fair, honest and periodic elections in which candidates freely compete for votes and in which virtually all the adult population is able to vote' (1991, 29). Similarly, Diamond, Linz and Lipset, in their study of democracy in developing countries, define democracy as a system of government that meets three essential conditions: meaningful *competition* for political power amongst individuals and organised groups; inclusive *participation* in the selection of leaders and policies, at least through free and fair elections; and a level of *civil and political liberties* sufficient to ensure the integrity of political competition and participation (1995, xvi). This is itself a refinement of Dahl's much-cited definition of democracy (which he called 'polyarchy') as a process of participation and contestation which approximates rather than fully satisfies democratic ideals (Dahl 1971, 1–7), and will be the working definition of democracy used throughout this book.

This model of democracy, with its focus on republican ideals of contestation and participation, becomes difficult in societies divided along deep social cleavages such as ethnicity. Critics of democracy in multi-ethnic societies assert that 'open competitive politics facilitate the politicisation of ethnic communities and the consequent danger of ethnic extremism and violent destabilisation of the political order' (Esman 1994, 41). As concepts, 'ethnicity' and 'ethnic conflict' are, if anything, even more slippery than 'democracy'. An 'ethnic group' can be defined as a collectivity within a larger society which has real or putative common ancestry, memories and a common cultural focus such as language, religion, kinship or physical appearance (Bulmer 1986). Under this typology, ethnic identity can be seen, on the one hand, as being based on ascriptive and relatively immutable factors such as religion, tribe, race or language – a position often characterised in the scholarly literature as 'primordialism' – and, on the other hand, as being a more malleable function of constructed social identities formed by colonialism and by post-colonial developments. In reality, most examples of politicised ethnic identities and ethnic conflicts in the world today exhibit a combination of both 'primordial' ascriptive associations and 'instrumental' opportunistic adaptations, the latter often harnessed by unscrupulous would-be ethnic leaders or 'ethnic entrepreneurs', who mobilise supporters on the basis of crude but often effective ethnic appeals.[2] Such mobilisation of ethnic identities for political purposes can create a 'divided society', a term I use – following Rabushka and Shepsle (1972, 21) – to describe a society which is both ethnically diverse *and* where ethnicity is a *politically salient* cleavage around which interests are organised for political purposes, such as elections.

Democratic competition is inherently difficult in such cases because of the strong tendency towards politicisation of ethnic demands, which in turn often leads to the growth of zero-sum, winner-take-all politics in which some groups are permanently included and some permanently excluded. Politicians in divided societies face powerful incentives to play the 'ethnic card' and campaign along narrow sectarian lines, as this is often a more effective means of mobilising voter support than campaigning on the basis of issues or ideologies. A frequent result in multi-ethnic societies is that optimal outcomes for one player or group – electoral victory for one side on the back of a mobilised ethnic vote, for example – are accompanied by decidedly sub-optimal outcomes for the society as a whole (cf. Olson 1971), as identity politics becomes an

---

[2] There is a considerable literature on ethnicity and ethnic identity. See Geertz 1963; Young 1976; Rothschild 1981; Brass 1985; Horowitz 1985; Smith 1986; Esman 1994.

increasingly central part of the political game and the cycle of ethnic hostility and conflict unwinds. The 'bankruptcy of moderation' (Rabushka and Shepsle 1972, 86) in such cases greatly undermines the prospects of peaceful democratic politics taking root.

Although few scholars would argue that ethnic divisions are a positive facilitating condition for democracy, in recent years a revised focus on the possibilities and prospects for democracy in divided societies has become evident. At the base of this new wave of interest in democracy is a recognition that all societies are inherently conflictual to some degree, and that democracy itself operates as a system for *managing* and *processing* conflict, rather than resolving it (Przeworski 1991). Within certain circumscribed boundaries, conflict is considered legitimate, is expected to occur and is handled through established institutional means when it does occur. Disputes under democracy are never definitively 'solved'; rather, they are temporarily accommodated and thus reformulated for next time. Well-structured democratic institutions allow conflicts to formulate, find expression and be managed in a sustainable way, via institutional outlets such as political parties and representative parliaments, rather than being suppressed or ignored. Changing formal political institutions can result in changes to political behaviour and political practice, and the design of political institutions is thus of paramount importance to the management of conflict in any democracy.

Institutional engineering

Institutions are the rules and constraints which shape human interaction and, as a consequence, behavioral incentives. They reduce uncertainty by establishing stable and predictable structures for interactions between people, either as individuals or groups (North 1990). Just as economists see the key to institutions in their role in structuring markets, reducing transaction costs and facilitating exchange – 'they promote trades, and hence trade' – for political scientists, political bargaining and exchange 'is possible only against the backdrop of the stability provided by more deeply nested, institutionalised rules' – rules that generate stable, recurring, predictable patterns of behaviour (Goodin 1996, 4–23). Paradoxically, the stable and predictable behavioral patterns engendered by functioning institutions will often be a reaction to uncertainty and potential instability. In a well-institutionalised democracy, for example, the competitive nature of the political process is ideally characterised by a recurring uncertainty of outcomes, thus encouraging a 'rule bounded' commitment amongst political actors to the democratic process itself. The best example of this is at election time, where parties and individuals may 'win' or 'lose', but where the losers may win next time and the winners know that their victory is only temporary (Przeworski 1991, 10–14). The structural uncertainty of a democratic electoral process, where all outcomes are necessarily unpredictable and impermanent, is thus a basic precondition for the evolution and institutionalisation of behavioral norms of cooperation.

Heralding the appearance of a 'new institutionalism' in political science almost twenty years ago, March and Olsen argued that political institutions deserved a more autonomous role as subjects of academic study: 'democracy depends not only on economic and social conditions but also on the design of political institutions . . . They are political actors in their own right' (1984, 738). Such arguments, once novel, are now widely accepted, with most scholars today agreeing that institutional choices are of paramount importance for the longer-term prospects of democratic consolidation and sustainability (Diamond, Linz and Lipset 1995, 33), and that 'different institutional forms, rules, and practices can have major consequences both for the degree of democracy in a democratic system and for the operation of the system' (Lijphart 1991d, ix). This recognition of the importance of institutions has been accompanied by an emerging concern in the discipline with the importance of *engineering* political rules so as to improve the operation of political processes and institutions (Horowitz 1991a, Ordeshook 1996). For the political engineer, institutions change outcomes, and changing formal political institutions can result in changes in political behaviour and political practice. This message has been echoed by a number of recent studies, reflecting an emerging scholarly orthodoxy concerning the importance of political engineering and institutional design.[3]

Most of this book deals with the implications of such political engineering for the management of conflict by virtue of one key institutional choice – the electoral system. I argue that certain electoral systems, under certain circumstances, will provide rational political actors with incentives towards cooperation, moderation and accommodation between themselves and their rivals, while others will lead logically to hostile, uncooperative and non-accommodative behaviour if individuals act rationally. By giving politicians in ethnically divided societies reasons to seek electoral support from groups beyond their own community, well-crafted political institutions – particularly electoral systems – can influence the trajectory of political competition, exerting a centrist pull upon electoral politics and a moderating, cooperation-inducing influence upon

---

[3] See, for example, Taagepera and Shugart 1989; Shugart and Carey 1992; Lijphart 1994; Sartori 1994; Harris and Reilly 1998.

the conduct of politics more generally. A key challenge of institutional design in such circumstances is thus to create an environment in which cooperative interaction and mutually beneficial 'win–win' exchanges are possible, so that norms of cooperation and negotiation can become habituated amongst political actors. In showing how such 'electoral engineering' can work to manage conflicts, this book introduces a normative prescription for the design of political institutions in divided societies that I call 'centripetalism'. As the name suggests, a centripetal political system is one in which the focus of political competition is directed at the centre, not at the extremes. Centripetal institutions are designed to encourage moderate, centrist forms of political competition, rather than the polarising extremes and centrifugal patterns that characterise so many divided societies.

The theory of centripetalism

Centripetalism envisages democracy as a continual process of conflict management, a recurring cycle of dispute resolution in which contentious issues must ultimately be solved via negotiation and reciprocal cooperation, rather than simple majority rule. We know from the seminal work of Duncan Black (1958) that many of the issues which confront democracies are not resolvable by majority decision, but rather 'cycle' through an endless series of unstable temporary majorities. In plural societies split along several cleavage lines, the intermixture of ethnic identities with non-ethnic or cross-cutting issues *should* ostensibly create the potential for diverse coalitions of interest – but the possibilities of such cross-ethnic coalitions are often undermined by the dominance of overarching group identities and loyalties in forming political identities. In such situations, differences need to come to be seen not as irreconcilable sources of conflict, but as part of a broader collective action problem, a problem which potentially can be overcome by bargaining and reciprocal trade-offs. The goal is not consensus but accommodation, via positional shifts that can only be uncovered by the process of active engagement, discussion and negotiation. Under this scenario the role of democratic institutions, as the mediating agents which can process divergent interests and preferences into centripetal outcomes, becomes paramount.[4]

At the heart of the case for centripetalism as a form of conflict management is thus the need to create incentives for accommodation

---

[4] For more on this idea of democratic liberalism as 'compromise by negotiation' see Bellamy 1997.

between competing interests in societies riven by deep-seated ethnic or other cleavages. One of the most feasible paths to such inter-group accommodation is to present political parties and candidates campaigning at elections with incentives to cooperate across ethnic lines. Most of this book is devoted to empirical analysis of the institutional foundations of such arrangements across a variety of societal contexts, ranging from elections in the traditional societies of Papua New Guinea and Fiji to modern industrialised states like Northern Ireland and Australia. A common theme across all cases is that, even in deeply divided societies, when office-seeking politicians and their supporters are presented with sufficiently strong institutional incentives to engage in cross-ethnic (or cross-issue) behaviour, they will act upon these incentives, and that the changes in their behaviour can effect much larger changes on the nature of political competition as a whole. For example, electoral systems that encourage reciprocal vote transfer deals between rival candidates representing antagonistic social groups can, as I will show, have a major impact upon the nature of electoral politics, vastly increasing the prospects for the consolidation of moderate, centrist political competition.

An additional benefit of such institutional designs is the opportunity they offer for cross-agent communication. Via the creation of voluntary 'bargaining arenas', whereby rival politicians come together to negotiate vote-trading deals in the search for electoral success, institutional conduits for inter-ethnic communication can facilitate recurring positive-sum exchanges between competing actors. Theorists of bargaining and co-operation have emphasised the importance of regular, face-to-face meetings in building trust and developing cooperation and understanding. Even in competitive situations, regular, reciprocal interactions are, *in and of themselves*, likely to facilitate cooperation (Axelrod 1984). Laboratory experiments have found that disputants who engage in face-to-face dialogue can achieve more satisfactory outcomes than those who communicate in other ways (Raiffa 1982), and that situations in which subjects are permitted to communicate directly with each other generate both higher levels of cooperation and lower levels of defection than when such communication is not permitted.[5] Similarly, in their influential work on inter-ethnic cooperation, Fearon and Laitin (1996) found numerous examples of peaceful inter-ethnic relations being facilitated by recurring exchanges and effective inter and intra-group channels of communication. By encouraging reciprocal bargains between convergent interests, such exchanges can increase mutual confidence and help address the ethnic 'security dilemma' that lies at the heart of so many communal

---

[5] See Green and Shapiro 1994, 89–90, for a summary of these.

conflicts (Posen 1993). In such cases, the *process* of negotiation itself builds possibilities of future cooperation, regardless of the significance of the matters under discussion.

Unfortunately, the political environment in most divided societies offers few incentives for campaigning politicians to engage in this kind of cooperation-inducing dialogue. In most election campaigns, for example, office-seeking politicians have little to gain and much to lose by engaging in negotiations with their rivals. After all, candidates are engaged in direct competition for a finite number of votes, and more votes for one side can never be an advantage for another, while the social restraints on even participating in face-to-face dialogue with ethnic adversaries can easily be characterised as displays of weakness and 'selling out' to opposing interests. The standard form of behaviour is therefore mutual avoidance, a situation often exacerbated by adversarial campaign rhetoric directed against political rivals. Rejection of common ground becomes a self-fulfilling prophecy, as the less often leaders meet, the less they are able to explore their common concerns and possibilities for cooperation. This creates a vicious cycle, as 'outbidding' by ethnic entrepreneurs, who push the mean political position further away from the moderate centre towards the extremes, becomes a familiar pattern. The consequences can be devastating: moderate forces are quickly overwhelmed by more extreme voices, leading to an ongoing cycle of violence and retribution – 'precisely because a moderate ethnic center is often unable to sustain itself against the centrifugal forces unleashed by the heated rhetoric of ethnic chauvinism' (Sisk 1995, 17).

This problem is exacerbated by the mono-ethnic nature of political parties in most divided societies. A recurring feature of democratisation in plural societies – particularly in conflictual multi-ethnic countries like the former Yugoslavia – is the rapid emergence of nationalist parties, who draw their support exclusively from one ethnic group or region, and who are often committed to the realisation of separatist agendas. Contrast this with idealised Western conceptions of democracy, which are based upon implicit assumptions about the presence of free-floating, 'swinging' voters and political parties fighting for the middle ground. The Downsian model of political competition, on which so much contemporary theory is based, makes such assumptions transparent: under plurality elections on a left–right policy spectrum, both voters and parties can be expected to converge on the middle ground, making elections a contest for the support of the 'median voter' (Downs 1957). Parties will thus adjust their policy platform to attract votes from this group, so that electoral competition becomes a fight for the moderate centre. Unfortunately, divided societies tend not to conform to this ideal model. Instead, political parties in divided societies are normally ethnic parties, and voters are normally ethnic voters, who are no more likely to cast their vote for a member of a rival group than rival ethnic parties are to court their support. Under such conditions of 'polarised pluralism' (Sartori 1976), the logic of elections changes from one of convergence on policy positions to one of extreme divergence. Politics becomes a centrifugal game. With no median voters, competition for votes takes place at the extremes rather than at the centre. The result is an increasingly polarised political process, in which strategic incentives for office-seeking politicians often push them in the direction of encouraging ethnic hostilities and perceptions of group insecurity. Terrible communal violence is often the outcome.

Scholars argue that the key to regulating ethnic conflict is thus to change the conditions that encourage it, via alternative institutional designs. Creatively crafted electoral rules hold particular promise, because they structure the incentives and pay-offs available to political actors in their search for electoral victory, making some types of behaviour more rewarding than others. One core strategy, as advocated by Donald Horowitz (1985, 1991a&b), is to design electoral rules that make politicians reciprocally dependent on the votes of members of groups other than their own. To build support from other groups, candidates must behave moderately and accommodatively on core issues of concern. In ethnically divided societies, this means that electoral incentives can promote much broader changes in political behaviour: even small minorities have a value in terms of where their votes are directed, as small numbers of votes could always make the difference between victory and defeat for major candidates. As much of this book discusses, one of the most promising strategies for inducing such 'vote-pooling', and the positive-sum exchanges that go with it, is to put in place electoral institutions that enable politicians to campaign for the 'second-choice' votes of electors – the presumption being that, particularly in ethnically divided societies, the first choice will almost always go to a coethnic rather than a candidate from a rival group.[6]

Parties and candidates who adopt conciliatory policy positions and make compromises with other parties are more likely to pick up such secondary votes than parties who choose to maintain a narrowly focused, sectarian approach. Those who are broadly attractive and can successfully sell themselves as a good 'second-best' choice to others will tend to be rewarded with a greater share of these votes; those who have polarised support will generally not. To attract second-level support, candidates

---

[6] This approach has some commonalities with broader 'theories of the second best' in economics and political science. See Goodin 1995, 52–5.

may need to make cross-ethnic appeals and demonstrate their capacity to represent groups other than their own. In other cases, where a moderate or non-ethnic 'middle' part of the electorate exists, candidates may need to move to the centre on policy issues to attract these voters, or to accommodate fringe issues into their broader policy. Either way, elected candidates will be dependent to a certain extent upon the votes of groups other than their own core support base for their electoral success, and can be expected to serve the needs of these groups as well as their own ethnic group if they are to establish their positions and gain re-election. As we shall see, negotiations between rival candidates and their supporters for cross-ethnic vote transfers can also greatly increase prospects for transfer votes flowing from ethnic parties to non-ethnic ones – thus encouraging, even in deeply divided societies, the formation and strengthening of a core 'moderate middle' sentiment within the electorate as a whole.

Timothy Sisk has labelled this approach to electoral engineering as 'centripetalism', 'because the explicit aim is to engineer a centripetal spin to the political system – to pull the parties towards moderate, compromising policies and to discover and reinforce the centre of a deeply divided political spectrum' (1995, 19). Following Sisk, I use the term 'centripetalism' to describe a political system or strategy designed to focus competition at the moderate centre rather than the extremes – primarily by presenting rational, office-seeking politicians with incentives to seek electoral support from groups beyond their own ethnic community. However, in contrast to Sisk's narrower definition derived from Horowitz's work, the term centripetalism in this book refers to a normative theory of institutional design designed to encourage three related but distinct phenomena in divided societies:

(i) *electoral incentives* for campaigning politicians to reach out to and attract votes from a range of ethnic groups other than their own, thus encouraging them to moderate their political rhetoric on potentially divisive issues and forcing them to broaden their policy positions in the hope of attracting broader multi-ethnic electoral support;

(ii) *arenas of bargaining*, under which political actors from different groups have an incentive to come together to bargain and negotiate in the search for cross-partisan and cross-ethnic vote-pooling deals, negotiations which may then lead on to discussion of other more substantial issues as well; and

(iii) *centrist, aggregative political parties* or coalitions of parties which seek multi-ethnic support and present a diverse range of policy options to the electorate and which, via cross-ethnic voter appeals, vote transfers and inter-ethnic coalitions, are able to make and sustain cross-ethnic bargains based upon programmatic policy platforms.

Electoral engineering for conflict management

The possibilities of engineering the development of a political system via institutional design has ancient antecedents in political science, but was perhaps given contemporary prominence by Sartori (1968), who urged political scientists to take up the challenge of becoming participants in the building of political institutions via 'constitutional engineering' – that is, purposive attempts to induce particular political outcomes by the design of political institutions – as, he argued, economists had long been involved with the economy. Political development, particularly in new democracies, could be aided by the adoption of institutions which constrain the centrifugal tendencies which affect many newly created nations. Electoral systems represent a particularly important element in this process because they are 'the most specific manipulable instrument of politics' (Sartori 1968, 273). This oft-quoted formulation is now widely accepted: Lijphart, for example, reflects the scholarly consensus when he writes 'if one wants to change the nature of a particular democracy, the electoral system is likely to be the most suitable and effective instrument for doing so' (1995a, 412).

There are many ways of studying elections and electoral systems. At the most basic level, electoral systems can be viewed as either dependent or independent variables. In other words, we can look at the way electoral systems are shaped by their political environment – for example, the reasons behind particular electoral system choices, such as those investigated by Stein Rokkan (1970) in his influential analysis of the adoption of proportional representation in continental Europe. Alternatively, we can look at the consequences of electoral system choices upon other parts of a political system – for example, Rae's (1967) seminal investigation of the effects of electoral laws on political parties. Particularly important for this second line of investigation has been the proportionality or otherwise of different electoral systems – that is, the correspondence between votes won in an election with seats won in parliament. The seats–votes relationship, which one influential work went so far as to depict as 'the Rosetta Stone' for unlocking a true science of politics 'in the sense of a cumulation and interlinkage of quantitatively testable theory' (Taagepera and Shugart 1989, 246), has long been something of a *sine qua non* of the entire electoral studies field.

Given this focus, it is perhaps not surprising that discussions of the effects of electoral systems which do not focus on proportionality and the seats–votes relationship remain rare in the electoral studies literature, and that much scholarly work on elections and electoral systems has limited usefulness for those investigating the peaceful management of conflict by democratic means. Conversely, ways in which the engineering of electoral rules can inter-relate with other elements of a political system – for example, how incentives presented by particular electoral systems can encourage or discourage certain types of behaviour on the part of politicians and candidates – are central to the concerns of this study but not well covered in the general literature. The result has been a rather unbalanced academic literature that is increasingly divorced from the real-world concerns of political engineers, and in which mathematical calculations of fairness have predominated over some of the subtler impacts of electoral system choices on political behaviour. While the future of electoral systems research will likely involve a move away from seeing proportionality as the dominant criterion by which electoral systems are evaluated – and towards a more integrated approach which looks at the effects of electoral systems on factors such as coalition building, incentives to cultivate a personal vote, localisation of politics and strategic incentives for voters – such concerns remain on the margins of traditional electoral research.[7]

In a similar vein, the analysis of elections in this book differs from the usual academic approach to this subject in treating elections as a drawn-out process of campaigning and positioning for electoral support, rather than just a one-off event focussed on the act of voting. Typically, both scholars and the mass media tend to treat an election as an *event*, a zero-sum contest, which consists of 'winners' (successful candidates and particularly governing parties) and 'losers' (those unelected or in opposition), and which acts primarily as a mechanism for choosing representatives and hence for forming governments. Elections are, in effect, a political version of a horse race. A more profitable analytical approach, particularly when looking at the impact of alternative electoral system designs, is to view the electoral process not just as an event, but as a *multicandidate game* – contested not just by candidates and parties, but their supporters as well – in which different strategies of cooperation or antagonism between the players can increase or decrease their prospects for success. This approach sees elections not just as a means of choosing representatives and forming governments, vitally important though that is, but also as a public spectacle (Edelman 1988) which, by virtue of the heightened atmosphere and scrutiny of the political process generated, can help establish patterns of political behaviour that resonate beyond the boundaries of the electoral contest itself.

Because of the formative role of elections in shaping broader norms of political behaviour, scholars and practitioners alike are increasingly in

---

[7] For some partial exceptions see Katz 1997 and Bowler and Grofman 2000.

agreement that representative institutions such as electoral systems have a powerful role in promoting both democracy and conflict management.[8] In addition, the basic elements of an electoral system such as the electoral formula and the structure of the ballot, as well as determining the translation of votes into seats, also impact upon issues of concern to divided societies such as 'ethnic alignments, ethnic electoral appeals, multi-ethnic coalitions, the growth of extremist parties, and policy outcomes' (Horowitz 1985, 628). In societies where ethnicity represents a fundamental political cleavage, particular electoral systems can be designed to reward candidates and parties who act in a cooperative, accommodatory manner to rival groups, or they can punish these candidates and instead reward with electoral victory those who appeal only to their own ethnic group. But what electoral designs can best encourage these types of virtuous interactions to occur?

Types of electoral systems[9]

While the choice of electoral system is one of the most important institutional decisions for any democracy, most electoral systems are not consciously and deliberately chosen. Often, the choice of electoral system is essentially accidental: the result of an unusual combination of circumstances, of a passing trend, or of a quirk of history. The impacts of colonialism and the effects of influential neighbours are often especially strong. Yet in almost all cases the effects of a particular electoral system choice have a profound effect on the future political life of the state concerned, as in most cases electoral systems, once chosen, tend to remain unchanged for long periods as political interests quickly congeal around and respond to the incentives presented by the system.

There are countless electoral system variations, and countless ways to classify them. As noted earlier, one standard approach is to group systems according to how proportional they are: that is, how closely the ratio of votes to seats is observed in electoral outcomes. Such a classification gives us ten main formulas which fall into three broad families: plurality-majority systems, semi-proportional systems, and proportional representation (PR) systems. These constitute the major electoral systems used for national elections in the world today.

---

[8] For an overview of these, see Harris and Reilly 1998.
[9] This discussion draws on a similar section in Reynolds and Reilly *et al.* 1997.

Plurality-majority systems

The five types of plurality-majority systems comprise two plurality systems (first past the post and the block vote), and three majority systems (the two-round run-off, the alternative vote and the supplementary vote). As the name suggests, the distinguishing feature of all majority systems is that they are structured so as to ensure that the winning candidate gains an absolute majority (i.e. more than 50 per cent), not just a plurality (i.e. more than any other contestant), of eligible votes.

Under a *first past the post* (FPTP) system, the winner is the candidate who gains the most votes, but not necessarily an absolute majority of the votes. FPTP electoral contests are held in single-member districts. Voters choose their favoured candidate with a tick or a cross on the ballot paper, and the winner is simply the candidate who gains a plurality of votes. FPTP is the world's most commonly used electoral system for both presidential and parliamentary elections. Countries using this system include the United Kingdom, the United States, India, Canada and most countries that were once part of the British Empire.

The *block vote* is the application of FPTP in multi-member rather than single-member electoral districts. Voters have as many votes as there are seats to be filled, and the highest-polling candidates fill positions regardless of the percentage of the vote they actually achieve. This system is used in some parts of Asia and the Middle East. A further variation on the block vote is the 'party block' system used in Singapore, where voters choose between parties rather than candidates, and the highest-polling party wins all seats in the district.

The most common form of majority system, the two-round or *run-off* system, takes place in two rounds of voting, often a week or a fortnight apart. The first round is conducted in the same way as a normal FPTP election. If a candidate receives an absolute majority of the vote, then he or she is elected outright, with no need for a second ballot. If, however, no candidate has an absolute majority, then a second round of voting is conducted, usually as a run-off between the two highest polling candidates from the first round, and the winner of this round is declared elected.[10] This system is widely used for presidential elections, and also

---

[10] A variant on this procedure is used for legislative elections in France, the country most often associated with the two-round system. For these elections, any candidate who has received the votes of over 12.5 per cent of the registered electorate in the first round can stand in the second round. Whoever wins the highest numbers of votes in the second round is then declared elected, regardless of whether they have won an absolute majority or not.

for legislative elections in France, most former French colonies, and some parts of the former Soviet Union.

The *alternative vote* (AV) is another type of majority system. Like elections under FPTP, AV elections are usually held in single-member districts. Unlike FPTP, however, AV enables electors to *rank* candidates in the order of their choice, by marking a '1' for their favoured candidate, '2' for their second choice, '3' for their third choice, and so on. The system thus enables voters to express their preferences between candidates, rather than simply their first choice. If no candidate has an absolute majority of first preferences, the candidate with the lowest number of first preference votes is eliminated and his or her ballot papers redistributed to remaining candidates according to the lower-order preferences marked. This process of sequential elimination and transfer of votes continues until a majority winner emerges. The AV system, which this book discusses in considerable detail, is currently used for parliamentary elections in Australia and Fiji, and for presidential elections in Ireland. As much of Chapter 4 discusses, it was also used in Papua New Guinea from 1964 until 1975.

AV can also be used in multi-member rather than single-member constituencies. Multi-member AV operates quite differently to single-member AV. The use of AV in multi-member districts effectively requires each seat to be filled by a separate election, but with the same electorate voting at each. While the first vacant seat is filled in the same way as a single-member AV election just described, for the successive seats the ballots showing a first preference for an already elected candidate are transferred to the remaining candidates before the seat is filled. In effect, this means that under conditions of party identification and disciplined voting patterns, the same party can easily win every seat with a bare majority of the vote, resulting in highly lopsided and disproportional outcomes. This system has been used on only a few occasions, most notably for elections to the Australian Senate between 1919 and 1946.

A final type of majority system, the *supplementary vote* (SV), can be seen as a mid-point between AV and the two-round run-off. Under this system, voters mark their preferences on the ballot paper in the same way as under AV. However if no candidate has a majority of first preference votes, the election is decided by simultaneously eliminating *all* candidates bar the top two from the count, and redistributing all available preference votes marked for one or the other of these two leaders to determine the winner. SV is thus an instant run-off system which takes place in one round, rather than the two rounds needed for run-off elections where there is no majority victor from the first round. While this system has been used in a number of sub-national jurisdictions (most notably, in May 2000, to elect the first mayor of London), the only national-level use of this system today is for presidential elections in Sri Lanka, as will be discussed in some detail in Chapter 5.

Semi-proportional systems

Semi-proportional systems translate votes cast into seats won in a way that falls somewhere between the proportionality of PR systems and the majoritarianism of plurality-majority systems. The two main semi-proportional electoral systems are the *single non-transferable vote* (SNTV), and *parallel* (or mixed) systems. In a SNTV system, each elector has one vote but there are several seats in the district to be filled, and the candidates with the highest number of votes fill these positions. This means that in a four-member district, for example, one would on average need only just over 20 per cent of the vote to be guaranteed election. This system is used today only in Jordan and Vanuatu, but is most often associated with Japan, which used SNTV until 1993. *Parallel* systems, by contrast, use both PR party lists (see below) and single-member districts running side-by-side (hence the term 'parallel'). Part of the parliament is elected by proportional representation, part by some type of plurality or majority method. Many countries use parallel systems to combine two divergent system types, such as PR and FPTP in Russia, or PR with SNTV in Taiwan.

Proportional representation (PR) systems

There are three main variants of PR systems. *Party list PR* systems, the most common type of proportional representation electoral system, requires each party to present a list of candidates to the electorate. Electors typically vote for a party rather than for a candidate; and parties receive seats in proportion to their overall share of the national vote. Winning candidates are usually taken from the lists in order of their respective positions. This system is widely used in continental Europe, Latin America and southern Africa. *Mixed member proportional* (MMP) systems, used in countries like Germany, New Zealand and Mexico, attempt to combine the positive attributes of both majoritarian and PR electoral systems. A proportion of the parliament (approximately half in the cases of Germany and New Zealand) is elected from single-member districts, while the remainder is constituted by PR lists, with the PR seats being used to compensate for any disproportionality produced by district seat results.

Finally, the *single transferable vote* (STV) form of PR uses multi-member districts, with voters ranking candidates in order of preference on the ballot paper in the same manner as the alternative vote. After all first-preference votes are tallied, the count begins by determining the 'quota' of votes required to elect a single candidate.[11] Any candidate who has more first preferences than the quota is immediately elected. If no-one has achieved the quota, the candidate with the lowest number of first preferences is eliminated, and his or her second and later preferences are redistributed to the candidates left in the race. At the same time, the surplus votes of elected candidates (i.e. those votes above the quota) are redistributed at a reduced value according to the second, third etc. preferences on the ballot papers, until all seats for the constituency are filled. At the national level, this system is used in Ireland, Malta, the Australian Senate and, as will be discussed in some detail in Chapter 6, in Northern Ireland.

Preferential voting

Of these ten forms of electoral system used in the world today, three enable electors to *rank-order* candidates in the order of their choice on the ballot, and are thus known as 'preferential' systems: the alternative vote (AV), the supplementary vote (SV), and the single transferable vote (STV). The first two of these, AV and SV, are quintessential majority systems, requiring successful candidates to gain not just a plurality but an absolute majority of votes. STV, by contrast, is a system of proportional representation which, depending on the number of members to be elected in each district, allows even small minorities access to representation. Despite these distinctions, all preferential electoral systems share a common feature: they enable electors to indicate how they would vote if their favoured candidate was defeated and they had to choose between those remaining. It is this particular feature that distinguishes preferential voting from other electoral system options.

In this book, the term 'preferential' will be used when referring to any of the three major voting systems which utilise preference marking. The acronyms AV, SV and STV will be used when discussing a particular system. There are, however, differences in nomenclature between different regions which should be kept in mind. In Australia (where voters must rank-order *all* candidates on the ballot paper at national elections) the alternative vote is usually known as the 'preferential vote'. In Papua New

---

[11] The formula used divides the total number of votes in the count by one more than the number of seats to be elected, and then adds one to the result. For example, if there are 6,000 votes and five members to be elected, the quota for election is 6,000/(5+1), +1, or 1,001 votes.

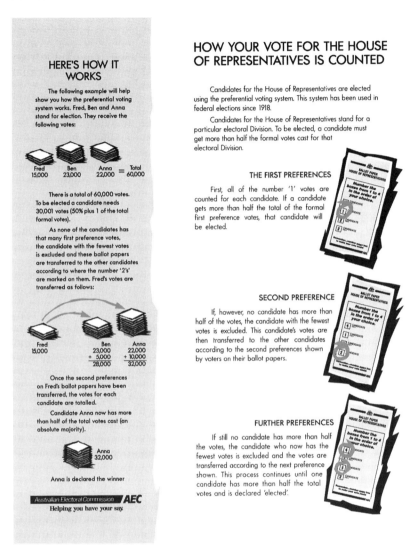

Figure 1.1 The alternative vote in pictures (courtesy of the Australian Electoral Commission)

Guinea (where the marking of preferences was optional) the system is also known as the 'preferential vote' or sometimes the 'optional preferential vote' (OPV). In the United States, it is increasingly known as 'instant run-off voting', or IRV for short. These are all usually synonymous with the term 'AV', which will be used whenever possible in this book.

Centripetalism versus consociationalism

Most scholarly advocates of constitutional engineering agree that the electoral system is a key mechanism in shaping the wider political arena. Horowitz, for example, argues that 'the electoral system is by far the most powerful lever of constitutional engineering for accommodation and harmony in severely divided societies, as indeed it is a powerful tool for many other purposes' (1991a, 163). Lijphart says that 'the electoral system has long been recognized as probably the most powerful instrument for shaping the political system' (1991a, 91). Sisk writes that electoral systems 'play an important role in "engineering" the results of democratic voting, and along with other institutional choices can have a profound impact on the nature of political parties and the general character of democracy' (1993, 79). Beyond this consensus on the importance of electoral systems, however, there is profound disagreement among theorists as to which electoral systems are most appropriate for divided societies.

Two schools of thought predominate. The scholarly orthodoxy has long rejected majoritarian approaches and instead argued that some form of PR is all but essential if democracy is to survive the travails of deep-rooted ethnic divisions. For example, Arthur Lewis's study of the failure of post-colonial democracy in countries such as Ghana, Nigeria and Sierra Leone in the late 1950s and 1960s prompted him to argue that divided societies need PR to 'give minorities adequate representation, discourage parochialism, and force moderation on the political parties' (1965, 73). Such arguments foreshadowed, in part, the electoral recommendations of *consociational* approaches to managing ethnic cleavages in divided societies. Consociationalism emphasises the need for divided societies to develop mechanisms for elite power-sharing if democracy is to survive. These are encapsulated in four key features: grand coalition governments in which all significant groups are represented; proportional representation of different groups in the distribution of legislative seats and in the civil service; segmental autonomy via federalism or similar devices; and a power of veto over key decisions by minority groups (Lijphart 1977). The scholar most associated with the consociational model, Arend Lijphart, developed this prescription from a detailed examination of the features of power-sharing democracy in some continental European countries (the Netherlands, Belgium and Switzerland), and there is disagreement over how far these measures can work (if at all) when applied to ethnic conflict in developing countries (see Horowitz 1991b, 451–76; Sisk 1996, 27–45). However, there is little doubt that consociationalism represents the dominant – and according to Lijphart, the only – model of democratic government for divided societies (see

Lijphart 1991c). In terms of electoral systems, consociationalists argue that some form of proportional representation is all but essential for divided societies, as this enables all politically significant ethnic groups, including minorities, to 'define themselves' into ethnically based parties. Consociational prescriptions for electoral system design focus on the need for party list PR, usually in large districts. This is based on the tendency of PR to produce multi-party systems and hence multi-party parliaments, in which all significant segments of the population can be represented, and on the empirical relationship between proportional electoral rules and 'oversized' or grand coalition governments, which are a fundamental feature of the power-sharing approach on which consociationalism is based (Lijphart 1990, 10–13).

In contrast to this orthodoxy, centripetalists argue that the best way to mitigate the destructive effects of ethnicity in divided societies is not to simply replicate existing ethnic divisions in the legislature, but rather to utilise electoral systems which encourage cooperation and accommodation between rival groups, and therefore work to break down the salience of ethnicity rather than foster its representation in parliament. The theoretical basis for this approach owes much to arguments put forward by Donald Horowitz in *Ethnic Groups in Conflict* (1985) and *A Democratic South Africa? Constitutional Engineering in a Divided Society* (1991a), which cite numerous cases of electoral engineering. Some electoral systems, such as that used for presidential elections in Nigeria, require the winning candidate to gain support from different regions, thus helping to break down the claims of narrow parochialism or regionalism. Others, such as Lebanon's, attempt to defuse the importance of ethnicity by pre-assigning ethnic proportions in parliament and in each constituency, thus requiring parties to present ethnically mixed slates of candidates for election and making voters choose between them on issues other than ethnicity.

However, the most powerful electoral systems for divided societies, according to Horowitz, are those which actively attempt to transcend the political salience of ethnicity by promoting accommodation and bargaining across group lines. Preferential systems, by enabling electors to rank candidates in the order of their choice on the ballot, can provide parties and candidates in divided societies with an incentive to 'pool votes' via the exchange of preferences between their supporters. Of the preferential systems, Horowitz favours the Australian alternative vote (1991a, ch. 5) and the Sri Lankan supplementary vote (1985, 639–42) – both majority systems rather than proportional ones. He does not reject proportional alternatives out of hand, noting that if the choice is between PR and FPTP, then proportional systems are to be preferred, but that

'STV is a far better choice than list-system PR' (1985, 171, 173). Properly designed, these kinds of preferential systems can help to harness the forces of moderation at the local level: rather than relying on political leaders to behave accommodatively after an election, they can encourage the formation 'of electoral coalitions *by constituents* as they specify their second or third preferences beyond their narrow group interests' (Sisk 1995, 38, emphasis in original).

In his 1991 book, Horowitz recommended an AV electoral system as the centrepiece of a selection of accommodation-inducing structures (including federalism and a strong elected president) for the post-apartheid era in South Africa. According to Horowitz, the use of AV could provide parties and candidates in divided societies such as South Africa's with a strong incentive to search for the political middle ground. Parties which broadened their support base in search of lower-order preference votes from supporters of other parties would be more likely to win seats than parties which were unable to garner such secondary support beyond their primary voter base. In order to gain this type of support, major parties and groups would have to attract at least some secondary votes from minorities – by, for example, adopting favourable policy positions on key areas of interest to these groups. This could in turn provide an incentive towards moderation and accommodation between rival ethnic groups,

> by making politicians reciprocally dependent on the votes of members of groups other than their own. The dependence is only marginal, of course, but it will sometimes be the margin of victory. Since parties must pool votes before they pool merely seats, they must find ways before the election to communicate their ethnically and racially conciliatory intentions to the voters. After the election, they must deliver on those commitments or risk electoral retribution. (1991a, 196)

These proposals represented a considerable challenge to the scholarly orthodoxy concerning appropriate electoral systems for divided societies, and (perhaps not surprisingly) there is little evidence that Horowitz's proposals received serious consideration in South Africa itself prior to its transitional 1994 election. Most South African political actors believed preference voting was simply too complicated for what was, for most of the population, a first-generation election (Sisk 1993, 89).[12] However, the debate about the most appropriate electoral system choice for South

---

[12] The case for AV has not been revived in future discussions of electoral options for South Africa, although Horowitz has continued to argue more generally for the importance of accommodative electoral institutions which encourage vote-pooling. See, for example, Horowitz 1991c; Horowitz 1993.

Africa – which at the time was clearly a key test case for constitutional engineering worldwide – encouraged the first real examination by many scholars and policy-makers of the case for preferential voting in divided societies.

Most commentators saw many more weaknesses than strengths. Critics concentrated on four themes – all of which I will return to at length in the concluding chapter of this book. The first was a perceived dearth of practical examples of preference voting in action: Sisk, for example, wrote that 'although vote pooling is theoretically compelling, there is simply insufficient empirical evidence at the level of national politics to support claims that subsequent preference voting can lead to accommodative outcomes' (1996, 62). Specific critiques of AV focussed on its propensity to deliver disproportional electoral outcomes and minority exclusion when compared to PR systems (Lijphart 1991b, Reynolds 1995) – although most of these arguments focussed less on standard single-member AV than its unusual multi-member variant, which did indeed produce dangerously disproportional results when used in the Australian Senate (Lijphart 1997; Reilly and Maley 2000). A number of critics argued that AV actually acts in practice much like other majoritarian electoral systems such as the run-off and FPTP, meaning that there is no more incentive to compromise under AV than under these systems. Lijphart, for example, queried whether 'the incentives for moderation inherent in the alternative vote are much greater than incentives in other majoritarian systems' and suggested that differences between the two are likely to be negligible (1995b, 863). A final objection was that AV would fail to encourage integrative behaviour in some regions because the demographic distribution of ethnic groups meant that majority communities would easily win any election, rendering inter-communal vote-pooling redundant (Reynolds 1995).

Horowitz responded that his proposals had never been properly put to the test (as quoted in Sisk 1996, 491–509). In this he, like his critics, was wrong. As this book will show, there is a considerable range of evidence from Australia, Papua New Guinea, Fiji, Northern Ireland and elsewhere that demonstrates vote-pooling in action. However, much of this material remains relatively obscure, and it is true that until now little *empirical* evidence has been put forward in support of the integrative effects of preference voting in ethnically divided societies, resulting in substantial criticism of Horowitz's arguments (see Sisk 1996, 44, 62; Diamond and Plattner 1994, xxiv). One of the purposes of this book is to provide this missing evidence, and to expand the range of cases scholars can examine when attempting to assess the debate over electoral engineering for divided societies.

Another purpose is to illustrate the scholarly and real-world history of centripetal approaches to the management of democratic conflicts. Three theoretical schools of thought in particular have contributed to the development of centripetal theory. The first pillar of centripetalism is the theory of bargaining and cooperation mentioned earlier. The second is the work by many political scientists on the nature of social cleavages (Lipset 1960; Rae and Taylor 1970), and the institutional expression of such cleavages in terms of party system formations and the direction of political competition (Downs 1957, Sartori 1976). The third pillar of centripetalism is the work by theorists of democracy in divided societies, particularly the analysis of the problems of elections in ethnically divided societies advanced by Horowitz (1985, 1991a) and Sisk (1995, 1996). Similarly, while scholars like Horowitz have been influential exponents of vote-pooling prescriptions, discussions of preference-swapping as an electoral mechanism for interest aggregation and conflict management have considerably older antecedents. The first prominent public exponent of vote-transfer electoral systems, John Stuart Mill, considered Thomas Hare's proposal in 1859 for a transferable vote 'a scheme of almost unparalleled merit for carrying out a great principle of government' which, via the 'aggregate of minorities', would ensure that the 'very best and most capable of the local notabilities would be put forward by preference' (1972 [1910], 265–9). The introduction of preference voting in Australia in the early years of the twentieth century, detailed in Chapter 2, was designed to counter the possibilities of vote-splitting between aligned interests and to encourage and reward collaboration or coalition arrangements between parties (Graham 1962; de Garis 1977). The British electoral activist Enid Lakeman campaigned over many years for the STV form of preference voting which, she argued, enables 'political considera-tions [to] gradually assume more importance and racial ones less, without the elector ever being faced with a conflict of loyalties' (1974, 136). And in the then Australian territory of Papua and New Guinea, both a 1968 United Nations Visiting Mission and Australian electoral advisors ex-pressed the opinion that preferential voting systems were necessary mechanisms for aggregating the interests of smaller ethnic groups and circumventing possible tribal conflicts.[13]

Conclusion

The following chapters proceed to evaluate the arguments for and against centripetalism and vote-pooling by examining *all* cases of preferential

---

[13] See United Nations Visiting Mission 1968; Electoral Commission of Inquiry into Electoral Procedures 1970.

electoral systems applied in ethnically divided societies around the world, as well as a number of other cases where preferential systems have been used in non-divided societies. This spreading of the net is the most reliable way of generating empirically sound conclusions about the performance of preferential voting institutions across different social contexts (King, Keohane and Verba 1994). Because many scholars have (incorrectly) perceived a lack of empirical examples of preferential voting in action, most assessments of centripetal strategies for conflict management to date have been based not on observations of actual cases but on speculative hypotheses (Horowitz 1985), models (Lijphart 1991a) or simulations (Reynolds 1999). This book therefore evaluates the case for centripetalism and preferential electoral methods by examining the electoral history of *all* the divided societies which have utilised such institutions – Papua New Guinea from 1964 to 1972, Northern Ireland since 1973, Sri Lanka since 1978, Estonia in 1990, Fiji in 1999 – plus Bosnia and some other, non-divided cases from Australia, Europe and North America. Importantly, most of the evidence herein either post-dates (in the case of the 1999 elections in Fiji and Sri Lanka), was not examined (in the case of Australia), or was apparently unknown to (in the case of Papua New Guinea) the various proponents and opponents of centripetalism cited above.[14]

The chapters proceed in rough chronological order, starting with an account of the historical development of preferential voting in Chapter 2 and, in Chapter 3, an examination of the impact of preferential voting in Australia, which has utilised all three preferential systems, and which is by far the longest-running example of such systems in action. Although Australia is an ethnically diverse society, it is not an ethnically divided society (in the sense of ethnicity representing a fundamental political cleavage around which political interests are formed and mobilised), and so cannot be used to directly evaluate arguments for or against centripetalism as a strategy for managing ethnic conflict. However, Australia does offer the case which best illustrates the way preference swapping can promote tangible policy changes on the part of parties and governments. It also enables us to examine the way political actors adapt their strategies to the incentives of the system over time in a stable and well-institutionalised political environment, and how preferential systems can be used to combat the rise of extremist parties who *do* attempt to mobilise support around ethnic issues, as occurred with the rise of the extremist One Nation party in the 1990s.

---

[14] Although preliminary evidence on some of these cases was earlier put forward in two journal articles: Reilly 1997a and 1997b.

In many ways, the most important test of centripetalism comes from the case examined in Chapter 4, Papua New Guinea. An ethnically fragmented state in the South Pacific, Papua New Guinea's first three elections – in 1964, 1968 and 1972 – were conducted utilising the AV preferential system, inherited from Australia, its colonial administrator until independence in 1975. These three elections represent a key – and almost completely unknown – example of a vote-transfer institution applied to a politically nascent, fractionalised and divided society. Papua New Guinea also offers an instructive lesson in the consequences of electoral system change, having abandoned AV for a FPTP system at independence, with literally devastating consequences for the fragile political system. Two additional cases from the Asia-Pacific region are examined in Chapter 5: Fiji, which in 1999 held its first election under an AV electoral system, and Sri Lanka, which has used a SV system to elect its president since 1978. Following this, Chapter 6 examines the other cases of preferential voting systems around the world, including the use of STV in two ethnically divided European states, Estonia and Northern Ireland, as well as the broader use of AV and SV systems elsewhere in Europe and North America.

As detailed in Chapter 7, examination of the experience of these different cases suggests that, while vote-pooling does indeed appear to have encouraged viable steps towards inter-ethnic cooperation and conflict management in some countries, not all preferential systems are equally effective at promoting accommodation in divided societies, and even apparently minor technical differences between systems can have major effects in terms of outcomes. This chapter also looks at the theoretical pros and cons of preferential voting. The final chapter summarises the collected evidence and attempts to draw out the lessons for constitutional engineers of when – and when not – centripetalism may represent a viable strategy of constitutional engineering and conflict management. One conclusion is that the application of the centripetal model is highly dependent upon demographic and sociostructural conditions, particularly the size, number and geographic dispersion of contending ethnic groups, and is likely to work well only under certain social conditions. Political engineering is contingent upon many variables, and understanding the way such variables interact with institutional design is a crucial part of crafting viable and sustainable political systems.

2

The historical development of preferential voting

The story of the historical development of the various systems of preferential voting represents a fascinating study in the way institutions evolve and adapt over time. While a rank-ordering of preferences between different alternatives are a fundamental part of any decision-making process, it was not until the eighteenth century that electoral methods for such choices began to be formalised. Preferential voting as a concrete electoral system, rather than a theoretical decision-making rule, originally evolved as a compressed form of run-off election, in which a second round of voting takes place if no candidate secures a majority in the first round; the key to preference voting is its ability to aggregate preference rankings in one round, rather than having to go through successive sequences of elections. The possibilities of such aggregations of rank-orders, via assigning weighted scores to each preference rank, was originally suggested by the French mathematician Charles de Borda in the eighteenth century in relation to decision-making procedures for assemblies and committees,[1] but was vigorously criticised by one of the giants in the field of voting theory, the Marquis de Condorcet, who instead advocated exhaustive pairwise comparisons between each candidate, rather than Borda's rank-order aggregations (McLean and Hewitt 1994, 45). While 'Condorcet voting' has often been advocated as an ideal model for choosing between two alternatives, it is not a practical option for mass elections. Run-off elections, by contrast, are theoretically hard to defend but have the crucial practical advantage of ensuring that whoever is

---

[1] Although several earlier formulations have been uncovered. See McLean and London 1990.

elected will have received the mandate of an absolute majority of the voters. It was this feature, so conspicuously absent from plurality electoral systems such as FPTP, that encouraged nineteenth-century electoral reformers to think of ways of merging majority outcomes with the simplicity of a single election. To do so required some method of rank-ordering candidates on the ballot, such as the systematic comparison of preference schedules suggested by de Borda in 1770 for elections to the Academy of Sciences in Paris.

It was not until the expansion of the suffrage in the nineteenth century, followed by the near-simultaneous invention of STV by Thomas Hare in England and Carl Andræ in Denmark in the 1850s, that preferential voting came to be considered as a feasible electoral reform option for national elections. By enabling each voter to indicate, via a new form of ballot structure, his or her strength of feeling *between* candidates, preferential voting came to represent many broader democratic ideals in vogue in the second half of the nineteenth century, such as the growing acceptance amongst elites that people behaved in politics as rational individuals, forming their own opinions and considering their own interests, and that such diversity of opinion between thinking individuals was to be encouraged rather than repressed. In short, preference voting was, as Birch has noted, a logical expression of the individualist phil-osophy of Victorian liberalism[2] – a point strikingly underlined by John Stuart Mill's 'virtual intoxication' with STV, which he enthusiastically, although unsuccessfully, advocated as an electoral reform in the United Kingdom and elsewhere (Hart 1995, 55).

From run-off elections to preference voting

Run-off elections have much older antecedents than preferential ones, and were commonly used for parliamentary elections in many countries until the end of last century.[3] But they have three central advantages in common with preferential voting procedures: they encourage candidates to broaden their support base in search of a majority; they limit the impact of vote splitting; and they can 'manufacture' majority support for one candidate or another. These factors together provide a powerful institutional incentive towards centrist politics – but, it must be noted, only in those cases where no candidate garners a majority in the first

---

[2] For a discussion see Birch 1964, 63–4.
[3] In Great Britain attempts were made in 1872 and 1882 to introduce the run-off; and it was briefly tried in New Zealand and New South Wales in the early part of this century. See Steed 1975, 40, 43.

round. In such cases, a run-off round of voting can encourage the two top candidates from the first round to broaden their appeal on partisan issues for the second-round run-off. When the run-off winner assumes office, this should lead to greater responsiveness and moderation on policy positions than would be the case if the winner had a plurality of votes alone.

One of the most graphic examples of the moderating impact of run-off elections under conditions of deep societal divides was its use in combating the rising forces of the Ku Klux Klan in several American states last century. According to Bullock and Johnson:

> The rise of the Ku Klux Klan in the South spurred interest in the run-off provision in at least one state as a way to consolidate anti-Klan voters behind a more moderate candidate in a second primary. If nominations were made simply by plurality vote, a candidate relying on the solid support of the Klan (or some other extremist group) could conceivably snatch victory from the hands of a crowded field of contenders – including some candidates more widely acceptable to the electorate – with only a small percentage of the total vote. (1992, 6)

This example also illustrates a second advantage of run-off elections: it reduces the possibility of several candidates who may draw support from similar political bases 'splitting' their vote between them. Diverse interests which compete with each other in the first round election can, if necessary, coalesce behind successful candidates in the lead up to the second round. The 1924 adoption of the run-off in Arkansas, for example, was a reaction to the fear of splitting the anti-Klan vote in a straight plurality election contest (Bullock and Johnson 1992, 6). Of course, as pointed out earlier, if the original support base is so fractured that none of the candidates from that group make the run-off stage, then the vote-splitting advantage is negated. Nonetheless, a second round of voting almost always encourages bargains and trade-offs between parties and candidates.

For this reason, academic analysis of the effects of electoral laws has often discussed majority preference voting systems like AV and run-off systems in tandem. Some scholars, for example, praise the run-off as a 'two-shot' system which enables voters to have a second choice or even change their mind between the first and second round (Sartori 1994, 63). Others argue that both run-off and plurality elections promote similar vote-pooling incentives to preferential voting ones, and thus that the transfer of support from one party to another is an 'implicit feature of the French second ballot or the Anglo-American first-past-the-post system' (Laver and Schofield 1991, 204). While this may be true in non-divided societies, it does not appear to hold in cases of deep ethnic division, as it assumes that electors vote strategically, and that minor-party voters will be prepared to ignore their first choice and instead vote for a candidate with a better chance of winning, or that likely losers will pull out of the race. Such assumptions are not realistic in divided societies, where the depth of ethnic identity and antagonisms makes it extremely unlikely that such strategic considerations will occur.

Despite this, some scholars have advocated run-off elections as a means of minimising the influence of extremist or 'anti-system' parties (Fisichella 1984). A major problem encountered when applying this system in divided societies is that coalitions do not tend to be formed until after the first round of voting, when it is clear which candidates are likely to proceed to the next round. This greatly affects the depth and timing of cross-ethnic appeals: candidates needing to reach out to other groups for additional support will only do so after their 'base' support levels have become clear at the first round of an election. By this time, ethnic stances are likely to have hardened and cross-ethnic appeals may well be too late and lacking in credibility. The result is a much weaker (and later) set of incentives for accommodative behaviour than is the case with preferential systems, and it is therefore not surprising that run-off elections are seldom used or advocated for divided societies.[4]

For this reason, run-off elections in the United States, despite their earlier role in combating racist forces such as the Klan, have increasingly come to be seen as unfavourable to minority-race candidates in general, and to black candidates in particular, because of the widely held belief that minority candidates who win a plurality of first-round votes are often structurally penalised in the second round when confronting a white candidate, although the empirical evidence for this widely held view is rather shaky (Bullock and Johnson 1992). Another major disadvantage of such elections is the pressure they place on the electoral administration by having to hold a second election a week or two after the first, thus increasing costs, instability and uncertainty (Reynolds and Reilly 1997, 44). Nonetheless, both AV and run-off systems have traditionally been lumped together by political scientists as the two examples of 'majority formulae' found in Western countries (see Rae 1967, 107–10) – not because of any structural similarities, but rather because both strive to achieve a majority victor in each case. Lijphart, for example, argues that AV 'may be thought of as a refinement of the majority run-off formula in the sense that weak candidates are eliminated one at a time (instead of all

---

[4] My thanks to Larry Diamond for this point.

but the top two candidates at the same time) and that voters do not have to go to the polls twice' (1994a, 19).

Because run-off elections were developed in response to the requirements of decision-making assemblies, which often needed to make choices between a number of alternatives via sequential elections, the simplest way to conduct them was via successive 'eliminations': that is, at each stage the lowest-ranked candidate or option dropping out and successive rounds of voting between those remaining being repeated until a majority winner emerges. Such a system of successive elections entails an implicit rank-ordering of preferences between the different choices presented (Rokkan 1968, 15). While the exhaustive repetition of run-off elections, sequentially eliminating lowest-placed candidates one-by-one until a majority winner is found, continues to be used in a number of important decision-making assemblies today (the International Olympic Committee's means of choosing the venue for the Olympic Games being perhaps the best known of these), it is an impractical method for mass-suffrage political elections, where a sequence of run-offs needs to be compressed from several elections into one. The solution was what Rokkan described as 'the great innovation' of British electoral reformers: the single transferable vote (1968, 15). The following three sections describe the evolution of the three primary forms of preferential voting used at mass elections – STV, AV and SV – that developed from this basic idea.

The single transferable vote

The first serious proposal for applying the preferential ballot to nation-wide elections was put forward by Thomas Hare in 1856 as part of his manifesto for a new form of proportional representation, *The Election of Representatives, Parliamentary and Municipal.*[5] Hare's proposal for a 'single transferable vote' (STV) envisaged the entire United Kingdom as one vast constituency in which all candidates for the parliament would simultaneously stand and be chosen. Voters would have to separately choose between (and rank-order on their ballots) several thousand candidates. Despite its obvious impracticalities, Hare's scheme was publicly championed by his mentor John Stuart Mill, who called it 'among the very greatest improvements yet made in the theory and practice of government' (quoted in McLean and Urken 1995, 46). Mill was so enamoured of Hare's proposal that he wrote that Hare had 'for the first time, solved the difficulty of popular representation; and by doing so, to

---

[5] All references here are to the 4th edition: Hare 1873.

have raised up the cloud and gloom of uncertainty that hung over the futurity of representative government and therefore of civilisation'. As noted earlier, the core principles of the system were also independently invented around the same time by Carl Andræ in Denmark, and STV's first national-level application was for the Danish federal assembly, the Rigsraad, lasting from 1855 until 1864.

As detailed in Chapter 1, STV uses multi-member districts with voters ranking candidates in order of preference on the ballot paper (i.e. 1, 2, 3, etc.) in the same manner as the alternative vote. After the total number of first preference votes are tallied, the count then begins by establishing the 'quota' of votes required for the election of a single candidate. Any candidate who has as many or more first preferences as the quota is immediately elected. If no-one has achieved the quota, the candidate with the lowest number of first preferences is eliminated, with his or her second preferences being redistributed to the candidates left in the race. At the same time, those votes for elected candidates above the quota are also transferred according to the preferences marked. Because it is not possible to determine which votes actually elected the candidate and which votes are surplus, at Australian elections all the elected candidates' ballot papers are transferred at a reduced value, known as the 'transfer value'. The transfer value of each elected candidate's ballot papers is worked out by dividing the number of surplus votes by the total number of that candidate's ballot papers. This process continues until all vacancies have been filled.

The 'Hare system', as it was known, was to be much admired but much modified by future electoral reformers (such as, in Australia, Catherine Helen Spence and Andrew Inglis Clark) as they attempted to fashion a functioning electoral system from Hare's ambitious but impractical basic model. One of the few parts of Hare's original scheme for STV *not* to require modification was the idea of the *transferability* of preferential votes 'from one candidate to another until it reaches a candidate whom the elector has named' (Hare 1873, 121–2). This transferability of votes from both excluded candidates and those elected candidates with a 'surplus' of votes formed a central part of Hare's scheme for a nationwide system of proportional representation. From the outset, the proposal that votes should be transferable was criticised as being overly complex and beyond the understanding of ordinary voters. A recurrent concern was that the method by which lower-order preferences were transferred presupposed that these carried the same weight or value as a first preference, which may not in fact reflect the true value which voters placed on their lower-order rankings. Hare saw it instead as a 'vast augmentation of their electoral power' and criticised as mischievous and patronising those who argued that STV was beyond the capacity of the average elector (1873, viii). Like Mill, Hare was not reluctant to ascribe wider benefits to his electoral proposal, seeing it as 'bringing to the duty of voting reflection, judgement and moderation' (1873, 122) which 'by the opportunity the voting papers afford of separating, distinguishing, and bringing out every form of political opinion, will give an immeasurable increase of force and strength to the representative principle' (1873, 127).

This polemic approach to STV continued into the academic study of electoral systems in the twentieth century. Taagepera and Shugart see the 'missionary zeal of early twentieth-century electoral reformers' as having stunted the growth of genuinely comparative research on the subject of electoral systems, defining the debate as increasingly an argument between the proponents and opponents of proportional representation in general, and its STV variant in particular (1989, 49–50).[6] This division between pro- and anti-PR approaches has also obscured the relationship between many proportional and non-proportional systems – such as, for example, the way that AV actually developed not as a majoritarian system, but as a variant of STV proportional representation.

The alternative vote

The alternative vote was developed as an adaptation of STV so as to enable its use in single-member rather than multi-member electorates. It had been pointed out as early as 1863 that Hare's original STV proposal made elections in single-member districts all but impossible due to the overly high quota for election in Hare's version (see McLean and Urken 1995, 46–7). The next step was to find a way of reworking the preferential mechanics proposed by Hare into a practical package for the election of a single member. Although the essentials of the system were originally proposed (and dismissed) by Condorcet, the first documented example of such a method appears to have been carried out by Professor W. R. Ware of Harvard College in 1871. In a letter to Hare (published as Appendix M to the fourth edition of *The Election of Representatives* under the heading 'The Preferential Vote') Ware detailed the efficacy of Hare's method when used for a mock election by Harvard students to

---

[6] Even apparently analytical works such as (in the United Kingdom) Bogdanor's *What is Proportional Representation?* (1984) or (in Australia) Wright's *Mirror of the Nation's Mind* (1980), are unable to escape the lure of becoming implicit (or in Wright's case explicit) advocates of STV.

select their four favourite writers – Shakespeare winning handsomely (Hare 1873, 351–5). Ware also showed that Hare's method could be utilised to fill casual vacancies (and thus obviate the need for by-elections) by re-examining the ballots cast for a retiring member and distributing the second and later preferences accordingly.[7] Ware used this example to show that 'contrary to the generally received opinion, the system of preferential voting is applicable to the choice of a single candidate' (Hare 1873, 353). Ware's experiment demonstrated that, where no candidate has an absolute majority, the sequence of elimi-nation of the lowest-placed candidate and the transfer of his or her votes to continuing candidates could work just as well for single-member elections as for Hare's more complex scheme of proportional representation: thus the alternative vote was born.

It was not until its adoption for state elections in Western Australia in 1907, however, that AV was used for legislative elections, having been brought to prominence in Australia by E. J. Nanson, professor of mathematics at Melbourne University from 1875 to 1922 and an influen-tial campaigner for electoral reform in Australia and internationally. In 1882 Nanson published a widely circulated pamphlet explaining the mechanics of the 'Ware method' as he called it, which he praised for its lack of susceptibility to strategic voting and for its relative simplicity, making it 'extremely suitable for political elections' (Nanson 1995 [1882]). By the late 1890s, with the framing of the Australian constitution in progress, Nanson concentrated his efforts on influencing the choice of electoral system for the new federal parliament. It was clear that political pressures would ensure that the House of Representatives utilised single-member electoral districts, and Nanson was at pains to ensure the selection of AV, which he saw as being 'far superior' to other single-member systems like FPTP (he also campaigned unflaggingly for the adoption in the Senate of STV, which would have been his favoured system for the House of Representatives as well were multi-member electorates utilised there). In a series of articles in the *Age* and *Argus*, collectively published in 1900 under the title *The Real Value of a Vote and How to Get it at the Coming Federal Elections*, Nanson emphasised 'the absolute necessity of insisting that no candidate be elected in a single electorate unless he poll an absolute majority of the votes', initially advocating the 'contingent vote', as SV was know in Australia at the time (1900, 32). Intriguingly, Nanson claimed that 'there is nothing new in preferential or contingent voting. This method was used in France and Switzerland 130 years ago' – a claim which presumably refers to

---

[7] This is how casual vacancies are filled under the STV system used in Tasmania.

Condorcet's writings, which Nanson was known to have read. However, Nanson went on to emphasise that even better than the contingent vote was a procedure which entailed an exhaustive use of preferences – the alternative vote, a system which was, at that time, unused anywhere in the world (1900, 7, 12).

Following the successful federation of the Australian colonies in 1901, Nanson's campaign for preferential voting had a significant influence upon the first draft electoral bill presented to the new Commonwealth parliament in 1902, which provided for AV in the House and proportional representation in the Senate. The government's stated aim in introducing AV was 'to bring out in the most certain way possible the choice of the majority of the electorate' (quoted in Reid and Forrest 1989, 98). The progressive lineage of the proposed systems was clear from the ensuing parliamentary debates: references to John Stuart Mill, Thomas Hare, Helen Spence, Nanson and Andrew Inglis Clark were made by both supporters and opponents of the bill. As it was, the conservative opponents emerged victorious: both AV in the House and STV in the Senate were deleted during the passage of the bill, to be replaced with the 'safe' options of FPTP and the Block Vote (i.e. FPTP in multi-member constituencies) respectively. According to Reid and Forrest, with the wisdom of hindsight:

> it is easily seen now that the major proposals of 1902 were decades ahead of their time . . . it took seventeen years, until 1919, before the contingent (preferential) method of voting for the House of Representatives with single-member divisions was acceptable; and it took almost fifty years, until 1948, before the Parliament finally accepted a brand of proportional representation for the Senate's State-wide, multi-member electorates. In both cases the reforms came not as a result of the pursuit of principles of electoral justice, but from pragmatic considerations of party gain. (1989, 99)

The first attempt at resurrecting AV for the lower house came before the third federal election in 1906, when protectionist Prime Minister Alfred Deakin wrote to his Labor counterpart, Chris Watson, suggesting a deal to isolate the free-trade forces of George Reid:

> Have you thought of the exhaustive ballot – compulsory voting for every candidate. The lowest dropped out & his votes divided until someone gets a majority. With this our candidate & yours could not do each other anything like so much harm & one or other of us would win in several Reidite constituencies. Of course it must be compulsory voting for all candidates. It would be a great safety valve for both of us. What do you think? (Reid and Forrest 1989, 114)

Watson, whose rising Labor Party was the clear beneficiary of vote splitting amongst the non-Labor candidates, was not interested. The Deakin government introduced another bill for AV in August 1906, but it lapsed with the Parliament's dissolution. A Liberal private member's bill in 1911 met a similar fate (Reid and Forrest 1989, 115).

It was not until 1918 that AV was finally introduced for federal elections to the House of Representatives, after having previously been introduced at the state level by Liberal governments in Western Australia (1907) and Victoria (1911). The decision was prompted more by considerations of partisan advantage than by the finer points of electoral theory. The increasing incidence of minority Labor candidates beating a divided field of conservatives had prompted Sir Joseph Cook's short-lived Liberal government (1913–14) to appoint a royal commission into electoral matters, which recommended that AV and STV be introduced for elections to the House of Representatives and Senate respectively.

After Cook's defeat, the issue lay dormant until 1917 when the newly formed Nationalist Party, under the leadership of W. M. Hughes, was able to form a governing majority. Interest in preferential voting gathered pace in 1918 following a by-election for the seat of Swan in Western Australia, which was won in a FPTP contest by a Labor candidate with 35 per cent of the vote despite the three non-Labor candidates collectively mustering 65 per cent. When this result threatened to be repeated at another by-election, with a similar constellation of political forces, in the Victorian electorate of Corangamite later that same year, pressure for electoral reform from the non-Labor side of politics intensified. Under considerable pressure from the farming lobby, which threatened to split the Nationalist vote by standing its own candidates unless preferential voting reforms were introduced, the Hughes government moved to head-off a repetition of the Swan scenario by introducing AV for all House of Representatives elections. The consequences of this change will be discussed in some detail in Chapter 3. At this stage, however, it is sufficient to note that the introduction of AV was intimately related to the need to counter the possibilities of vote splitting and to encourage and reward collaboration or coalition arrangements between like-minded forces on the conservative side of politics (see Graham 1962, 164–81).

The supplementary vote

As described earlier, while AV is the application of STV to elections for a single office, the supplementary vote, while structurally similar to AV, is actually an attenuated form of run-off election. Under this system, candidates are rank-ordered on the ballot in the same way as AV, and any candidate who receives an absolute majority of first preferences is declared elected. However, the process of counting votes is different: if no candidate has an absolute majority, *all* candidates other than the two leaders on first preferences are eliminated, and the votes for eliminated candidates are redistributed to one or the other of the top two, according to the preferences marked, to ensure a majority winner. Supplementary voting is recognised in Australia as the forerunner to the alternative vote (see Wright 1980, 34, 58–61). It was first used in Queensland in 1892, where it was known as the 'contingent vote'.[8] Again, the original stimulus for change was a by-election in which aligned conservative forces split their vote under FPTP, and which led to a proposal that a run-off be introduced for Queensland elections to ensure that all winners enjoyed clear majority support. But concerns about the practicality of running two-round elections across the state's vast electorates and dispersed population centres led to a search for practical alternatives. One suggestion was to compress the two rounds of voting into a single election, so that in those districts where no candidate received a majority of first-round votes, 'all candidates but the two with the highest totals of votes should be excluded and the votes of their supporters should be transferred to either of the two top candidates for whom the voters had shown preferences' (Wright 1980, 58). The expression of 'contingent' preferences was not compulsory, and voters could number as many preferences as they wished.[9] SV was subsequently used for eighteen Queensland state elections, in a mixture of single-member and two-member electorates. It was replaced by FPTP in 1942, after growing Labor concern at the appearance of splinter groups and the loss of the safe seat of Cairns when preferences from the non-Labor side were successfully directed towards an independent Labor candidate.[10] A similar system had also been used around the same period for primary elections in several US states (see Chapter 6).

Following its abandonment in Queensland, the supplementary vote was effectively a 'dead' electoral system until its revival by Sri Lankan constitutional drafters in 1978. However, the system gained considerable publicity in Britain in 1993 when it was recommended by the Labour Party's Plant Commission as a reform to Britain's existing FPTP electoral

---

[8] The system was introduced by the conservative government of Samuel Griffith, who went on to become one of the primary drafters of the Australian constitution.

[9] New South Wales also experimented with the supplementary vote at one election, in 1927, before adopting the alternative vote.

[10] Queensland adopted the alternative vote in the 1960s, and in 1991 changed to an optional rather than compulsory expression of preferences.

laws. According to media reports, SV was devised by Labour MP Dale Campbell Savours as a clever compromise between a two-round run-off and the full alternative vote. One of the distinctive applications of SV in Britain is that voters are allowed only two preferences – a first choice and a 'supplementary' second one – marked with a cross in two columns on the ballot paper, rather than with numbers (Dunleavy *et al.* 1997). The Plant Commission described this as an achievable change to the British FPTP system which would be 'practical, straightforward and comparatively modest' (1993, 21), and which would temper some of the more extreme results of FPTP elections. Critics, of which there were many, by contrast focussed on the apparent novelty of 'a new system which had never been used elsewhere' (Norris 1995, 82), with one Conservative MP describing it as 'an idea dreamed up by a Labour MP which is not in existence anywhere in the world: it has no record' (Best 1993, 80). Despite widespread acceptance of their veracity, these claims were, of course, incorrect: the system has been independently 'invented' on at least four separate occasions in Queensland, the United States, Sri Lanka and most recently the United Kingdom, each time apparently without recourse to or knowledge of previous incarnations. Although apparently having lost prominence as a possible electoral reform at the national level, in 1998 it was adopted by the British government as the system to elect the new mayor of London.

Although superficially similar to AV, supplementary vote rules actually have quite different electoral impacts. A hypothetical example of how the system works in a four-candidate contest with two major-party candidates and two minor candidates is given in Table 2.1. The supplementary vote enables the Liberal and Independent Liberal candidates to defeat a Labor candidate who would have won under first-past-the-post.

Considering that SV elections (unlike AV ones) effectively require voters to guess who the top two candidates in any election will be in order to use their preferences effectively, it is perhaps not surprising that the expression of 'supplementary' preferences has always been optional wherever SV has been practised. However, this has meant that the system has rarely worked as planned: in Queensland, for example, few voters expressed second or later preferences, and consequently nearly all seats returned results identical to a FPTP contest (at sixteen elections between 1896 and 1935 the supplementary vote changed the final result in only seven seats). Similar problems, as we shall see, appear to bedevil the system in Sri Lanka. However, SV does afford voters the *possibility* of expressing some kind of choice between candidates on their ballot, and gives minorities the chance to have some influence on which majority candidate is selected. This should, in theory, provide a stake in the system

Table 2.1. *A hypothetical example of the supplementary vote (1)*

Candidate	First count	Second count	Result
Independent Labour	600	Eliminated – all second preferences to Labour	
Independent Liberal	2,000	Eliminated – 1,600 second preferences to Liberal; 400 to Labour	
Liberal	3,500	3,500 + 1,600 = 5,100	Liberal elected
Labour	3,900	3,900 + 600 + 400 = 4,900	
Total votes	10,000		
Majority needed to win	5,001		

for minority groups, who know that even if they do not have the numbers to elect their own candidate outright, they can influence which majority candidate gets elected via their supplementary preferences.

Discussions of SV elections are almost completely absent from the standard literature on electoral systems. None of the major comparative works on electoral systems of the past thirty years mentions the system.[11] On the rare occasions when a SV election is cited – usually by reference to Sri Lanka's presidential elections – the system is often misclassified as AV. Horowitz, for example, provides two definitions of the alternative vote, one of which is actually a description of the supplementary vote (1991a, 188). A similar error is made in Shugart and Carey's otherwise comprehensive volume on presidential systems, which compounds the error by comparing presidential elections in Ireland (where the specified electoral system is actually STV, which is identical to AV in single-member elections) with elections in Sri Lanka, which they assume to be an identical system (1992, 210). Even the *doyen* of the comparative study of electoral systems, Arend Lijphart, makes the error, mistakenly classifying Sri Lanka as an example of AV (1995a, 413). This could be dismissed as a semantic quibble of little importance, were it not for the fact that the two systems will often produce quite different results. If we take the example

[11] These include Rae 1967; Lakeman 1974; Taagepera and Shugart 1989; Lijphart and Grofman 1984; Grofman and Lijphart 1986; Shugart and Carey 1992; Lijphart 1994a.

Table 2.2. *A hypothetical example of the supplementary vote (2)*

Candidate	First count	Second count	Result
Independent Labour	600	SV and AV: Eliminated – all second preferences to Independent Liberal. Third preferences to Labour.	
Independent Liberal	2,500	SV: Eliminated – 1,950 second preferences to Liberal; 550 to Labour. AV: 2,500 + 600 = 3,100	AV: Independent Liberal elected (2,500 + 600 + 3,000 = 6,100)
Liberal	3,000	SV: 3,000 + 1,950 = 4,950 AV: Eliminated 2nd. All second preferences to Independent Liberal	
Labour	3,900	SV: 3,900 + 550 + 600 = 5,050 AV: 3,900 + 0 = 3,900	SV: Labor elected
Total votes	10,000		
Majority needed to win	5,001		

used earlier, but change the relative vote shares slightly, this is illustrated quite sharply (see Table 2.2). Under SV rules, the two Independent candidates are eliminated and their votes passed on to Labour or Liberal, with the result that the Labour candidate is narrowly elected, with 5,050 votes to the Liberal's 4,950. Under AV rules, by contrast, the Independent Labour candidate's preferences go to the other Independent, who now has 3,100 votes – more than the Liberal's total of 3,000. The Liberal is thus the next to be eliminated; her preferences ensure the easy election of the Independent Liberal over the Labour candidate.

The point of this example is that AV and SV are clearly distinct systems, and should not be confused or discussed as if one was a mere variation of the other. In fact, in conditions of high candidature, it becomes increasingly probable that the two systems will elect different candidates, because the votes of lower-placed candidates are more likely to see a candidate initially placed third or fourth (who would be eliminated under SV rules) gain enough preferences under AV rules to leap-frog one of the two leaders during the distribution of preferences.

Conclusion

Preferential voting was developed as a means of simplifying the sequential elections and run-off methods used in many forums in past centuries. But its adoption for mass elections, particularly in Australia, was primarily a response to the coordination problems created by too many politically aligned candidates standing for election under FPTP, and splitting their combined vote between them. The need to aggregate, rather than divide, common interests was thus a primary reason for preferential systems being adopted. Yet despite its eventual spread across all Australian jurisdictions, and its centrist influences on political competition there, for most of the twentieth century the Australian experience of preferential voting was neither emulated nor seriously evaluated as a useful model for other countries. Indeed, so far, the only countries outside Australia which have adopted the 'Australian' version of preferential voting – the alternative vote – are located in Australia's regional 'sphere of influence', the South Pacific. Thus the former Australian colony of Papua New Guinea inherited Australia's electoral laws almost unchanged for its first three elections between 1964 and 1972, before changing to first-past-the-post at independence in 1975. Similarly, the tiny Pacific island micro-state of Nauru, which came under Australian trusteeship following the First World War, also inherited Australian institutions at independence in 1968. And in 1997, the island state of Fiji, which had suffered two ethnically motivated military coups in the 1980s, adopted a range of Australian institutions, including the alternative vote, following a review of ways to encourage moderate multi-ethnic politics in that divided society. Effective understanding of the political effects of the electoral system in all of these cases also requires an understanding of the Australian institutions on which they are based, and of the subtle but powerful centripetal force that preferential voting has had upon Australian politics. This is the subject of Chapter 3.

3

Centripetal incentives and political engineering in Australia

Introduction

Australia is a particularly interesting case of centripetalism at work for three reasons. First, the Australian experience represents by the far the best-established and longest-running example of preferential voting in the world today, with all three of the major preferential electoral systems (AV, SV and STV) having been used for elections in various jurisdictions in Australia. All three systems were also developed or substantially refined in Australia, and the Australian development of electoral institutions there-fore represents one of the more distinctive national contributions to institutional design (McLean 1996, 369). Having been a feature of Australian politics since the early years of last century, preferential voting has become an embedded and well-institutionalised factor of Australian elections. Since 1963, all state, territory and federal jurisdictions have utilised preferential voting of one sort or another. The Australian experience thus enables us to examine the effects of preferential voting upon political competition over a long period in a stable political environment.

The second distinctive feature of Australia for investigation of divided societies is its combination of high degrees of ethnic diversity with low levels of inter-ethnic conflict. Australia has one of the world's most ethnically diverse populations, with approximately 40 per cent of the population being overseas-born or the offspring of overseas born immi-grants, most of whom come from non-English speaking countries in southern Europe, the Middle East and Asia. According to one source, 'Australia has the highest proportion of foreign born in the population of any advanced industrial democracy, with the possible exception of Israel' (Bowler *et al.* 1996, 468). Despite this level of ethnic diversity, ethnic relations in Australia have been characterised by relatively high levels of inter-communal harmony and integration, without 'the sharp-edged and sometimes violent racial tension which is found in Britain, Germany or the United States' (Jupp 1991, 51–2). Kukathas argues that Australia represents

> an attractive model of a modern multi-cultural society . . . its migrants have come from all parts of the world to contribute to a population marked by ethnic, linguistic and religious diversity. Yet while this diversity is no less substantial than that found in other multicultural societies such as the United States – and is more considerable than that found in others such as Malaysia or Germany or France – it prevails in circumstances that are far more peaceful, and politically and socially stable, than those in any of these other countries. (1991, 167)

Australia has thus been relatively successful in integrating millions of recent arrivals into a democratic society – although considerably less so in achieving equality for its indigenous Aboriginal and Torres Strait Islander population. In general, ethnicity has not become politicised in Australia, and many studies emphasise the low political profile of both ethnic actors and ethnic issues in Australia compared to their prominence in comparable countries (see Jupp 1984). In the late 1990s, however, the rise of a racially exclusive extremist party – One Nation – led to an increase in inter-ethnic tensions between some elements of mainstream society and minority groups, particularly Aborigines and Asians, and presented a major challenge to the established political order. The way that Australia's major political parties responded to this challenge from One Nation, and effectively marginalised it via a successful electoral strategy of reciprocal cooperation and vote-pooling, makes an interesting case for students of centripetalism in divided societies that will be examined further in this chapter.

Third, the institutions and policies of contemporary Australia represent one of the best approximations of a complete package of centripetal political institutions amongst comparable democracies (see Horowitz 1985, 597–600). Australia combines a federal system of government which disperses power geographically; preferential voting systems for state and federal elections; three levels of government (federal, state and local) contributing to devolution; formal and informal offices representing ethnic interests; government policies aimed at reducing inequalities for underprivileged groups (particularly Aborigines and immigrants from non-English-speaking backgrounds); and an accepted government policy of 'multiculturalism' which urges ethnic group integration but not assimilation (Jupp 1991). Australia's relatively benign ethnic situation would thus appear to offer some positive empirical evidence for the relationship between these dispersive and integrative institutions and policies and a harmonious multi-ethnic society, even if the direction of causation is far from clear (see Jupp 1991, 51).

Centripetal politics in Australia

While Australia offers much useful evidence for an investigation of the affects of preferential voting, its comparative value is limited for the purposes of assessing the key arguments made for centripetalism. Despite being an extremely diverse society with high degrees of ethnic pluralism, diversity does not mean division. With the notable exception of Aboriginal Australians, who continue to have drastically lower living standards than all other groups in the population, ethnicity and politics have tended to remain largely detached from each other. At the end of the twentieth century, Australia is clearly not an ethnically *divided* society in the sense of ethnicity being a politically salient cleavage – indeed, its harmonious inter-ethnic relations would scarcely be possible if this were so. This was not the case at the beginning of the twentieth century, however, when the new country was beset not just by the ongoing stark divide between the settler and indigenous populations, but by deep Protestant–Catholic divisions inherited from the main settler origin countries of Britain and Ireland. Along with a clear distinction between rural and urban interests, between the forces of labour and capital, and between free-traders and protectionists, this religious cleavage formed the basis of an emerging party system. The social bases of Australia's political parties, formed in the early decades of the twentieth century, have evidenced more continuity than change since then, and continue to exert a strong influence upon the overall shape of Australian politics.

Following the federation of the six British colonies into the Commonwealth of Australia in 1901, the previously amorphous party structure began to achieve a more coherent form. This was reflected in the emerging party system, with the Irish-Catholic Australian Labor Party – which has historically acted as a classic social-democratic party and, in recent decades, as a progressive liberal one as well – pitted against the Anglo-Protestant Liberals and Nationals, who have traditionally represented the interests of the urban middle classes and rural property owners respectively. 'No-one who reads the history of religious conflict in Australia', wrote one authority, 'can fail to be impressed by how important the link between religion and party politics once was' (Aitkin 1982, 162). Over the course of this century, however, the salience of these cleavages have weakened dramatically, and despite ongoing tensions between indigenous and settler Australians, and increasingly between urban and rural areas,[1] ethnicity as a mobilising force in Australian politics has, for the most part, been conspicuous by its absence.

Because of this, the Australian experience of preferential voting cannot be used to directly evaluate arguments for or against the centripetalist case regarding the relationship between preference-swapping arrangements under AV elections and policy moderation in divided societies. Australia does, however, offer the case which best illustrates the way preference-swapping can promote tangible policy changes on the part of parties and governments, and is thus worthy of investigation on this score alone, particularly when one examines the impact of preference voting at contemporary elections, such as the 1990 federal poll. Indeed, I will argue in this chapter that an important effect of preferential voting has not been its majoritarian, 'winner-take-all' qualities but rather its moderating, 'consensual' influence upon Australian politics.[2]

In this respect, perhaps the most important consequence of the use of preferential voting in Australia is the way that it has provided the ever-cautious national electorate with the means to punish perceived extremism of any ideology, providing strong incentives for the major parties to keep their focus on the middle ground at all times. In addition, the mechanics of preference distribution has resulted in the institutionalisation of negotiations between major and minor parties for second-preference support – 'preference-swapping' as it is known in Australian parlance – which, particularly in the context of STV elections to the Senate, has become a well-established practice of Australian politics. This in turn has encouraged the consequent development of well-institutionalised arenas of bargaining across party lines – with important, but subtle, influences on the political process and, as such practices become normalised over time, on the wider political culture.

Australia's long use of different varieties of preferential electoral systems also represents a particularly interesting case of the unintended consequences of electoral innovation. As detailed in Chapter 2, preferential voting for national elections was first introduced in the early decades of the twentieth century, primarily to combat the rising labour movement and counter the effects of vote splitting between conservative parties.

---

[1] Norris (1999, 12) argues that Australia's 'main centre–periphery ethnic cleavage was based on rural versus non-rural populations'.
[2] See Lijphart 1984 for the standard dichotomy between 'majoritarian' and 'consensual' forms of democracy.

Over the years, preferential voting has remained a significant, if sometimes subtle, influence on the development of Australian party politics. It
has (mostly) ensured the election of governments which enjoy the
majority support of the electorate. It has sustained the presence of some
minor parties, but also constrained tendencies towards party system
fragmentation. It has also enabled the development of partnership
arrangements between parties – with the long-running coalition arrangement between the Liberal and National parties being the most prominent,
but not the only, example. A less examined feature of preferential voting
is the way it has pushed the Australian political system away from
extremes and towards the 'moderate middle'. Indeed, preferential voting
for lower house elections has been described as a system for choosing 'the
least unpopular candidate' (Lucy 1985, 97). As such, it acts as an
exemplary case of the way some electoral institutions can promote
centripetal rather than centrifugal political incentives (Cox 1990). As this
chapter will show, preference voting has introduced a significant degree of
centripetal and 'consensual' practice to what is, on most indicators, a
highly adversarial political culture.

Preferential elections in Australia

As detailed in Chapter 2, Australia has, since 1918, used an AV electoral
system to elect its lower house, the House of Representatives, and since
1949, an STV system for elections to the upper house, the Senate. The
combination of these two distinct but related electoral systems has had a
major impact on the development of Australian party politics. For the
lower house, AV was adopted for Australian federal elections primarily to
counter vote splitting by enabling multiple aligned candidates to stand for
election to the same seat and aggregate their combined vote share. In its
first use at the national level, at the Corangamite by-election in 1918, it
did exactly that, enabling the election on preferences of a Victorian
Farmers' Union candidate over a Labor candidate who had led on first
preferences (see Graham 1962, 164–81). At the same time, the spread of a
distinctive feature of preferential voting elections in Australia – the
practice of party agents distributing 'how to vote' cards outside polling
booths – quickly served to institutionalise the new electoral arrangements
without placing excessive expectations on the interest or memory of
voters. 'How-to-vote' cards are leaflets, typically distributed outside
polling booths on election day by major parties, which contain the
parties' recommendations to their supporters as to how they should mark
their ballot papers and, in particular, who should receive lower-order
preference votes. Slightly over half of all voters claim to follow their

favoured parties' suggested preference ordering, although rates differ markedly between major party and minor party voters (see Bean 1997).

The immediate impact of the introduction of preferential voting on national politics was relatively modest, although it did provide an early spur for the coalition of urban and rural conservative interests, with the Liberal and National parties having been in a close electoral alliance at the federal level since 1922. But until the 1980s, most commentators on Australian politics tended to assess AV as being a minor variant of FPTP, in most cases giving outcomes near identical to that system in terms of election results and its impact upon the structure of party systems. Douglas Rae, for example, stated baldly that 'the Australian system behaves in all its particulars as if it were a single-member district plurality formula' (Rae 1967, 108). David Butler thought AV made little difference to Australian electoral results and had 'never been central in determining how governments have been chosen' (Butler 1973, 96). Writing in 1977, Colin Hughes agreed: it was 'unlikely' that AV would 'determine who governs Australia' (1977, 294). The common element in all these judgements is that they were predominantly based on observation of the Australian federal elections of the 1950s and 1960s where, with the notable exception of the Democratic Labor Party – a minor party breakaway from Labor whose preferences heavily favoured the conservative Coalition – preference distribution had little effect on electoral outcomes in the House of Representatives.

In the federal upper house, the Senate, the situation has been rather different. The Senate's members serve staggered six-year terms, with half of the membership facing election every three years (except when the Senate is prematurely dissolved). Despite broadly congruent powers between the two parliamentary chambers, winning control of the lower house is the focus of Australian election campaigns, as it is the lower house, the House of Representatives, where governments are formed and where major financial legislation is introduced. The Senate, by contrast, is theoretically a 'State's house', established to represent the constituent units of the federation. Convention in Australia holds that, since governments are formed on the floor of the House of Representatives, the Senate's role is limited by the 'mandate' of the House majority. But in constitutional terms the Senate is one of the world's most powerful upper houses, with the capacity to defeat lower house legislation and to initiate its own bills, barring those directly concerned with Commonwealth finances. As noted in Chapter 2, since 1949 the Senate has been elected by STV, with compulsory numbering of all preferences. Since 1983, electors have had the option of adopting a 'ticket vote', which constitutes one distinctive element of the Australian implementation of STV, and represents an open attempt on the part of the political parties to control the flow of their supporters' preferences. Under ticket voting, parties and aligned candidates may lodge prior to the election a full preference schedule or 'group voting ticket' which sets out where they would like to see their preferences allocated. A voter may vote either by numbering every candidate to indicate the order of his or her preference for them, in the standard preferential voting manner, or by marking one square to indicate that he or she wishes to adopt the full voting ticket lodged by the group. Where a voter adopts a group voting ticket, his or her ballot paper is deemed to have been marked in accordance with the complete preference ordering specified in the group voting ticket. There is thus a major difference in the simplicity of the task facing a person wishing to cast a ticket vote, and that facing a person who wishes to determine his or her own preference ordering. The ticket voter has to mark but one square on the ballot, while the person wishing to depart from group tickets must rank-order every candidate, which can number over sixty separate candidate choices. The net effect, not surprisingly, has been a steady increase, since its introduction, in the use of ticket voting. At the 1998 election, for example, fully 95 per cent of all voters chose to adopt their favoured parties' preference ordering by ticket voting, rather than manually numbering each candidate on the ballot themselves (Reilly and Maley 2000).

While ticket voting certainly represents an unusual Australian innovation, the most striking long-term effect upon Australian politics of the introduction of STV has been on the representation of minor parties in the Senate, where the introduction of STV dramatically increased both the representation and the influence of minor parties in federal politics. It also greatly changed the role of the Senate, which since 1949 has developed as a powerful check on majoritarian government, moving away from its formal constitutional role as a chamber which represents the interests of the states, towards one which places much more emphasis upon its deliberative and legislative review functions. Minor parties have now held the balance of power continuously since mid-1981 (and, except for the period from 1976 to 1981, since 1962), creating a new and powerful role for the Senate as the voice of minority opinion in federal politics. As a consequence, for most of the post-war period successive governments have had to gain the support of one or more independent or minor party senators to pass legislation.

Because of the increasing importance of minor parties, in recent decades preference voting has come to play a much more important role in Australian elections than in previous years. It is important to emphasise that most preference-trading activity at Australian elections takes place in the context of 'cross-house' preference deals, whereby a minor party exchanges its preferences in lower house seats in return for the major party's preferences in the Senate (Sharman and Miragliotta 2000). This has been particularly important for prominent Senate minor parties such as the centre-left Australian Democrats and environmental parties such as the Greens, whose dispersed support base mean they are unlikely to win seats in the single-member lower house AV elections but have, by virtue of proportional representation, become well-established players in the Senate. Because all parties distribute 'how-to-vote' cards which direct voters as to how the party would like to see them allocate their preference votes, the rising power of minor parties facilitated by proportional representation in the Senate also gave them a new and powerful role in influencing the outcomes of elections to the lower house, via the instructions they give to their supporters. For example, minor parties with a secure presence in the Senate can trade preference allocation pledges from other parties in return for reciprocal preference directions to their own supporters at lower house elections.

As the number of minor parties has increased, so the issue of which major party will receive their preference votes has become increasingly important. This has been reflected in the increasing number of lower-house seats which are not won outright on first preferences, but are effectively decided by the distribution of preference votes. In the 1960s, preferences had to be distributed in about 25 per cent of all seats; this figure rose to 30 per cent in the 1970s and 1980s, and over 50 per cent in the 1990s. The 1998 election saw the highest ever rate of preference distribution at an Australian federal election, with two-thirds of all seats 'going to preferences' to determine the outcome. The actual rate of winners being different to that of a straight FPTP system, however, has remained low, at an average of 6 per cent of all seats. Yet even this rate of outcomes being affected can have significant impacts: had a FPTP rather than an AV system been in use, the results of the 1961, 1969 and 1990 elections would probably have been reversed. Table 3.1 outlines the extent to which preferences have been distributed (column 1), and as a consequence results different to FPTP recorded (column 2), at all Australian federal elections since 1960.

What have been the wider impacts of this system? For most of this century, AV has had two positive effects for the non-Labor parties in particular: it has facilitated the coalition arrangement between the Liberal and Country (now National) parties by enabling them both to stand candidates in some seats without the danger of vote splitting, and it has enabled the preferences of one small party, the now-defunct Democratic Labor Party, to flow predominantly against the Australian Labor Party

Table 3.1. *Proportion of seats where preferences distributed and outcomes changed at House of Representatives elections, 1963–1998*

Election Year	Preferences distributed (%)	Outcomes changed (%)
1963	19.2	6.6
1966	25.0	4.0
1969	32.0	9.6
1972	39.2	11.2
1974	26.0	7.9
1975	18.9	5.5
1977	36.2	3.1
1980	32.0	4.8
1983	24.8	1.6
1984	29.7	8.8
1987	36.5	2.7
1990	60.1	6.1
1993	42.2	8.2
1996	39.2	4.7
1998	66.2	4.7

Source: Hughes 1997, 166–7, updated to 1998.

and hugely assist the Liberal–Country Coalition maintain control of government throughout the 1960s. Indeed, of the 100 cases in which outcomes were changed due to preference distribution between 1969 and 1996, 81 went in favour of the Coalition (Hughes 1997, 166). In the 1980s and 1990s however, the partisan impact of AV appeared to turn around, with minor party preferences playing a crucial role in the 1990 Labor victory in particular (Hughes 1990, 140–51). In fact, the result of this election is the best example of preferential voting's ability to aggregate aligned interests, rather than dividing them, although it has not been until relatively recently that the full potential of preference distribution as an instrument for influencing policy decisions has been evident. As the 1990 election was probably the high point to date of interest in the effects of preferential voting, it is worth looking in some detail at this case.

Case study: the 1990 federal election

During the campaign for the 1990 federal election, it became clear that the incumbent Labor government was trailing the Liberal–National

Coalition in opinion polls, and that it appeared to be heading for certain electoral defeat. At the same time, however, the polls consistently showed that voter support for left-of-centre minority parties such as the Australian Democrats and Greens had reached historic heights. Labor, under the influence of senior strategist Senator Graham Richardson, assiduously courted the second preference votes of the supporters of these parties in the lead-up to the election, both indirectly via interactions with the major environmental lobby groups and directly via media appeals to minor party voters. Richardson has told the story:

> At the seminar for campaign directors and electorate staff . . . I outlined for the first time to a major party gathering the need to chase preference votes from the greens and the Democrats. I pointed out that according to surveys conducted over the past two years, the environment had come from twelfth to second place as an issue of public importance. Our surveys were consistent with all the others, and my message was that we could drag reluctant voters to our side by a preference strategy that stressed our impressive record on the environment. I urged our local campaigners not to campaign against green candidates but to pursue them for preferences which, overwhelmingly, they would want to give us. (Richardson 1994, 257–8)

Policy initiatives palatable to minor party voters were announced, and the then prime minister, Bob Hawke, used important sections of an address to the National Press Club to plead directly for second preferences:

> I want to say to those who intend to vote for third party and independent candidates that they should consider with the greatest care where they direct their second preferences. This is a vital election and it is – I make no bones about it – a tight election. And so I say specifically to them – if you do not want Medicare gutted, the capital gains tax scrapped, more uranium mining, a uranium enrichment industry in Australia, up-front tuition fees, mining in Kakadu, then your preference between the two major parties must be Labor. (Quoted in Warhurst 1990, 31)

Labor repeated this message in a national radio and television advertising campaign, appealing directly for the second or third preferences of minor party supporters, offering policy concessions on key issues and arguing that the Labor Party was far closer to their core interests than the major alternative, the Liberal–National Coalition (see Hughes 1990, 140–51). To see how this type of campaign for second preferences worked in practice, consider the victory of the Labor Party's Neville Newell in the seat of Richmond, in northern New South Wales. Newell scored only 27 per cent of the first preference vote. The Coalition candidate (and then leader of the National Party) Charles Blunt won over 41 per cent of first

Table 3.2. *Allocation of preferences in division of Richmond, 1990*

Candidate	First count	Second count	Third count	Fourth count	Fifth count	Sixth Count	Final Count
Gibbs (Australian Democrats)	4,346	4,380	4,420	4,504	4,683	Excluded	Excluded
Newell (Australian Labor Party)	18,423	18,467	18,484	18,544	18,683	20,238	34,664 (Elected)
Baillie (Independent)	187	Excluded	Excluded	Excluded	Excluded	Excluded	Excluded
Sims (Call to Australia Party)	1,032	1,053	1,059	1,116	Excluded	Excluded	Excluded
Paterson (Independent)	445	480	530	Excluded	Excluded	Excluded	Excluded
Leggett (Independent)	279	294	Excluded	Excluded	Excluded	Excluded	Excluded
Blunt (National Party)	28,257	28,274	28,303	28,416	28,978	29,778	33,980
Caldicott (Independent)	16,072	16,091	16,237	16,438	16,658	18,903	Excluded

Source: Australian Electoral Commission, 1990.

preferences, and looked set for an easy victory. However, the count saw a combination of preferences from minor parties and independents, especially the anti-nuclear campaigner Helen Caldicott, flow through to Newell and enable him to win the seat with 50.5 per cent of the full preference vote.

Newell won the seat because he was able to secure over three-quarters of Caldicott's preferences when she was excluded at the seventh count. Caldicott herself had received the majority of preferences from the other independent candidates. This scenario was repeated in numerous other electorates, helping Labor claim a solid national victory. The Labor Party in Richmond, as in other seats, was thus the beneficiary of a strategy aimed at maximising not just its own vote but also the preferences it received from others: the 'second preference' strategy, as it became widely known. This strategy was markedly successful: with minor party support levels at an all-time high of around 17 per cent, Labor was the beneficiary of around two-thirds of all lower-order preferences from Democrat and Green voters – a figure which probably made the difference between it winning and losing the election (Papadakis and Bean 1995, 103–4). This was thus a 'win-win' situation for both groups:

the ALP gained government with less than 40 per cent of the first-preference vote, while the minor parties, who did not win any lower house seats, nonetheless saw their preferred major party in government and committed to favourable policies in their areas of concern.

Wider impacts

As has been pointed out already, elections held under AV rules enable the votes of several aligned candidates to be accumulated, so that diverse but related electoral interests can be marshalled successfully without the vote being 'split' several ways. The long-standing coalition agreement between the Liberal and National parties in Australia is probably the best example of this arrangement working in practice. This allows both Coalition parties to independently stand candidates in so-called 'three-cornered contests' against Labor, enabling them to direct preferences to each other: the common tactic of 'preference-swapping', as preference-based vote-pooling strategies are known in Australia. It is questionable, in fact, whether the Coalition agreement could have been maintained under a different electoral system which did not allow preference-swapping. Because preferential voting is one of the few electoral systems which sets up a coalition formation phase *before* elections rather than after them, it thus encourages the intertwining of coalition formation with the politics of electoral competition. Conversely, there is evidence that AV allows voters to punish parties that fragment internally, giving political leaders powerful incentives to maintain party unity (Jackman 1992).

Preference distribution in Australian politics has almost never facilitated the common collaboration of the two major parties, Labor and the Coalition, against a common foe. One graphic exception to this rule, however, was at the 1998 federal election, due to the rising power of Pauline Hanson and her One Nation party. Ms Hanson was an endorsed Liberal Party candidate at the 1996 election in the Labor stronghold seat of Oxley, in the outer suburbs of Brisbane. After making a series of uncomplimentary remarks about Australia's Aborigines in the lead-up to polling day, she simultaneously achieved national media notoriety and Liberal disendorsement. Nonetheless, she appeared on the ballot as a Liberal candidate and was elected with a huge swing in her favour. She went on to form a new political party, One Nation, whose ideology represented a distinctively Australian version of the populist right-wing racist parties that had appeared in many European countries during the 1990s. One Nation campaigned on a platform of ending immigration, removing benefits and subsidies to Aborigines and other disadvantaged groups, drastically cutting taxation rates, raising tariffs, ending all foreign aid and removing Australia from international bodies such as the United Nations.

Following a protracted period of national and international media attention, the major parties decided effectively to eliminate what they saw as a dangerous aberration in the political system by bringing their combined forces to bear against One Nation in general, and Hanson in particular. One potent way of doing this was via the suggested distribution of preferences that the parties recommended to their supporters via the general media and the instructions on their 'how-to-vote' cards. At the 1998 election in the federal seat of Blair, which Hanson contested as One Nation leader, both major parties (i.e. Labor and the Liberal–National Coalition) instructed their supporters to place her *last* in their order of preference when marking their ballot (in contrast to the more familiar tactic of suggesting their major party opponent – from Labor or the Coalition, as the case may be – be placed last). The result was an instructive lesson in the capacity of the 'moderate middle' under AV to defeat an extremist candidate who commands significant core support but ultimately repels more voters than he or she attracts. Coming first in a nine-candidate field before the distribution of preferences, Hanson achieved the highest first preference total with 36 per cent of the vote. But she received very few preference transfers from other candidates. As the count progressed into its final exclusion, with the elimination of Labor candidate Virginia Clarke, fully 73.7 per cent of Clarke's preferences went to a Liberal, Cameron Thompson, who thus won the seat with 53.4 per cent of the overall (preference-distributed) vote, even though he was only the *third* highest polling candidate on first preferences (14,787), being outpolled by both Hanson (24,516) and Clarke (17,239). This pattern was repeated in less dramatic fashion in other seats around the country, and saw One Nation largely eliminated from federal politics (although it did win one seat in the Senate). By contrast, the almost certain result under FPTP would have seen Hanson beating a divided field of more moderate candidates and taking a seat in the federal parliament. This example demonstrates the capacity of AV to privilege centrist interests and centripetal political strategies in a potentially divisive situation.

A possibly even more important consequence of the major parties' decision to direct preferences away from One Nation came in the New South Wales Senate contest. Due to the conservative parties' decision to direct preferences away from One Nation, a newcomer – Aden Ridgeway of the Australian Democrats – gained a Senate seat following the exclusion of the National Party's Sandy McDonald, when preference votes from the National Party and other excluded candidates flowed predominantly away from One Nation and, by default, towards the Democrats. This in itself was an unusual outcome, as on most indicators the rural-based National Party's policies and voter base have much more in common with the 'rural poor' supporters of One Nation than with the urban, centre-left Democrats. But even more significant was the fact that Ridgeway is an Australian Aboriginal. He thus became only the second indigenous Australian (after Neville Bonner) to be elected to the federal parliament.[3] As such, Ridgeway was widely credited as playing a mediating role as a representative of indigenous culture and interests *vis-à-vis* white society. Few commentators, however, noticed the irony of Ridgeway's presence being a consequence of the Coalition's decision to eschew One Nation preference votes, to the extent that Ridgeway's election meant that a Labor candidate rather than a National was elected to the final New South Wales Senate vacancy via the transfer of the Democrats' 'surplus' preference votes. Fewer still noticed that if a standard, non-preferential form of proportional representation – such as a party list PR system – had been used, One Nation would have gained the final Senate seat and Ridgeway would have missed out.

This type of self-denying political behaviour on the part of the major parties remains relatively unusual, however. In most cases, preferences are used to aggregate common interests on either the labour or conservative sides of politics rather than align those interests against a common enemy. Indeed, most analyses of the effects of AV in Australia have tended to concentrate almost exclusively on its partisan impacts. Some commentators have seen the system as an instrument for maintaining the dominance of the two major parties and for restricting the role of minor parties in the lower house to one of influencing the policies of the major parties rather than gaining election themselves (Hughes 1977, 294). Others claim that it can enhance the power and position of minor parties, especially if they have the potential to hold the balance of power between two major parties (Aitkin, Jinks and Warhurst 1989, 150). There is widespread agreement that AV has facilitated coalition arrangements, such as that between the Liberal and National parties, and that it works to the advantage of centre candidates and parties, encouraging moderate policy positions and a search for the middle ground: 'generally, the preferential voting system, in combination with compulsory voting, helps "centre" parties to be influential' (Bean 1986, 65). Graham (1962) argues

---

[3] His impact in national politics was immediately apparent in the drafting of a proposed new preamble to the Constitution (which included a much discussed reference to aboriginal 'custodianship' of Australia's land prior to European colonisation) and, soon after, in the drafting of a statement of regret by the government for the 'stolen children' policies – Aboriginal children forcibly removed from their parents to live with white families – of previous decades.

that the advantage AV gives to centre parties has actually been its most distinctive (and, in the Australian context, unexpected) feature.

Conclusion

A core normative argument in favour of all preferential voting systems is that by granting voters the capacity to indicate a range and gradation of preferences between parties and candidates, rather than a single 'one-shot' choice, incentives are created for office-seeking politicians to campaign for these secondary preference votes and thus to bargain, cooperate and compromise in search of electoral victory. While this type of behaviour does occur in Australian elections, it is often seen as a secondary aspect of political activity by the news media and the general public alike. But Australian politicians, like those elsewhere, respond to the rules of the electoral game, and to the incentives or constraints inherent in these rules. Whereas most electoral systems act as a zero-sum game, in which there is rarely an incentive to bargain (much less cooperate) with rival candidates, under some circumstances preferential voting can encourage precisely this type of behaviour, thus operating as a positive-sum game for many players. Labor's victory on the back of minor party preferences at the 1990 election was one example of this; the major parties' collaboration to defeat One Nation by preference-swapping at the 1998 election was another. The sometimes fiery and aggressive rhetoric of Australian politics has often distracted observers from recognising just how much cooperative behaviour there is between parties – via preference-swapping deals, for example – and how close the major parties are on most substantive policy issues. It would appear that preferential voting, particularly in its AV form, provides significant institutional encouragement for these centrist tendencies.

In theory, on a left–right policy spectrum such as Australia's, presuming that preferences are 'single peaked', AV should provide the strongest centrist incentives of all the preferential systems, due to its majority threshold for victory and the bottom-up sequence of elimination of excluded candidates. At Australian elections, for example, in any three-way contest between candidates A (right wing), B (centre) and C (left wing), the centre candidate, B, should be the second choice of those who vote for both A and C. As a result, candidate B will usually have high prospects of receiving preferences from each of his or her two rivals and would therefore stand an excellent chance of winning every contest from which either candidate A or C was excluded. One analysis thus concluded that the application of AV in a system of right, centre and left parties 'results in a high proportion of centre victories in constituencies where political forces are evenly balanced. In the long run, such victories could have the cumulative effect of exaggerating the electoral and parliamentary strength of the centre party' (Graham 1962, 186). While the benefits of victory for such 'centrist' parties in normal situations of competitive elections are debatable, their benefits in deeply divided societies, which are often characterised by an absence of moderation and a lack of centrist politics, are much clearer. And it is to divided societies that we now turn in the next three chapters, examining the impact of preferential voting in Papua New Guinea, Fiji, Sri Lanka, Estonia and Northern Ireland.

4

The rise and fall of centripetalism in Papua New Guinea

One of the abiding influences of colonial rule tends to be the transfer of political institutions from the metropolitan power to the newly autonomous or independent colony. This tendency is well illustrated by the choice of electoral systems by new, post-colonial democracies since the Second World War: nearly all the former British colonies in the developing world at independence adopted Westminster-style systems of government featuring first-past-the-post electoral systems, just as the former Spanish, Belgian and Dutch colonies initially imitated the PR electoral rules of their colonisers (see Reynolds and Reilly 1997; Reilly and Reynolds 1999). Australia's modest twentieth-century experience as the administering trustee for successive League of Nations and United Nations mandates over the South Pacific 'external territories' of Papua New Guinea and Nauru was consistent with these trends.[1] The state of Papua New Guinea (see Map 1), which comprises roughly half of the world's second largest island, New Guinea, and about 600 smaller islands, was formed by the merger at independence of the Territory of Papua, which had been under Australian rule from 1906, with the Trust Territory of New Guinea, which had been a German colonial territory from 1884 to 1914, and had thenceforth been administered by Australia – first under military rule, then under a League of Nations mandate granted in 1920, and later under United Nations trusteeship from 1945. The two territories were jointly administered by Australia as an administrative union until independence in 1975. Papua New Guinea adopted the Australian electoral system of the

---

[1] For one of the few discussions of politics in Nauru, see Crocombe and Giese 1988.

alternative vote, slightly modified for local conditions,[2] for its first three elections in 1964, 1968 and 1972, before moving to a FPTP system at independence in 1975.

As Horowitz (1985, 602) has noted, now and then political systems create quasi-experimental conditions under which propositions can be tested. In many ways, Papua New Guinea represents such an approximation of experimental conditions, by virtue of its historical isolation (most of the country had no contact with the outside world until the 1930s), the strength of its traditional society, and its general lack of exposure to external influences. This meant that the series of nationwide elections which began in the 1960s, as part of the Australian administration's preparation for self-government and independence was, for many Papua New Guineans, the first national event in which they had participated. Even today, in some remote areas, the five-yearly cycle of candidate selection, campaigning and polling may be one of the only times that many villagers have an opportunity to interact with the state.[3] The most important reason for our examining Papua New Guinean elections, however, is because its use of a vote-pooling electoral system (AV) for the first three elections, and the subsequent change to a non-vote-pooling system (FPTP), provides an excellent model of a quasi-experimental research structure. While there were several significant changes to other variables at the same time as the change of electoral system in Papua New Guinea (in particular, the attainment of independence and the withdrawal of the Australian colonial apparatus), the major elements of a competitive political system such as an elected legislature, mass suffrage elections, and a nascent party system were already in place prior to the change of electoral rules. In addition, a number of the Papua New Guinean political actors quoted in this chapter experienced elections under both systems, and are thus in a position to compare their experiences accordingly. It is therefore possible to make meaningful and specific comparisons about the effects of the two electoral systems in a way that would not be possible under a country-by-country study.

For all of these reasons, Papua New Guinea functions as what Eckstein (1992, 117–76) calls a 'crucial case study' for the evaluation of

---

[2] Papua New Guinea's *Electoral Ordinance 1963* was, for the most part, a direct copy of the Australian *Commonwealth Electoral Act 1918*, a situation which led to unexpected problems when it was realised that the optional AV system used in Papua New Guinea was incompatible with the requirement, lifted from the Australian act, that a candidate must receive an absolute majority of all ballot papers, including exhausted ballot papers, to be elected. See Hughes and van der Veur 1965, 412–16.

[3] I am indebted to Hank Nelson for this point.

centripetalism. It also demonstrates the very different impacts of AV and FPTP in ethnically diverse societies. This distinction is important because the two systems, which actually possess markedly different institutional incentives, are often lumped together and classified as analogous 'majoritarian' procedures in the electoral studies literature. Lijphart, for example, states that AV and FPTP are both 'a perfect reflection of majoritarian philosophy: the candidate supported by the largest number of voters wins, and all other voters remain unrepresented' (1984, 150). While indeed similar in many ways, the effects of these two systems in terms of the incentives they provide for accommodative political behaviour are sometimes very different – in fact, in some ways they can be seen as polar opposites when applied to a highly fragmented social and political structure. This chapter examines how these two electoral systems have encouraged very different types of election campaigning, political behaviour and political outcomes.

Democracy and ethnic conflict in Papua New Guinea

Like its national symbol, the *kumul*,[4] Papua New Guinea is a rare bird which combines two unusual features for the purposes of comparative study. First, Papua New Guinea has one of the longest records of continuous democracy in the developing world, with highly competitive national elections having been held without interruption since 1964. Having attained self-government in 1973 and independence in 1975, Papua New Guinea is also one of the founding members of Huntington's 'third wave' of democracy (1991, 24), and an unusual example of an economically underdeveloped 'Third World' country which has nonetheless been able to maintain democratic government and meaningful elections. With a population of approximately 4 million people, predominantly of Melanesian race, Papua New Guinea is also an extraordinarily culturally fragmented country. With no common history of statehood, 'its people are fragmented into hundreds of often mutually antipathetic ethnic groupings' (Hegarty 1979, 188). At the latest count, approximately 840 distinct languages were spoken in Papua New Guinea – around a quarter of the world's stock – reflecting enormous cultural divisions. Given this, Papua New Guinea is almost certainly the world's most ethnically fragmented state in terms of the sheer numbers of independent ethno-linguistic groups: 'in a very real sense the country is a nation of minorities' (Minority Rights Group 1997, 682). Observers of Papua New Guinea politics have long argued that its ethnic fragmentation represents

---

[4] The Pidgin word for 'bird of paradise'.

a 'formidable and intractable' impediment to nation-building (Premdas 1989, 246), and that Papua New Guinea's '10,000 micro-societies' and hundreds of language groups, the largest of which numbers only 150,000 people, presents an almost insurmountable barrier to stable democracy (Griffin 1974, 142–3).

Modern representative politics has been strongly influenced by the fractionalised nature of Papua New Guinea's traditional society, which is based around several thousand competing 'clans' or extended family units. The combination of extended democratic government with exceptionally high levels of ethnic fragmentation thus offers tremendous potential for studies of the relationship between democracy, political institutions and ethnic conflict. In addition, while it is a relatively rare example of democratic longevity in the developing world, on many indicators the quality of Papua New Guinea's democracy has been in steady decline since independence. Representative democracy in Papua New Guinea has increasingly come to be characterised by a diffuse and fragmented party system, high candidacy rates, very low support levels for some successful candidates, vote splitting, low party identification on the part of the electorate, high turnover of politicians from one election to the next, frequent 'party-hopping' on the part of parliamentarians and, as a consequence, weak and unstable executive government. No-confidence motions have become a staple feature of Papua New Guinea's parliamentary politics – to the extent that to date *every* elected government since independence has been deposed on the floor of parliament without reference to an election. Table 4.1 details the changes of executive government since independence.

Despite the relative obscurity of Papua New Guinea for academic scholarship, there has been an invaluable series of election studies published after each of the country's general elections to date (these are Bettison *et al.* 1965; Epstein *et al.* 1971; Stone 1976; Hegarty 1983; King 1989; Oliver 1989; Saffu 1996) – although these studies have concentrated overwhelmingly on a seat-by-seat description and analysis of election campaigns, with minimal attention paid to formal election rules or the way these rules influence styles of political competition. This reflects the preoccupations of the respective authors and editors: Papua New Guinean elections are often interpreted as clashes between traditional culture and the modern world of representative politics, the 'counterpoint between traditional and modern bases for status-competition' in the words of one observer (Strathern 1976, 283). Taken together, however, the election studies enable us to chart the effects of the introduction and then the rejection of centripetal incentives in a divided, fragmented and adversarial new democracy.

Table 4.1. *Changes of executive government in Papua New Guinea,*
1975–2000

Year	Previous prime minister	New prime minister	Reason for change
1975	–	Michael Somare	Independence
1977	Somare retains prime ministership after general election		
1980	Michael Somare	Julius Chan	No-confidence vote
1982	Julius Chan	Michael Somare	General election
1985	Michael Somare	Paias Wingti	No-confidence vote
1987	Wingti retains prime ministership after general election		
1988	Paias Wingti	Rabbie Namaliu	
1992	Rabbie Namaliu	Paias Wingti	General election
1994	Paias Wingti	Julius Chan	Judicial decision[a]
1997	Julius Chan	Bill Skate	General election
1999	Bill Skate	Mekere Morauta	No-confidence vote

Note: [a] The judicial decision was the result of events in September 1993, when
the then prime minister, Paias Wingti, organised a constitutionally questionable parliamentary manoeuvre: a surprise resignation and immediate parliamentary re-election after 14 months in office in order to circumvent a
constitutional provision permitting votes of no confidence after 18 months in
office, thus gaining another 18 months of valuable governing time. In August
1994, the Supreme Court ruled that the resignation was valid but that the
constitutional requirements of the re-election had not been met, thus forcing
a new election by the parliament which enabled Wingti's former deputy, Sir
Julius Chan, to return to the prime ministership.

Ethnicity and elections

Agreeing on what constitutes an 'ethnic group' in Papua New Guinea is
no easy task. Some scholars define an ethnic group as a collection of
people who see themselves as a distinct cultural community, often sharing
a 'common language, religion, kinship, and/or physical characteristics
(such as skin colour); and who tend to harbour negative and hostile
feelings towards members of other groups' (Lijphart 1995b, 853). This is
quite a broad definition of ethnicity, including as it does reference to
factors such as race and religion. Other authors contrast this with a
'narrower definition' of ethnic identity which denotes a community
claiming common origins, possessing distinctive and valued cultural
markers such as custom, dress and, especially, language, and expecting to
share a common destiny (Esman 1994, 15). This narrower definition may

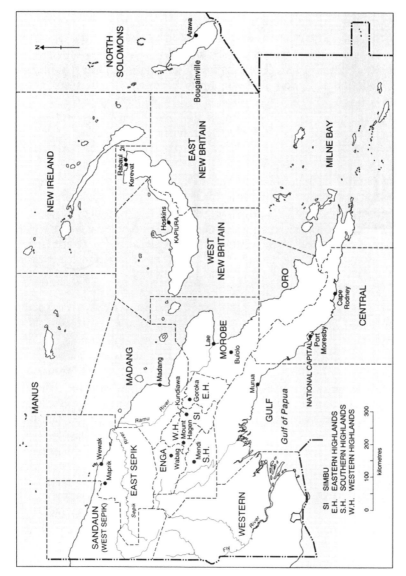

Map 1 Papua New Guinea

63

be more applicable to Papua New Guinea, where groups are divided less on overt ascriptive criteria such as race or religion than on kinship, custom, language and regional ties. Levine writes that 'if ethnic communities are understood to be groups possessing a distinctive language, custom and memories – traits that give its members a sense of unity and cause them to distinguish themselves from (and be distinguished by) others – then Papua New Guinea may have more than one thousand such ethnic groups within its borders' (1997, 479).

Part of the difficulty of defining what constitutes an ethnic group in Papua New Guinea is the sheer variation of its ethnic structure, which limits the ability to make generalisations. For example, in lowlands areas the population of ethno-linguistic units normally ranges from a few hundred to four or five thousand, whereas in the highlands regions, home to most of Papua New Guinea's population and its most competitive and violent inter-ethnic relations, these groups may number up to 60,000 persons (de Lepervanche 1973, 1065). For our purposes, an ethnic group constitutes any of these larger or smaller cultural-linguistic groupings which can be distinguished on the basis of a common identity and perceptions of common origin and concerns.

At the root of PNG's unusual social structure are unilateral descent groups often known as clans – ascriptive extended family networks which are the primary, and sometimes the only, unit of political and social loyalty in many areas (see Hogbin 1973, 23). Considering the lack of overt racial distinction between them, the depth of cleavages between clan groups is often striking, and can be partly explained by two related factors: geography and language. Papua New Guinea has some of the world's most dramatic terrain, with a vast range of mountains and valleys running though the middle of the mainland ('the highlands'), and an extensive arc of populated volcanic islands off the coast – all of which create severe difficulties in terms of access, transport and isolation. Accordingly, 'most groups developed their own physical and cultural identity in isolation . . . communities living on different sides of the same highland valley sometimes speak languages as distinct from one another as Spanish is from Italian' (Souter 1963, 49). While few groups were entirely isolated, and many had 'ally' clans with which they conducted trade and marriage, relations between many of them were characterised as much by hostility as by cooperation. Traditional contact in the highlands, for example, often took the form of intermittent tribal warfare between clan groups (see Reay 1982, 630–6). Moreover, within the main language groups themselves, there are often deep and bitter internal divisions (see de Lepervanche 1973, 1066).

There has been little detailed assessment of the total number of ethnic groups in Papua New Guinea, but estimates from informed observers are in the region of 5,000–7,000 separate groups.[5] This means that Papua New Guinea is one of the most heterogeneous societies anywhere in terms of the number of distinct polities (which continue to be based, overwhelmingly, on ascriptive ethnic identities), with estimates of the number of separate political units ranging from 2,000 to 18,000.[6] If a larger unit of base measurement is used, such as 'tribes' (i.e. aligned or related clan groupings), then we are still dealing with an extremely fragmented society: a rough average of 2,000 members per tribe against Papua New Guinea's total population of approximately 4 million people gives a figure of around 2,000 separate tribes. Even using conservative figures, we are dealing with a level of fragmentation that makes divided societies elsewhere look relatively homogeneous by comparison.

Despite this extraordinary degree of fragmentation, ethnic identity in Papua New Guinea, as elsewhere, tends to be manifested as a mixture of primordial and constructed factors.[7] Many analyses of ethnicity in Papua New Guinea, for example, emphasise the extent to which ethnic identities are both a salient feature of traditional society and also a reaction to colonialism, modernisation and independence (see Premdas 1989, 246). Unsurprisingly, descriptions of 'traditional' ethnic identities in Papua New Guinea tend to privilege primordial characteristics of ascription, competition and dynamism. Parker and Wolfers characterised the traditional situation in Papua New Guinea as one in which

> political entities . . . were both relatively unstable and small. Not many effective political units contained more than a few hundred people, although on occasions thousands might co-operate for a specific battle, or in trade and ceremonial exchange. Membership of even the smallest primary groups was unstable – as people married in and out, disputes arose between rival leaders, and inter-group warfare forced some members of each group to choose between the claims to their loyalties of, say, their residential or their kin group. (1971, 16)

Primordial factors remain salient at virtually all levels of Papua New Guinea politics. Political loyalties tend to be focussed primarily at the level of family, clan and regional allegiances, rather than along party or ideological lines: 'most Papua New Guinea people maintain a mind-set of primary attachment and loyalty to their clan and tribal group' (Standish

---

[5] Personal communication, Dr Bill Standish, Research School of Pacific and Asian Studies, Australian National University, 28 September 1996.
[6] Personal communication, Dr John Burton, Research School of Pacific and Asian Studies, Australian National University, 24 December 1996.
[7] For a discussion of this typology in the scholarly literature, see Esman 1994, 9–16.

1994, 60). Ethnicity thus taps deep levels of socialisation, experience and culture, with the result that 'instinctive loyalty, as well as considerations of personal and family security and of group sanctions, tie individuals to their ethnic community, especially under conditions of intergroup tension and conflict' (Esman 1994, 15). The political consequences of ethnicity in Papua New Guinea tend to be manifested in different ways from the extended family, clan and tribal level up to regional allegiances, even extending to those based on the colonial divisions of the state between Papua and New Guinea (Parker and Wolfers 1971, 16–17). The strength of ethnic attachments is thus dependent to a significant extent upon social context. Demographically, Papua New Guinea is also fragmented not just at the clan, village and immediate region level, but also along the overarching geographical axes of south coast (Papua), north coast (New Guinea), highlands and islands as well – and identities often extend into these larger regional levels in addition to the clan or village ones (Standish 1994, 60).

Discussions of ethnic conflict and politics often focus on the concept of political cleavage – alignments of a population around particular social dimensions which are conducive to conflict between them (see Rae and Taylor 1970). In Papua New Guinea, the nature of such cleavages tends to be manifested at several levels. The most important conflicts to date have been at the macro level, in terms of ethno-nationalist movements and secessionist struggles (see Premdas 1977; May 1982). By far the most persistent and deadly of these has been the long-running civil war on Bougainville, which has claimed several thousand lives to date (see Regan 1998). Most conflicts in Papua New Guinea, however, are manifested not at the ethno-nationalist level, but at the local level, as violence between Papua New Guinea's many small, competitive ethnic groups. The nature of ethnic conflict between these groups is traditionally played out locally, often via inter-tribal fighting, rather than as part of an ethno-nationalist quest or a competition for regional or national hegemony, although it is no less deadly for that. Over 100 people are killed every year in tribal fights in Papua New Guinea (Dorney 1990, 310). Reports have estimated that around 20 per cent of the population is affected by such violence, with a marked concentration in highlands regions (Clifford, Morauta and Stuart 1984, 94–5). Recently, guns have supplanted more traditional weapons in tribal wars, thus raising the stakes and increasing the deadliness of such clashes (Dorney 1990, 310–11). Barnes claims that 'a characteristic of Highlands cultures, and perhaps of Melanesia as a whole, is the high value placed on violence' (as quoted in May 1982, 641), and it is notable that conflicts between clan groups in many parts of Papua New Guinea are considerably more violent than those between communities in 'deeply divided' states such as Malaysia, Fiji, Trinidad and Tobago and many other plural societies.

The imposition of representative government via competitive national elections has tended to sharpen ethnic distinctions, as the salience of ethnicity in Papua New Guinea 'tends to come to the fore . . . during national election campaigns' (Howard 1989, 45). It is thus perhaps not surprising that, particularly in recent decades, ethnic violence has increased at election time (Strathern 1993, 51). Elections in Papua New Guinea often have the effect of underlining the significance of basic clan or village-level ethnic attachments. Premdas notes that 'the general electoral pattern since the introduction of universal adult suffrage in 1964 and through subsequent elections . . . has underscored unequivocally that ethnic identity, usually at the *ples tok* [i.e. village language] level, is the foremost determinant of voter preference' (1989, 251). Especially in pre-independence elections, there appears to have been a high correlation between ethnic affiliation and voting behaviour. Parker's analysis of the 1968 election found that most indigenous candidates 'commanded a more or less automatic bloc vote. Its core was usually to be found in their own or their more notable relatives' kinship or clan groups' (1971, 316). More recent elections, however, have illustrated the increasing importance of other factors – such as education and familiarity with the skills and occupational experience of the modern world – as influences upon voting choice (Saffu 1989). But post-independence elections have also encouraged a 'retribalisation' of ethnic groups, in which the commodification of the voting process has led increasingly to rigidified ethnic group boundaries and inter-ethnic armed conflict (Strathern 1993, 48). Elections are thus one of the primary ways in which traditional enmities are mobilised in contemporary Papua New Guinea, even though in most cases contestation is very much for election to office itself, rather than larger concerns such as policy implementation, government formation or national ideology (Dinnen 1996; Standish 1996). Traditional clan, tribe and *wantok* affiliations remain for the most part ascriptive and competitive categories, sometimes violently so, and continue to represent the primary, but far from the only, explanation of voting behaviour. In this sense, the politicised nature of ethnic conflict in Papua New Guinea via clan contests for electoral victory is comparable to the less fragmented cases of ethnic groups in conflict found in many other countries.

One of the most striking aspects of the relationship between ethnic conflict and elections in Papua New Guinea is the way in which the electoral system itself appears to have played a key mediating role. As this chapter discusses, it became clear relatively soon after the introduction of AV in 1964 that the vote-pooling capacity of preferential voting made it

particularly well suited to Papua New Guinea's fragmented social structure. By enabling electors to make a second or third choice of candidate
beyond their first, preferential voting allowed ethnic voters to reconcile
two divergent aims: the need to vote for their own 'local' ethnic candidate
(who almost invariably received the first preference) and the desire to
vote, using secondary preferences, for the candidate of their choice (who
would often be someone from outside their own immediate area). Despite
these useful characteristics, the electoral system was changed to FPTP at
independence in 1975. Given Papua New Guinea's highly fragmented
clan-based society, this led to a very different kind of electoral competition, with little incentive for cross-ethnic voting and increasingly high
levels of dummy candidature, vote splitting and electoral violence. This
chapter suggests that there is clear evidence that the move away from a
vote-pooling electoral system has been an important institutional impetus
for these trends, and consequently that the electoral system itself has acted
as a key variable in first suppressing, and then encouraging, the mobilisation of tribal politics at elections.

The alternative vote in Papua New Guinea

The introduction of AV in Papua New Guinea was a straightforward
example of an institutional transfer from colonial power – in this case,
Australia – to colony noted earlier. As early as 1962, the first report of the
Australian parliament's Select Committee on Political Development in
Papua New Guinea, which was charged with making recommendations
on the then territory's future representative institutions, reported that it
favoured an AV electoral system as 'giving the fairest result' for a tribal
society like Papua New Guinea's (Hughes 1965, 36). This recommendation, which was readily accepted by both the colonial administration in
Papua New Guinea and the Australian government, saw preferential
voting effectively transplanted from a Western society to a developing-
world one (Hughes and van der Veur 1965, 406). In no sense was the
introduction of AV an example of conscious constitutional engineering;
as Wolfers noted at the time, the principal *raison d'être* for the introduction of preferential voting was that it was the system used in Australia
(1968b, 29). In 1970, however, the Electoral Commission of Inquiry into
Electoral Procedures (ECIEP) argued that AV was particularly well suited
to Papua New Guinea's fragmented social structure, because if voters 'are
unable to gather enough votes to have their "local" man elected then their
next preference is a man who can adequately represent them in the House
because he is literate, articulate and able to move freely throughout the
electorate [and] represent all groups without prejudice' (ECIEP 1970, 2).

The adoption of AV in Papua New Guinea was thus an example of the law of unintended consequences at work: in many ways, the social conditions present there were, as we shall see, almost uniquely well suited to the use of a system which aggregated fragmented political choices to produce an overall majority victor.

AV was first used to elect members of Papua New Guinea's (largely appointed) Legislative Council in the early 1960s under what was known as the 'College Electoral System'. This involved electors physically queuing up behind the candidate of their choice in what the chief electoral officer called a system of 'open preferential voting':

> If, on a count, no candidate had an absolute majority, i.e. more than half the voters present lined up behind him, then the candidate with the least number of voters behind him moved away and his supporters redistributed themselves amongst other candidates ... this physical act of distributing one's person to the candidate of one's choice and, if he be eliminated, to one's next choice, was simple and understandable in the eyes of the voter. (Chief Electoral Officer 1968, 32)

While simple, such a system ignored the basic precept of the secrecy of the ballot, and was not practical for mass-suffrage elections. Papua New Guinea's first three national elections in 1964, 1968 and 1972 were therefore held under the optional preferential vote (OPV), a slight modification of the 'full preferential' AV method used for federal elections in Australia. Electors were required to express a first preference (defined as the number 1) for a candidate, and then given the option of marking as many further preferences (2, 3, 4 etc.) for other candidates as they so chose. Given Papua New Guinea's clan-based social structure, this meant that the first preference vote would almost invariably go to the candidate representing the voter's own ethnic group, but that 'After casting his first preference, and being virtually committed to do so . . . from within his ethnic group, the voter then feels free to make his own judgement of the remaining candidates in order of preference' (ECIEP 1970, 1).

In practice, low literacy rates meant that most electors were not capable of independently numbering preferences themselves, so the institution of the 'whispering ballot' – electors verbally expressing their preferences to a polling officer, who would mark the ballot paper for them – was extensively used (see Wolfers 1968b, 25). In a further departure from Australian practice, it was reasoned that it would not be necessary to compel voters to express preferences for all candidates (hence the description of the system as 'optional preferential'), as a direct imitation of the Australian system would have seen numbering mistakes render a ballot paper invalid – which would have had dramatic ramifications considering Papua New Guinea's low literacy rates.[8] Similarly, the Australian system of compulsory voting was not introduced 'because of the novelty of the elections and the problems of terrain and climate' (Hughes and van der Veur 1965, 406). With those important exceptions, the remainder of the Territory's electoral ordinance was a direct copy of the Australian electoral act.

Not surprisingly, the complexity of preference marking was an ongoing source of concern at Papua New Guinea's first nationwide election in 1964. Reay, for example, found that 'the bulk of electors never grasped the mechanics of the distribution of preferences and many placed misguided interpretations on orders of preferences' (1965, 151). Nevertheless, in the highlands electorates she was studying, electors 'were well accustomed to choosing between two alternatives and many compounded sets of such choices to construct their first two preferences' (1965, 155). Despite difficulties, investigations found that voters valued being able to split and aggregate their choices in this way. An official inquiry into electoral procedures found that:

> practically without exception people . . . placed emphasis on the right of the elector to exercise his choice of preferences, as far as he wished to go . . . Questioning . . . failed to produce evidence that the majority of voters could not intelligently cast preferences and that they did not understand the value of such preferences. Rejection of 'First Past the Post' by the majority stemmed from their fear that the 'big line' or preponderance of one particular ethnic group, would always win the election and 'boss' them. It was obvious to the Commission that this is a very real fear, and quite definite rejection of 'First Past the Post' by the majority of the people is based on this fear. (ECIEP 1970, 2)

A standard practice was to cast a first preference for a local clan candidate, and then a second preference for a knowledgeable outsider – 'preference votes given probably favour the educated Papuan or New Guinean who has come from another district, or the expatriate candidate' (ECIEP 1970, 2). Scholars at the time observed that, in general, 'a remarkable proportion of the voters was able to indicate a rational, that is, a rationally ordered, set of preferences' (Wikfers 1966, 79). Disciplined preference-seeking campaigning by some candidates took full advantage of this.

---

[8] The Papua New Guinea Electoral Commission supported a move to full preferential voting after the initial first-past-the-post elections in 1977. They argued that the optional nature of preference marking under the optional preferential system meant that 'voting results tend to swing towards that' of first-past-the-post (see Papua New Guinea Electoral Commission 1983, 78).

Case study: Kaindi and Henganofi electorates, 1964

A number of electoral strategies based on winning preference votes were reported at the 1964 elections, with probably the most successful exponent being that employed by the expatriate candidate Bill Bloomfield, in the electorate of Kaindi, who emerged as the winner of the seat after the preferences of seven candidates had been distributed. Without a strong local support base or home area, Bloomfield campaigned extensively, translated his speeches into local language and emphasised that if electors did not want to give him their first preference 'then give me number two'. It was an extremely effective strategy which saw him carry a seat that he would have had no chance of winning on first preferences (see Hughes and van der Veur 1965, 409). Table 4.2 shows the extent of preference-swapping with indigenous candidates that Bloomfield achieved in winning the seat.

While preferences were distributed in the majority of electorates in 1964, the final result was different to a FPTP contest in only 5 of the 44 electorates: Henganofi, Tari, Kaindi, Markham and South Markham Special. Henganofi provided a classic example of the way the use of preferences by supporters of aligned candidates can overcome a single dominant plurality winner (see Table 4.3). Candidate Bono, with massive support from his own region but negligible support elsewhere, lost to candidate Ugi, situated in the centre of the electorate and attracting a less partisan but considerably broader range of support. Ugi was well behind on first preferences, but gained the majority of all other candidate's preferences to win the seat.

As Wolfers noted, Ugi's victory was a 'quite remarkable' example of the way inter-group preference-swapping could result in the election of a broadly acceptable candidate, and the outcome 'was a tribute to the highly rational voting of his supporters, who were able to make a complex system of voting produce the desired result' (1966, 79).

The real significance of these examples of strategic preference-swapping was the pointer they give to a characteristic that emerged more strongly in later elections: regional alliances and cooperation between candidates. In the following election in 1968, for example, the presence of preferential voting began to stimulate alliances for mutual support between two or more candidates in a number of different electorates. Parker noted in the 1968 election study that 'most chapters give examples of mutual aid amongst candidates in the course of campaigning. The commonest form of this was the sharing of transport and of "platforms" at election meetings' (1971, 321). In a verdict that could not be repeated in regard to contemporary elections, the field teams in 1968 saw such cooperative

Table 4.2. *Result of the count in Kaindi electorate, 1964*

	Sue Kate	Bill Bloomfield	Anani Manlau	Ninga Yamung	David Iti	Mangi Iom	James Gould	Monbong	Isom Kala	Exhausted[a]	Total votes
First pref. votes for each candidate	1,842	4,583	3,372	1,188	5,425	369	254	801	1,377	–	19,211
254 votes of GOULD transferred	1,852	4,686	3,388	1,208	5,440	388	Excluded	824	1,392	33	19,211
388 votes of IOM transferred	1,913	4,720	3,397	1,225	5,456	Excluded	–	939	1,460	101	19,211
939 votes of MONBONG transferred	1,964	4,984	3,422	1,379	5,476	–	–	Excluded	1,592	394	19,211
1,379 votes of YAMUNG transferred	2,075	5,341	3,501	Excluded	5,517	–	–	–	1,708	997	19,211
1,780 votes of KALA transferred	2,596	5,796	3,595	–	5,793	–	–	–	Excluded	1,431	1,9211
2,596 votes of KATE transferred	Excluded	7,373	3,974	–	6,015	–	–	–	–	1,849	19,211
3,974 votes of MANLAU transferred	–	9,007	Excluded	–	6,407	–	–	–	–	3,797	19,211

Note: [a] An exhausted vote comprises a ballot where preferences have not or cannot be assigned to a continuing candidate, hence 'exhausting' before the full distribution of preferences.
Source: Chief Electoral Officer 1964b.

Table 4.3. *Allocation of preferences in Henganofi electorate, 1964*

Candidate	First count	Second count	Third count	Fourth count	Final count
Forapi	787	–	–	–	(787)
Posi	1,758	12	–	–	(1,770)
Punupa	3,708	73	41	–	(3,822)
Bono	8,028	12	35	224	8,299
Ugi	3,925	667	1,362	3,274	9,228
Exhausted	–	23	334	324	681

Source: As for Table 4.2

campaigning techniques 'as an example of a peculiar mildness – compared to the practice in industrial countries – that seemed to characterise electoral competition in New Guinea' (1971, 321).

Preference-swapping amongst candidates was similarly more prevalent in 1968 than in 1964, with 59 of the 84 elected seats being decided on preferences, including 12 seats which were ultimately won, after preference distribution, by candidates who had not led on the primary count. In Goroka, for example, where 16 candidates stood, the system enabled Sabuemei Kofikai, who came third on the primary count, to win on preferences, as 'he was clearly the popular compromise – his name figured near the top of almost every ballot paper' (Wolfers 1968b, 29). Wolfers argues that in such highly contested highlands seats, 'the preferential system has the most obvious relevance in that it may assist in forging a compromise among groups of people who would not, initially at least, consider helping an outsider' (1968b, 29). Shrewd candidates found that they could pick up votes by campaigning outside their 'home' areas, particularly in areas which fielded no local candidate (a number of non-local candidates were elected to seats in Central Province in this way). In other regions, little or no preference-swapping took place – especially in those regions where the candidates themselves (not to mention the electorate) had not grasped the mechanics of a preferential count, such as in most of the Milne Bay electorates (Gostin, Tomasetti and Young 1971, 97, 105). In the ten Western Highlands seats, over half of those who voted cast a single preference – although the rates varied widely between electorates, from 98 per cent in one district to 4 per cent in another (Colebatch *et al.* 1971, 263–4). The most likely explanation for this difference was the variation in official procedures used to elicit preferences from voters, whereby some polling officials (in imitation, perhaps, of Australian practice) directly solicited all preference orderings while others were less insistent (Wolfers 1968b, 29). Official leaflets and radio education programmes encouraged voters to fill in all their preferences, but the only explanation for this advice was that it was 'for the good of the country', a rationale that obviously left room for interpretation (Colebatch *et al.* 1971, 263).

In general, with most voters giving their first preference to their local clan candidate, second preferences at the 1968 election tended to go to candidates from geographically proximate tribes or, where possible, to expatriate candidates, who were often seen by voters as a better alternative than an indigenous member from a rival tribe. In the Western Highlands regional seat, for example, 93 per cent of votes cast for the most popular indigenous candidate, Philip Wamell, gave their second preference to an expatriate. For many candidates, the basic electoral strategy seemed to be to gain as many first preferences as possible from their home area, and then to expand this base as far as possible by soliciting second preferences from the supporters of others with whom they had some form of geographic connection or traditional alliance (Colebatch *et al.* 1971, 264–9). This was also a common strategy at the next elections in 1972, with alliances between candidates representing different areas within an electorate – for example, a town versus a village – cooperating to exchange preferences between themselves (see Holzknecht 1976, 202).

The importance of these preference-swapping alliances between aligned candidates is that they were the harbingers of the first forms of organised, cooperative political activity that began to emerge in Papua New Guinea at the 1968 elections. Thus Parker cites a Pangu Party alliance between different candidates in Central Province, and similar behaviour on the part of the expatriate-based 'All People's Party' in Madang, as evidence for 'the promise of widening political horizons' and increasing political development in Papua New Guinea (1971, 333). While political parties at this time were little more than 'personal associations between individuals who felt they had common political views and aspirations' (Parker 1971, 333), their growth into more coherent entities can be attributed, at least in part, to the associative qualities manifest in the type of accommodative campaigning encouraged by preferential voting, which enabled formal alliances and coalition arrangements to be sustained at the electoral level via preference exchanges. Indeed, the dominant political party throughout the 1970s, Pangu, based its campaign strategies in some regions around the disciplined exchange of preferences across clan lines between candidates, with numerous endorsed candidates standing and swapping preferences in each seat (Stone 1976a, 57; Lucas 1976, 227).

The last Papua New Guinea election held under AV rules took place in 1972, and records of campaigning from that contest provide some of the most detailed accounts of preference-swapping arrangements leading to accommodative behaviour. What stands out from many accounts, according to Saffu, was how accommodating and civil candidates were towards one another in their inter-personal relations: 'Although candidates could afford to be sporting in the pre-independence days when the stakes were not so high, the contribution of the optional preferential system to the avoidance of mudslinging could have been substantial' (1996a, 34). In the contest for the Kula Open seat in Milne Bay, for example, candidates in one area 'refrained from criticising each other' and instead 'often asked for second or third preferences' in a rival's home area (Leach 1976, 489). The eventual winning candidate often did not ask for a first preference at all, merely requesting 'a second or third vote if the people wanted to vote for others first' – and subsequently received a healthy share of other (eliminated) candidates' preferences and won the seat (Leach 1976, 487). Also important were candidates' direct appeals for not just second preference votes, but for third and fourth preferences as well. In highlands areas, humorous requests for these were made in the idiom derived from the distribution of pork at festivals whenever a candidate appeared outside his immediate area of strength: ' "I just want to know if you will give me a little piece of backbone and skin", they would say, and were duly assured that this would be forthcoming, i.e. that either second or third preferences would be given to them' (Leach 1976, 277). Similar appeals were made in many other electorates (see, for example, Pokawin 1976, 409; Holzknecht et al. 1976, 236; Allen 1976, 152).

Case study: Dei electorate, 1972

A good example of disciplined preference-swapping arrangements between hostile groups comes from Strathern's (1976) account of the contest for the Dei electorate in 1972. Dei was a new electorate in the Western Highlands which had been created in 1972 after tribal fighting in the former electorates became a problem. Despite inter-tribal violence immediately before the election, during the campaign most candidates enunciated 'a simple dogma of homogeneity and equality among all those standing' (Strathern 1976, 265), and this moderate philosophy, so different from the fiery rhetoric of later contests, was reflected in formal preference-swapping arrangements entered into by rival tribes in the electorate (Kombukala, Minembi and Tipuka being the dominant tribes):

First, leaders of one tribe (Kombukala) were said to have held a meeting to select their own candidate, and to have invited a small number of Minembi leaders and possibly one or two Tipuka men with whom they had connections. Beer was offered to the guests, and the Minembi and Kombukala leaders agreed that their two candidates could exchange preferences. (Strathern 1976, 276)

The 'arenas of bargaining' which preference-swapping incentives can create are well illustrated by accounts such as this, where previously hostile tribal leaders sat down and negotiated with each other for preference support. Even where the likely gains from preference-swapping were only marginal, candidates nevertheless took the time to meet and discuss ways of harnessing this potential advantage. This process also worked in reverse, with dispossessed groups wooing potentially friendly candidates – including the eventual winning candidate, Parua Kuri of the Tipuka tribe (Strathern 1976, 276). Kuri engaged in the most widespread and accommodative campaigning of any candidate, reaching out further to more rival tribes than any of his competitors. Significantly, he also forged close connections with a traditional ally tribe via 'intensive ties of ceremonial exchange' and, in a further example of rational preference-swapping, urged his supporters to cast their preferences for a member of a hostile rival tribe, Warike Wama, as well as for himself. Not surprisingly, when Wama was eliminated at the final count, a healthy proportion of his preferences went to Kuri himself, who won the seat accordingly. What Strathern typified as Kuri's 'growing importance in widening spheres of politics' was facilitated by an electoral system that was able to reflect the complexity of both traditional and modern alliances, and enabled him to succeed by utilising tactics which emphasised negotiation and coopera-tion rather than simple monoethnic appeals (1976, 277–83).

One of the most striking features of the 1972 elections was the extent to which candidates who managed to establish broad, cross-tribal support bases increasingly utilised the mechanics of preference distribution to defeat opponents who would have easily won a FPTP contest. For example, in one highlands electorate comprising seven major tribal groups each speaking a different dialect, the eventual winning candidate concentrated his early campaigning in areas where he had *no* traditional alliance or denominational ties, and in fact gained 41 per cent of his primary votes from such areas (Kuabaal 1976, 350–72). The pre-dominance of such strategies in the highlands, the home of Papua New Guinea's most fluid, aggressive and competitive traditional societies, was particularly marked. Despite making up only 32 per cent of all seats in 1972, 56 per cent of non-plurality winners came from highlands electo-rates (i.e. those in the provinces of Chimbu or the Eastern, Southern or

Table 4.4. *Cases where leading candidate on first preferences was defeated after distribution of preferences, 1964–1972*

Year	No of cases	Electorates involved	Percentage of all elected seats
1964	5	Kaindi, Henganofi, Tari, Markham, South Markham Special	9
1968	12	Central Regional, Finschhafen, Goilala, Goroka, Gumine, Ialibu, Kandep-Tambul, Kerowagi, Nawae, Sinasina, Sohe, Tari	14
1972	16	Bulolo, Hagen, Henganofi, Ialibu-Pangia, Kandrian-Gloucester, Koroba-Kopiago, Kundiawa, Lagaip, Lufa, Nawae, Nipa, North Fly, Okapa, Poroma-Kutubu, Sinasina, Tambul-Nebilyer	16

Source: Chief Electoral Officer (1964a, 1968, 1973).

Western Highlands). As will be detailed below, since 1975 it has been these same highlands provinces where modern electoral contests are most highly contested, and where minority victories have been most prevalent and electoral violence most extreme under FPTP. Table 4.4 sets out the electorates in which preference distribution ensured that the dominant plurality winner did not win the seat in 1964, 1968 and 1972.

While one would expect the highlands to figure prominently in terms of overall preference distribution because of the high numbers of candidates and clan groups in evidence there, it is less predictable that so many highlands candidates were able to win seats on the basis of preference support which they would have lost under FPTP. The strength of traditional ties rather than some form of party or policy-based affiliation is often the best explanation for their victories. For example, in Paypool's account of the campaign in Ialibu-Pangia, an electorate in the Southern Highlands province, the two most prominent candidates, Turi Wari and Koke Itua, who came from different regions of the electorate, Ialibu and Pangia, collaborated closely during the campaign, with each campaigning for the other in his home area. Voters from the two areas invariably gave their first preference to their clan candidate, but those who decided to express preferences for a candidate from the rival area almost invariably chose Turi or Koke – the former winning the seat after eight counts, with Koke coming second (Paypool 1976,

288–90). Similar practices were followed by two young candidates in the Wabag Open electorate who 'campaigned hard on a common policy' and 'shared their preferences' (Iangalio 1976, 302–3); by two United Party candidates in Kavieng who 'established a certain co-operation and mutually recommended each other as number two choice on the ballot paper' (Stagg 1976, 423); by rival candidates in the island province of Manus (Pokawin 1976, 413); and in many other electorates. In other cases in the Chimbu province of the highlands, candidates with similar religious affiliations swapped preferences, and traditional allegiances appeared to take precedence over party connections. As was the case in the Dei election, however, the candidate with the most widespread support base won the seat (Standish 1976, 326, 345–6). The important point here is that where accommodative behaviour is rewarded, traditional allegiances can be utilised in much the same way as more modern, policy-based connections.

Of course, just as there were many cases where preference-swapping deals were instituted, there was also a considerable number of successful candidates who, judging that they would receive majority support on first preferences, instructed their supporters to mark a '1' only. Sometimes this was because they felt that preference instructions would confuse their supporters; sometimes it was because they were confident of winning the seat outright (see, e.g., Pokawin 1976, 413). Often, this assumption proved to be a miscalculation: assurances of support are easy to give, but not always reliable in the exchange-focused environment of Papua New Guinea electoral politics, in which bloc votes are commodities to be exchanged, bought or sold. The dangers of candidates instructing their supporters to mark only a first preference were graphically illustrated in the contest for one Papuan seat in 1968, where one of two collaborating expatriate candidates 'deliberately and persistently instructed' his Goilala supporters not to allocate any preferences beyond their first, 'fearing that the preferential system might confuse them and cause them to lodge informal votes'. When the expatriate was eliminated his running mate consequently gained few preferences, allowing an indigenous candidate to win the seat instead (Groves, Hamilton and McArthur 1971, 309). Similarly, in Manus in 1972, lack of a preference-swapping strategy almost turned a sure victory against an ageing incumbent candidate into a loss: a group of younger candidates 'were unable or unwilling to work together and, failing to appreciate how the preferential system could be exploited to achieve their objective, might well have failed' (Stone 1976b, 535). In another Manus seat, by contrast, the eventual winning candidate was the only one to campaign for second preferences, of which he received the lion's share, winning on the third count (Pokawin 1976, 412–13).

All of these examples illustrate the way rational candidates were able to use the mechanics of preferential voting to improve their chances of success by reaching out to voters from other clan or tribal groups. To do this, they had to overcome not just traditional enmities, but also the novelty of asking for support from areas in which they had little prior profile. Possibly the most important strategy to gain preference votes was therefore the need to travel from village to village, in order to be seen by all the different clans and tribes in an electorate. Anthony Voutas claimed that walking from village to village was the most crucial single factor in his 1968 election victory, writing that 'in areas where there was no "favourite son" candidate, I gained heavily. Where there was a "favourite son" candidate, I generally gained second or third preferences' (1970, 499). Similarly, the successful candidate in the Chimbu Regional contest, Iambakey Okuk, spent almost two years driving around his electorate prior to the 1972 election (Standish 1976, 326). Such accommodative practices are virtually unimaginable in many areas of Papua New Guinea today, where it is judged to be both dangerous and a waste of valuable resources to campaign outside one's immediate home areas (Standish 1994, 60).

Despite problems of literacy and numeracy, the percentage of voters in Papua New Guinea utilising preferences increased with every election between 1964 and the last AV election in 1972. In addition, the incidence of preferences deciding outcomes increased over time. At the 1964 elections, while preferences were distributed in the great majority of electorates the final result was different to that provided by FPTP in only 5 of the 44 electorates. In 1968, due to the distribution of preferences, 12 electorates (out of a total of 84) returned results different to straight plurality contest. By 1972, preferences changed the result in 16 out of 100 elected seats – in other words, 16 per cent of seats returned different members than would have been the case under FPTP.[9] This figure, which is considerably higher than that recorded at any national election to date in Australia, reflects the increasing understanding of the mechanics of preference voting at each election, and with it the increasing recognition in Papua New Guinea of the utility of preference allocation as a means of defeating candidates with strong but localised support in favour of a more

---

[9] The Constitutional Planning Commission mistakenly stated that in 1972 'in only 13 electorates was the candidate who led on the first count defeated after preferences had been distributed'. In addition to being incorrect, the use of the word 'only' appeared to imply that this was a relatively small amount, when it in fact represents the highest rate of results being changed of *any* national AV election. See Constitutional Planning Commission 1974, 6/15–6/16.

Table 4.5. *Proportion of seats where preferences distributed and outcomes changed in Australia and Papua New Guinea, 1963–1996*

Australia			Papua New Guinea		
Election Year	Preferences distributed (%)	Outcomes changed (%)	Election Year	Preferences distributed (%)	Outcomes changed (%)
1963	19.2	6.6	1964	52.3	11.4
1966	25.0	4.0	1968	73.8	9.2
1969	32.0	9.6	1972	69.0	16.0
1972	39.2	11.2	–	–	–
1974	26.0	7.9	–	–	–
1975	18.9	5.5	–	–	–
1977	36.2	3.1	–	–	–
1980	32.0	4.8	–	–	–
1983	24.8	1.6	–	–	–
1984	29.7	8.8	–	–	–
1987	36.5	2.7	–	–	–
1990	60.1	6.1	–	–	–
1993	42.2	8.2	–	–	–
1996	39.2	4.7	–	–	–
1998	66.2	4.7			

Source: As for Table 4.3, plus Hughes 1997, 166–7, updated to 1998.

widely acceptable candidate. Table 4.5 compares the experience of the two countries.

While examples of accommodative campaigning from the pre-independence era are relatively common, it appears that few commentators specifically attributed this behaviour to the incentives presented by the electoral system. Of the numerous studies, mostly by Australian authors, detailing the period leading up to independence, only Ballard noted the fact that AV 'encouraged collaboration among candidates within an electorate' (1978, 11). Recent calls in Papua New Guinea for the re-introduction of preferential voting have, however, implicitly endorsed the argument that preferential voting encourages inter-group accommodation, although not always in the policy concession manner that advocates like Donald Horowitz anticipated. These arguments will be examined in detail later in this chapter. First, however, the effects upon political behaviour of the change of electoral system to FPTP will be examined.

First-past-the-post in Papua New Guinea

At independence in 1975, Papua New Guinea replaced AV with FPTP, on the grounds that AV was excessively complicated and, as a system introduced by the Australian administration, a colonial institution unsuited to the new country's needs and conditions. Other concerns focussed on the potentially lengthy time taken to achieve a result under AV rules, leading to increased tension and disputation, and the problematic nature of optional rather than compulsory preference marking (Wolfers 1968a, 70). By contrast, FPTP was seen as being a simpler system which, in most cases, would deliver the same results as AV anyway (Colebatch *et al.* 1971, 226, 261–4; Parker 1971, 352; Chief Electoral Officer 1973, 18). These judgements, based in part on the scholarly studies of Australian elections from that period, cited in Chapter 3, proved to be seriously mistaken in the context of Papua New Guinea's highly fragmented and competitive social structure. Because FPTP recast electoral politics as a zero-sum, one-shot contest between clans, most voters had little alternative but to express their choice in a 'friendly' versus 'antagonistic' pattern along predetermined ethnic lines. Rising levels of political violence, widespread dummy candidature and vote splitting – which in PNG usually takes the form of friendly candidates with little hope of winning standing in order to 'split' an opposition block vote – and increasingly unrepresentative elected members appear to have been a result.

The consequences of the new system were immediately apparent at the 1977 general election. Setting the pattern for all elections since then, a disturbingly high number of seats (forty-two – i.e. almost half the parliament) were won by candidates with less than 30 per cent of the vote, and the related factor of vote splitting first became a serious factor.[10] Hegarty noted that vote-splitting tactics in 1977 'heightened tension between clans and groups and in some cases polarised electorates to the point of violent conflict . . . this situation contrasted markedly with campaigning styles in previous elections where opposing candidates often toured their electorates together urging voters to cast preferences' (1983, 15). He went on to suggest that 'a continuation of such aggressive campaigning in future elections could well weaken the credibility of the electoral system' (1983, 15). Similarly, Premdas described the results of Papua New Guinea's first FPTP election as 'a great disappointment', arguing that

> the new electoral system encouraged candidates with the largest bloc of ethnic (clan) votes in an electorate to concentrate on his/her base alone

---

[10] For an illuminating discussion of the importance of vote (or issue) 'splitting' as a central political tactic throughout the ages, see Riker 1986.

rather than to seek co-operative exchanges for second or third preferences with candidates from other clans . . . In effect the first-past-the-post system did not encourage inter-clan and inter-community co-operation in a country which is notoriously socially and ethnically fragmented. (1978, 79–80)

The relatively new phenomenon of campaign violence in 1977 was a recurring concern, with the electoral authorities saying that the 1977 poll featured 'the most hectic and wild campaign activities that were ever seen in Papua New Guinea' (Papua New Guinea Electoral Commission 1983, 88). Looking at the 1977 elections in the Southern Highlands, Ballard found that the competitiveness induced by the new FPTP system left 'no incentive for collaboration through shared preferences'. As a result, the campaign 'was much more aggressive than in previous elections. In the past it was common for candidates to travel together [and] for them to ask people to "Vote for the best candidate; if you think I am the best, vote for me, but if you think someone else is best, give me your second preference"' (1983, 188). While some candidates continued to conduct their campaigns in this style, others resorted to open criticism of opposing candidates, a new phenomenon which quickly increased tensions. In combination with the large jump in ephemeral candidates attracted by the enhanced prospects of victory under the new system, this led to a much more aggressive contest than had been the case at previous elections (Ballard 1983, 192). Three factors of particular concern quickly became apparent: the increasingly high rates of candidature at each election; the success of increasingly unrepresentative and minimally supported candidates; and rising levels of inter-ethnic tension, intimidation and violence. Each of these distinguishing characteristics of contemporary Papua New Guinea politics is at least partly explicable by reference to the incentives for behaviour presented by the electoral system.

In terms of candidate numbers, the first post-independence elections in 1977 saw an explosion in the numbers standing for election – 881 candidates standing for 109 seats, representing a 44 per cent increase over the number contesting in 1972 and a 33 per cent increase in the average number of candidates per seat. Hegarty argued that the increase was 'largely due to the fact that, with independence, political power was at stake, and the fact that the first-past-the-post voting system gave candidates with a reasonably strong clan vote a chance of winning' (Hegarty 1983a, 13). As detailed in Table 4.6, rates of candidature have remained high, and increased, with every election to date.

Since independence, the increasing centrality of the state as a means of accessing resources and accumulating and distributing wealth has served to encourage more and more candidates to stand for election. Electoral

Table 4.6. *Candidates per electorate, 1964–1997*

Year	No of Electorates	No. of Candidates	Average per electorate	Percentage Increase
1964	54	298	5.5	–
1968	84	484	5.8	5.4
1972	100	611	6.1	5.2
1977	109	879	8.1	32.8
1982	109	1,125	10.3	27.2
1987	109	1,513	13.9	34.9
1992	109	1,654	15.2	9.4
1997	109	2,370	21.7	43.4

victory provides the surest way of gaining access to the resources of the state itself. The explosion in the number of candidates since independence was clearly not anticipated by the many influential players who supported a change to FPTP. With the number of candidates almost doubling in the ten years between 1972 (the last AV election) and 1982, official reports began to countenance a return to AV 'should the country's changing circumstances require it' (General Constitutional Commission 1983, 131).

The explosion of candidate numbers in the post-independence era in Papua New Guinea has many causes, but one of them is that almost anyone with a modicum of clan support who stands for election has at least a chance of victory under FPTP. Because most candidates rely, sometimes exclusively, on their own clan group for their primary support base, contests in electorates with many different clan groups of roughly equal size can produce winners with only a marginal plurality of votes over other candidates. This type of scenario is particularly common in regions like the highlands, where many similar-sized clans vie to have 'their' candidate elected, or in areas in which a high number of competing interest groups and issue dimensions are present, such as the National Capital District seats (see Griffin 1988). There is a clear relationship in Papua New Guinea between areas of greater group fragmentation and higher rates of candidature – corresponding to the theoretical expectations of the political science literature, which argues that the effective number of electoral candidates and parties in an election is a product of the interaction between social heterogeneity and electoral rules (see Ordeshook and Shvetsova 1994; Amorim Neto and Cox 1997; Jones 1997). By contrast, the pre-independence use of AV required successful candidates to gain an absolute majority of votes cast, and thus encouraged alliances between parties or candidates, since allied groups could each put up candidates without fear of splitting their combined vote.

One consequence of the very high levels of candidature under FPTP is that many successful candidates are elected on only a small plurality of votes, often well short of a majority: the 1987 elections, for example, saw one successful member in the highlands elected with 7.9 per cent of the vote; a figure which was surpassed in 1992 when another highlands seat was won on a bare 6.3 per cent of the vote. As well as undermining the overall legitimacy of both the electoral process and the elected legislature, such results point to a change in the meaning and nature of a 'constituency' in Papua New Guinea: for many members of parliament, their actual constituency is not their electorate but the much smaller sub-group within their electorate to which they owe their allegiance, and their parliamentary positions. Standish, for example, has written that 'it is assumed that "representatives" will only work for the benefit of a small minority who actually voted for them, which can be as low as 7 per cent under the first-past-the-post ballot' and that 'usually the majority . . . of voters opposed the winner, and often refuse to let their elected member visit them' (1994, 60). Former cabinet minister Anthony Siaguru has argued that this localisation of politics has reached such a point that, even if politicians want to expand their constituency service activities so as to more effectively represent their entire electorate, they cannot do so for fear of upsetting their clan base.[11]

Table 4.7 indicates the increasing numbers of successful candidates being elected with minority support. These figures show a clear increase in minority victories at each election since 1977. Winning members supported by an absolute majority of voters have declined from 19 in 1977 to just 4 in 1997. While only 11 members won with less than 20 per cent of the vote in 1977, by 1997 only 45 elected members could gain *more* than this level of support. In 1997, 15 parliamentarians were elected with less than 10 per cent of the vote each. As in previous elections, most of these candidates were independents from the highlands, where inter-clan fragmentation and competition is most prevalent and the inclusive and accommodative candidacy which was a feature of AV elections is now virtually unknown. While voting patterns in Papua New Guinea have always been largely parochial and clan-based regardless of the electoral system, the pre-independence AV system clearly rewarded candidates who cultivated the support of those outside their own local area. Strathern, for example, has argued that pre-independence elections were characterised by 'the idea of the politician as a collective advocate of the people'. By the

[11] Interview, Sir Anthony Siaguru, 25 July 1996.

Table 4.7. *Percentage of votes gained by successful candidates, 1977–1997*

Year	No of seats	Percentage of formal votes gained by winners					
		< 10	10–19	20–29	30–39	40–49	>50
1977	109	–	11	37	26	16	19
1982	109	4	20	33	20	14	18
1987	106	2	39	41	13	4	7
1992	108	9	45	33	14	3	5
1997	107	15	47	31	8	2	4

Source: Electoral Commissioner 1987; Electoral Commissioner 1997.

1980s, however, 'it was understood that politicians are in power to benefit themselves and their factions, and they concentrate on consolidating their existing power bases. As a result of armed conflict between groups these bases had become more, rather than less, rigidly defined and a process of neotribalisation was well under way' (Strathern 1993, 48–9). Recent elections in Papua New Guinea have also seen a high incidence of 'dummy' candidates being encouraged (and sometimes paid) to stand for a seat in order to split a strong block vote from an opposing clan (Dorney 1990, 59). By enabling a candidate with a very small support base to entertain hopes of winning, and by rewarding the placing of 'dummy' candidates and other vote-splitting devices (such as paying the nomination fees or electoral expenses of a friendly candidate from a different grouping in order to divide an opposition clan's block vote), FPTP in Papua New Guinea rewards tactics which militate against electoral alliances. This is another area where there is a clear difference between FPTP and the experience of elections under AV rules, where vote splitting is much less rewarding and where a majority rather than a plurality threshold for victory applies.[12]

---

[12] While this pattern of vote splitting is now widespread, it is not universal. In some areas, tribal groups negotiate candidature between themselves a year or more before the elections, ensuring both that candidate numbers are minimised and that clan groups deliver their 'block' votes to one or other candidates well before the election date. Some clans agree not to put up candidates so as not to split a vote; others agree to support a particular candidate. In this way, a form of vote-pooling takes place before the election. Note, however, that this vote-pooling relies on the ability of separate clan leaders to negotiate selective candidate withdrawal and deliver a block of votes from their clan to a particular candidate. See Burton 1989.

Another consequence of FPTP in Papua New Guinea is the way that the nascent party system that appeared to be developing under AV has been undermined. Because there is little incentive to form political alliances under FPTP, and good reasons not to, the spur towards party organisation evident at early elections has been replaced since independence with a trend towards party degeneration. The Papua New Guinea party system has been in steady decline since the early 1980s, being unstable (no government since independence has survived as elected for a full parliamentary term), fragmented (there were twenty registered parties prior to the 1997 election), highly personalised (parties tend to operate as parliamentary factions, based on one or two dominant personalities, rather than as coherent, broad-based vehicles for translating public preferences into government policy) and increasingly irrelevant (at the 1992 and 1997 elections, independents won over 50 per cent of the total vote). Because of this seemingly inexorable trend, elections in Papua New Guinea also represent a striking deviation from the precepts of 'Duverger's law' that FPTP electoral rules lead to a two-party system (Duverger 1954, 1984), or more generalised formulations that FPTP 'corresponds to a low number of parties' (Taagepera and Shugart 1989, 84). By 1997, the six 'core' parties of Papua New Guinea's political system had become almost irrelevant, winning just 22 per cent of the vote and less than half the seats (fifty-one) between them. By contrast, the major 'party' was in fact independent candidates, who gained 61 per cent of the total vote.

Electoral violence

The high rate of candidature under FPTP appears to be a factor contributing to the increasingly common phenomenon of electoral violence in Papua New Guinea, a phenomenon which includes 'intimidation of electors and electoral officials, particularly through the use of weapons; murders; unauthorised road-blocks; [and] snatching of ballot papers and ballot boxes' (Electoral Commissioner 1997, 7). Electoral authorities asserted that the 1997 elections were the most violent ever; similar statements have also been made after previous elections (see Papua New Guinea Electoral Commission 1983, 88). Threats of violence against the electoral administration is an increasing problem in Papua New Guinea, and recent elections in some of the more volatile highlands areas have provided detailed evidence of electoral officials being intimidated, sometimes at gunpoint, into issuing multiple ballot papers (see, e.g., Standish 1996, 277–322; Dinnen 1996, 91–5). Nonetheless, electoral violence between opposing candidates and their supporters remains the predominant form of election-related violence in Papua New Guinea.

Such disputes can take many forms, but many if not most incidents are related to ongoing inter-group conflict for which an election provides a temporary focus but not necessarily an underlying cause (Dinnen 1996). Many incidents are also the result of losing candidates and their supporters protesting the election result. One observer described the 1992 elections in the following terms:

> Elections are times of frenzied collective competition between dozens of candidates per electorate, each representing his group, offering inducements and making threats, with huge sums spent and much at stake . . . in many polling booths officials were coerced with weapons (axes, knives and pistols) to give out ballot papers in bulk and accept people blatantly voting ten or twenty times . . . One intending voter was chased from a booth and stoned to death, and five were killed in post-election disturbances, including at least four for voting 'the wrong way', that is against the desire of their communities. (Standish 1994, 70–1)

While a cause of great concern, this type of 'gunpoint democracy' is not a dominant pattern in Papua New Guinea as a whole – at least, not yet (see Saffu 1996a, 41). Indeed, there are clear regional and structural trends to election violence in Papua New Guinea: it is precisely in those highlands regions such as Enga, Chimbu and the Western and Eastern Highlands provinces, where clan voting and high candidacy are most pronounced, that electoral violence also appears to be a factor (see Standish 1996, 277–322; Dinnen 1996, 918).[13]

Most categorisations of electoral violence suggest that it is 'anti-system' behaviour which attacks the legitimacy of the democratic system itself (Electoral Commissioner 1997, 7). While the causes of such violence are clearly complex and multidimensional, electoral violence can also be seen as an example of rational (if anti-social) behaviour to the incentives presented by the FPTP electoral system: as ten or twenty votes sometimes separate the winner from the second-placed candidate, any action taken to influence only a small number of votes can have significant effects. Just as the small number of potential second preferences gained under an AV system can be the threshold between victory and defeat, so small numbers of votes forcibly gained (or, more often, forcibly withheld) under FPTP can prove crucial. Instances of a candidate's supporters hijacking and destroying ballot boxes containing ballots from 'hostile' regions of an electorate, as occurred in some areas after the 1992 election,[14] would presumably be a much less attractive strategy when a candidate has the possibility of picking up second or third preferences from a rival's home

[13] See also 'Polls officer warns against use of force', *The National*, 14 January 1997.
[14] As documented in Dinnen 1996, 94–5.

area. Such changes in the nature of campaigning have been among the most marked effects of the increasing incidence of election-related violence under FPTP. As noted earlier, pre-independence election studies indicated that the winning candidates in many electorates were those who cultivated the preferences of those outside their own local area. Today, such spreading of the net is almost inconceivable in many parts of Papua New Guinea, as the risks of campaigning in a hostile area tend to overshadow the (marginal) possibilities of picking up significant numbers of votes from rival areas. This is a particular problem in highlands regions, where increasingly candidates are virtually restricted by personal safety considerations to campaigning only in their home clans. For example, in the last three elections in 1987, 1992 and 1997, few candidates in the highlands campaigned beyond their own locality due to the very real possibility of violence if they ventured into a rival's clan or tribal region (Standish 1994, 1996).[15]

Papua New Guinea thus provides some evidence to support Arthur Lewis's oft-quoted contention that 'the surest way to kill the idea of democracy in a plural society is to adopt the Anglo-American electoral system of first-past-the-post' (Lewis 1965, 71). What it does not do, however, is support the wider application of this statement to all majoritarian systems in general. Indeed, what stands out from the Papua New Guinea case is the very real benefits of AV compared to alternatives like FPTP. These advantages are overwhelmingly focussed at the level of strategic coordination (Cox 1997). Recent anthropological research in the Western Highlands, for example, has concluded that traditional divisions between clans have been reformulated and reinforced by FPTP. As the importance of political office as a means of economic advancement has increased, so FPTP elections have increasingly become the source of inter-tribal tensions and violence. In particular, FPTP places tribes which have traditional alliances and allegiances with others 'in an inescapable bind' (Rumsey 1999, 325), as the electoral system forces them to make one all-or-nothing choice of loyalty rather than express the true complexity of their relationships. Alan Rumsey argues that the use of FPTP for recent elections in the Ku Waru region of the Western Highlands has hindered

[15] In other regions, particularly the larger and less developed electorates in the Gulf and Northern electorates, cooperative campaigning is still a factor today, although not always for cooperative reasons. Running a campaign in these areas requires considerable resources and energy, and constant expenditure on transport. In the Kerema Open electorate in the Gulf in 1987, for example, Oliver found that boat and road transport difficulties forced candidates to work together, with the most common combination being Open and Provincial candidates from the same party sharing travel costs (1989b, 167).

efforts at local-level peacemaking between rival tribes based on traditional ties, whereas an AV system would have been fully compatible with such local initiatives, and its reintroduction 'would help to remove certain obstacles to that path' (1999, 327). He concludes that the Ku Waru case provides a powerful argument in favour of the reintroduction of AV. Not surprisingly, this has become an increasingly discussed area of potential reform in Papua New Guinea.

The reintroduction of preferential voting?

As we have seen, questions about the suitability of FPTP for Papua New Guinea appeared immediately after the 1977 election, with both academics and government officials citing its tendency to encourage zero-sum campaign styles which enable ethnic clan voting blocs to dominate electoral competition. Serious consideration of the reintroduction of AV began after the 1982 election, when the effect of vote splitting and other negative aspects of the new electoral system became clearer. Reviewing the 1982 election, Premdas and Steeves wrote that FPTP 'was the focus of widespread criticism', as under Papua New Guinea's extremely heterogeneous social conditions 'votes cast could be so fragmented that candidates were not encouraged to campaign beyond their village or kin group because they could win by only a slim plurality' (1983, 993). The Papua New Guinea Electoral Commission similarly argued that while AV was time consuming and more complex than FPTP, it also ensured that 'popular feeling was canvassed'. FPTP was simple and easy to understand, but failed to 'encourage the people to look beyond their own linguistic group' and, by enabling candidates with a small but solid block of votes to win, did not 'contribute to creating national attitudes towards the general elections' (1982, 31–2).

Following the 1982 elections the new government attempted to reintroduce AV, arguing that it would result in the election of superior politicians with broader support bases. The minister responsible, Anthony Siaguru, wrote that:

> (people) consider themselves bound by social and family obligations to cast their first vote for their relative or a person from their own clan, house line or language group. It might not be that that person is the best candidate in the judgement of the voter! But he or she is obliged because of social traditions to vote for him. I know of elections in the past, when the optional preferential system was in use, where candidates went around the electorate saying 'Don't vote for me as your first choice. I know you will have to give your first choice to your line candidate. But give me second.' And they did get in on second preferences or third preferences.

They did it with far greater representative support than, say, the member who has got in with less than ten per cent of the vote. That is ridiculous! (quoted in Dorney 1990, 78–9)

However, in a good demonstration of the weakness of the PNG party system, the legislation for the proposed change was defeated in a back-bench revolt and consequently never put to parliament. Another attempt was made in 1986, when the then minister for justice, Warren Dutton, who had been elected under both electoral systems, argued that AV resulted in greater identification between the electorate and the elected member, and that under preferential voting 'even the people who had given me their sixth and last preference vote considered that they had in fact voted for me and therefore, I was their member and I would look after all of them rather than just the small group of people who gave me their first preferences' (Hansard (PNG), 27 November 1986). The failure of FPTP to encourage this link between the electorate and their MP was, he argued, a major weaknesses which encourages electoral violence and tribal fighting:

> I would state categorically that the reason why we have had so many Courts of Disputed Returns, why we have had instances of violence and other disruptions during elections, can be placed squarely on the first-past-the-post system . . . if we were able to pass these amendments I am prepared to guarantee that the elections that we will hold in 1987 would be more peaceful, more respected, and would return to Parliament members who were supported by the majority of the people in their electorates. (Hansard (PNG), 27 November 1986)

Dutton also argued that incumbent MPs would be the likely benefici-aries of a return to AV, as they would be better known than their opponents and therefore more likely to gain second preferences 'after the tribal obligations have been fulfilled by giving the first vote to the person of each and every tribe' (Hansard (PNG), 27 November 1986). If this argument was designed to appeal to members' collective self-interest (always a good strategy in Papua New Guinea), it was not successful. As in previous attempts, Papua New Guinea's unruly parliament could not be convinced of the utility of bringing in reforms which could endanger their own re-election prospects.

Following the 1987 elections the electoral commissioner entered the debate, addressing for the first time the possible benefits of a return to AV. Stating that previous election results had posed the question 'as to whether the nation has an efficient democratic process', the electoral commissioner argued that AV would reduce conflict, and that losers would more readily accept the result:

The question that has to be addressed is whether [AV] reduces conflict and generates greater acceptance of the final result because 'trading off' of preferences between candidates will occur. This spreads the sense of the winner's having relied on more electors than gave him/her their first option. In the final count of a preferential system the winner is seen as having an absolute majority over his nearest opponent. He can, therefore, be seen as having been invested with majority approval. First-past-the-post is simpler and should yield quicker results, but . . . a small solid block of votes from a *lain* or linguistic group can determine who wins. This does not engender responsibility to the whole electorate, nor, ultimately, national attitudes. (Electoral Commissioner 1987, 4)

It was not until 1993, however, that the first serious steps towards electoral reform in Papua New Guinea were undertaken, when Manus province returned to AV for their local elections, becoming the first province in the country to do so. The results were encouraging for proponents of AV: of the seventeen winning candidates, only one (the incumbent premier) was able to win the seat on first preferences, while six others gained absolute majorities after the distribution of preferences. Importantly for those who claim that AV would deliver results similar to a straight plurality contest, in five electorates the winning candidate was not leading on first preferences. As the electoral commission noted, under FPTP 'those five people who enjoyed a greater mandate by the people would never have got in' (1995, 6). An academic observer concluded that

in my view there is no question that the more elaborate and complicated mechanics of the optional preferential system presented no noticeable difficulties for either the voters or the electoral officials. It is also clear that the new voting system allowed all winners, except the Premier who won by an absolute majority on the first count, to improve . . . on the level of support they could claim to enjoy amongst their voters. In that sense, the cause for democracy and enhanced leadership has been served. (Papua New Guinea Electoral Commission 1995, 6)

While this experiment was clearly a success, it took place in conditions unlikely to be replicated across the rest of the country. Manus is a small island province with relatively good communications, high rates of literacy, an effective bureaucracy, a small centralised population and a relatively high degree of social cohesion. Few if any of these factors are typical of the rest of the country, particularly the mainland areas. Nonetheless, the success of the Manus experiment encouraged a further attempt to reintroduce AV at the national level immediately prior to the 1997 election – a move which was again scuttled by backbench resistance before it reached parliament. Despite widespread agreement on both the problem and the remedy, serious electoral reform in Papua New Guinea remains elusive: each move to return to AV over the past decade has been killed off by sitting parliamentarians, who inevitably (and correctly) see it as a threat to their future electoral prospects. The lack of party discipline in Papua New Guinea means that substantive electoral change has become almost impossible to achieve: those who have the most to lose are the very parliamentarians who are being asked to approve any new law.

Conclusion

Prescriptions for electoral engineering via manipulation of voting rules tend to be based on an underlying presumption of rational, self-interested behaviour on the part of political actors. This chapter has outlined how the campaigning behaviour of Papua New Guinea politicians and their supporters appears to have been influenced by the electoral system in place. Despite the very recent imposition of state structures and representative government, Papua New Guinea's politicians are no different to those elsewhere: they are rational actors who will respond to the incentives present under different electoral rules in order to facilitate their election, and when the rules of the game change, many will change their behaviour accordingly. While a general finding that politicians want to win and hold on to power is a truism, this argument has a special significance when applied to the study of political behaviour in Papua New Guinea, which – heavily influenced by anthropology – has often focussed on the exotic or colourful examples of political behaviour as much as the rational. To give but a few examples: the discussions of the 'election sickness' that swept the Gadsup after the 1964 elections (see Watson 1964, 111); election-related cargo cult movements such as the Johnson cult;[16] the election of the cult leader Yaliwan at the 1972 elections (with a record 87 per cent of the vote);[17] and the persistence of candidates who contest elections without receiving a single vote (not even their own) at recent elections[18] are all examples of apparently non-rational behaviour on the part of Papua New Guinea politicians and/or their supporters. But concentration on these incidents has tended to obscure what is an

---

[16] The Johnson cult was a well-publicised movement around the time of the 1964 elections, where a significant number of electors on the island of New Hanover apparently wanted to vote for US President Lyndon B. Johnson rather than the local candidate. The villagers had apparently been told that they were free to nominate whoever they liked for election and, perhaps with the abundance of American wartime supplies and equipment in mind, chose to nominate President Johnson. See Hughes and van der Veur 1965, 403–4.

[17] For a good discussion of the Yaliwan case, see Winnett and May 1983, 255–67.

[18] This has occurred in each of the past three elections.

underlying rationality on the part of Papua New Guinea's political actors
– most of whom, at both AV and FPTP elections, made optimal responses
to the electoral incentives in place in search of victory.

Tsebelis has argued that a successful rational choice explanation of a
political event 'describes the prevailing institutions and context in which
the actor operates, persuading the reader that she would have made the
same choice if placed in the same situation' (1990, 44). While not a study
in the rational choice genre, the conclusions to be drawn from this
chapter are very similar to those outlined by Tsebelis: namely, that if we
can show that the behaviour of political actors is an optimal response to
the institutional environment, it therefore follows that the prevailing
institutions are to some degree responsible for the behaviour of these
actors, and thus for political or social outcomes (Tsebelis 1990, 40). It is
clear that the increasing fragmentation of electoral competition and rising
levels of electoral violence in Papua New Guinea since independence have
been influenced by the change of electoral system. But this is not the full
story. The ongoing debate about the appropriateness of Papua New
Guinea's electoral structures is also directly related to serious questions
about regime stability and performance: for example, Papua New Guinea's first prime minister, Michael Somare, has claimed that Papua New
Guinea's FPTP electoral system is 'the root cause of the country's political
instability' (*Post Courier*, 4 May 1988). The failure of an electoral system
to produce accommodative, effective and (perhaps) legitimate government is thus seen as an issue that goes beyond one of government
function, to having wider implications for a country's security, stability
and long-term viability as a nation state.

The evidence from this chapter suggests that AV encouraged cooperative campaigning behaviour in many electoral contests in Papua New
Guinea's pre-independence period. Under AV, candidates from smaller
clans or those without a block vote were able to campaign outside their
home base area for other voters' second preferences, in the full knowledge
that first preferences would always go to the local clan candidate. In areas
where there was no clear majority candidate, accommodative campaigning practices were encouraged by the need to garner second
preferences which might have been relatively small in number but could
provide the necessary margin of victory. AV also enabled the votes of
several aligned candidates to accumulate so that diverse but related
electoral interests could be marshalled successfully without the vote being
split several ways. All of this led to clear centripetal incentives towards
cross-ethnic bargaining, multi-ethnic coalitions, and inter-ethnic moderation. When these incentives were removed, and political actors were faced
with a different set of strategic assumptions, their behaviour changed

accordingly. The result has been increasing levels of violence, increasingly unrepresentative members of parliament, a fragmenting party system and decreasing overall prospects for the consolidation of democracy in Papua New Guinea. It would be hard to find a clearer example of the importance of political institutions in general, or the case for centripetal strategies of institutional design in particular.

5

Electoral engineering and conflict management in divided societies (I): Fiji and Sri Lanka compared

As Chapter 4 has demonstrated, there is evidence that preferential voting, when used in Papua New Guinea's early national elections, encouraged a degree of collaboration and accommodation between rival candidates competing for elected office. However, the circumstances of the Papua New Guinea case are in many ways unique. Papua New Guinea's multitude of ethnic groups are typically small and isolated, with inter-group conflict being manifested at the local level rather than as a contest for state power; the elections in question took place at an early and relatively undeveloped stage of political competition; the electoral process was almost certainly administered more efficiently under the Australian administration than in the post-independence period; and the pervasive influences of colonial rule make it difficult to disentangle just how much of the political behaviour witnessed at these early elections can legitimately be interpreted as a valid response to the system itself as compared to the strictures of the colonial administration. For these reasons, one needs to be cautious in extrapolating too much from the Papua New Guinea example alone.

Unfortunately for comparative purposes, there are relatively few cases of similar electoral arrangements being used *over a substantial time period* in other ethnically divided societies which could help ascertain whether the apparently moderation-inducing effects of AV in pre-independence Papua New Guinea are likely to be replicable elsewhere. In addition, the failure of successive attempts at electoral reform in Papua New Guinea itself has so far removed what may have been the best chance of examining this issue in a contemporary context. For this reason, it is important to examine the available evidence from other divided countries

– less substantial though such evidence may be – which have adopted preferential electoral systems in order to encourage more moderate political competition, but where the systems have not, as yet, been fully tested.

There are two such cases: Fiji, which in 1997 introduced an AV electoral system for all future elections for this very purpose; and Sri Lanka, which has used a SV form of preferential voting to elect its president since 1978. These two cases provide important data to assess the possibilities – and limitations – of the centripetal model. Fiji and Sri Lanka also have the advantage, as far as comparative research is concerned, of both being relatively small and isolated islands in which a great deal of constitutional experimentation has taken place. In the natural sciences, studies of such discrete and isolated communities have had a profound impact on the development of scholarly understanding of evolution and geography, and upon Western conceptions of art, literature and philosophy (see Smith 1960; Withey 1987). But the same cases – because of their internal diversities, small-scale dimensions, and relative imperviousness to outside influence – can also play a hugely instructive role in the social sciences, providing 'laboratory-like opportunities for gaining deeper understandings' in fields like anthropology and political science (Douglas Oliver, quoted in Wesley-Smith 1994, 6). For example, as Larmour (1994) has noted, most Pacific Islands, by virtue of their small populations, locally focussed politics and other distinctive characteristics, approximate the size of the classic Greek city states that provide Western political theory with its earliest and most enduring images of participatory democracy in action.

The Fiji Islands

The Fiji Islands, an island group of approximately 750,000 people in the South Pacific (see Map 2), has been the site of one of the most comprehensive attempts at constitutional engineering in recent years. Fiji's primary ethnic conflict concerns relations between the indigenous population of Fijians, and the Indo-Fijian community whose forebears migrated to the islands from southern India over the previous two centuries. Fiji's indigenous population is characterised by a mixture of Melanesian and Polynesian features – indicative of the islands' geographical position at the interface between the two major population groups of the South Pacific region. By contrast, Fiji's Indian community are mostly the descendants of indentured laborers who came to the islands in the nineteenth century to work on sugar plantations under British colonial rule. While other groups such as Chinese, Europeans and

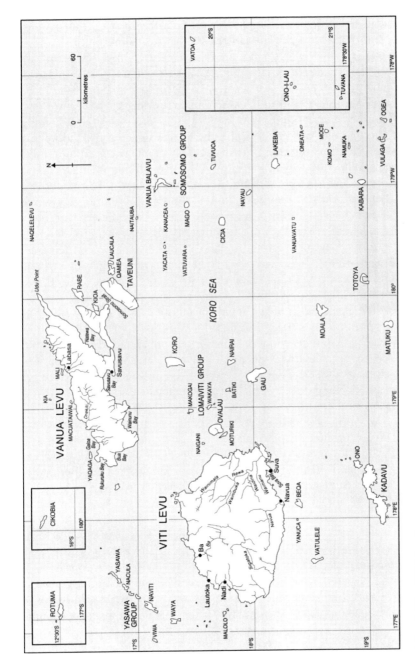

Map 2 The Fiji Islands

97

Rotumans (from the distant island of Rotuma, which forms a territorial part of Fiji) are also present, in essence Fiji's primary ethnic cleavage runs along a bi-polar division between these 'Indo-Fijian' (i.e. Indian) and 'indigenous Fijian' (i.e. Melanesian and Polynesian) communities.

Fiji society and politics have long been characterised by an uneasy coexistence between the two groups, with the Indo-Fijian population predominating in certain key sectors of the economy (particularly the sugar-cane industry), and indigenous Fijians owning 90 per cent of the land (much of it under long-term lease for sugar production) but holding limited economic power. Despite these economic and landholding disparities, the two communities are relatively evenly balanced in numerical terms. While the population ratios of the two groups are fairly similar – 50 per cent Fijian, 44 per cent Indo-Fijian according to a recent study[1] – there has historically been very limited informal social or economic interaction between the two communities. They speak different languages, observe different religions, work in different occupations, join different social groups, play different sports, and in most cases have little casual day-to-day contact. Intermarriage between the two groups, one of the best indicators of communal relations, is still extremely rare. Fiji is thus a classic example of what Furnivall described as a 'plural society', one in which 'different sections of the same community [live] side by side, but separately, within the same political unit' (1948, 304).

After achieving independence from Britain in 1970 and making what appeared to be a relatively successful attempt at consolidating a new multi-ethnic democracy, Fiji experienced two consecutive military coups in May and September 1987 which overthrew the elected government and installed a military-backed regime. The coups were prompted by the election in April 1987 of a government perceived by significant elements of the Fijian community, particularly the military, as being overly close to the Indo-Fijian community. The new government comprised a coalition of the National Federation Party, which drew its support predominantly from Indo-Fijians, and the Fiji Labour Party, with cross-ethnic support, headed by an indigenous leader, Dr Timoci Bavadra. The instigator of both coups, Major-General Sitiveni Rabuka, later claimed that the coups were carried out to prevent the bloodshed that would have resulted from outraged expressions of Fijian nationalism had the elected government continued in office (Dean and Ritova 1988). There has been considerable academic debate concerning the true motivations behind the coups (Ewins 1992), with some analysts seeing it as a racially motivated response by the indigenous Fijian community to the threat of Indo-Fijian domi-

---

[1] This was the figure used by the Constitution Review Commission (1996, 790–1).

nation (Scarr 1988), and others interpreting it as a more complex event encouraged by class interests, competition between chiefly and commoner indigenous Fijians, regional tensions and personal ambition (Robertson and Tamanisau 1988; Lal 1988; Lawson 1991).

What is clear, however, is that in transgressing what had been an unwritten law of Fiji's political life – that real political power must reside with indigenous Fijians, to balance a perceived Indo-Fijian control of the economy – the democratic process itself failed to successfully manage Fiji's deep-seated ethnic insecurities, and may in fact have provided a platform for them. This was significant, as attempts to engineer inter-communal harmony via engineering the electoral process had been tried several times in the past – indeed, Fiji's history is replete with them. From early colonial times, elections in Fiji have been based on communal representation, with seats allocated between the different communities on the basis of ethnicity. The colonial government in the United Kingdom reportedly viewed separate representation of different communities as 'natural and desirable', enabling differences to be isolated and the state itself to play the role of indispensable mediator of inter-communal disputes (Lal 1999). Until 1966, voters were separated on to communal rolls – that is, there was a separate electoral register for each community – and voted only for members of their own community, so that no possibility of cross-ethnic voting existed or occurred. This changed some-what at independence in 1970. Under Fiji's 1970 constitution, the ethnic balance of the 52 seat parliament was predetermined, with 22 seats reserved for Fijians, 22 seats reserved for Indo-Fijians and the remaining 8 seats reserved for 'General Electors' (i.e. Europeans, Chinese and others, who comprised only 5 per cent of the population and were thus proportionately over-represented in parliament compared to their numbers in the population). For the 22 seats reserved for each of the Fijian and the Indo-Fijian communities, in each case 12 were chosen purely by members of their own communal group, while the remaining ten were elected from 'national' seats, in which any elector could vote, even though the ethnicity of the candidate was predetermined. 'General Electors' had three communal seats and five national seats, thus holding something of an ethnic balance of power. The national seats were introduced with the explicit intention of encouraging a degree of cross-voting by voters from one ethnic community for candidates from another community, so that elected members from these seats would have to draw a degree of cross-communal support from all groups. Each elector therefore had no less than *four* votes at each election: one for their communal (co-ethnic) representative, and one for the national candidate from each of the three designated communal groups. An indigenous

Fijian voter, for example, would vote for a Fijian candidate in his or her communal electorate, and then cast three additional votes – one for a Fijian, one for an Indo-Fijian and one for a General Elector – in the appropriate national electorates. A FPTP electoral system was used for all seats.

The 1987 coups saw the abandonment of the 1970 electoral arrangements, and the introduction in 1990 of a new, ethnically biased constitution which enshrined a racial weighting in favour of indigenous Fijians in both civil rights and political representation, via an electoral system based exclusively on communalism. The new arrangements dispensed with the national seats, which had featured open competition on a non-racial basis for office, in favour of a purely communal system weighted heavily in favour of the indigenous community. The ethnic balance of the legislature was also shifted in order to guarantee indigenous Fijians an absolute majority of parliamentary seats (37 out of a total of 70 seats). By contrast, non-Fijians became a permanent minority: 27 seats were reserved for Indo-Fijians, 5 for General Voters and 1 for Rotumans (who had previously voted with Fijians). By under-representing the Indo-Fijian community, and reserving certain offices such as the prime ministership for indigenous Fijians, the 1990 constitution ensured that true inter-ethnic political competition was virtually impossible. The guarantee of a permanent majority of seats for ethnic Fijians turned the legislature into a classic in-group and out-group parliament: ethnic Fijians formed the government, while Indo-Fijians and others formed the opposition. International condemnation and the suspension of Fiji's membership in groups like the Commonwealth quickly followed.

The domestic consequences of this blatant ethnic gerrymander were predictable: inter-ethnic relations sank to new lows. In late 1994, following international pressure, economic difficulties and high levels of external migration by the Indian community, the Fijian government established a Constitution Review Commission (CRC) to review Fiji's racially based constitution and suggest alternative arrangements. The CRC toured Fiji extensively, holding meetings and public hearings across the country, and also embarked on extensive consultations internationally, holding public discussions and meetings with experts in Australia, Malaysia, Mauritius, South Africa, Great Britain and the United States. Their report, *The Fiji Islands: Towards a United Future*, published in 1996, proposed an entirely new non-racial constitution, with a revised package of electoral arrangements designed to encourage the development of multi-ethnic politics.

The commissioners, consciously or otherwise, adopted a centripetalist approach to the question of encouraging democracy in divided societies.

They viewed the electoral system as the most powerful tool by which the nature of Fijian politics could be influenced and engineered. After assessing and evaluating most major electoral systems against criteria such as the capacity to encourage multi-ethnic government; recognition of the importance of political parties; incentives for moderation and co-operation across ethnic lines; and effective representation of constituents, they recommended the adoption of a preferential AV electoral system in predominantly non-communal, multi-member constituencies (CRC 1996, 304). They posited politicians and political parties as key actors in the political system who would respond rationally to the various incentives and restraints imposed by the electoral system. Under this logic, as long as constituencies were ethnically heterogeneous and there was a number of political parties contesting the elections, politicians and parties would need to attract the second or third preference votes of voters from other ethnic groups to maximise their chances of electoral success. Candidates who adopted moderate positions and attempted to represent the 'middle ground' would, under this logic, be more electorally successful than extremists. By making politicians from one group reliant on votes from other groups for their electoral success AV could, the commissioners argued, encourage a degree of 'preference-swapping' between groups which could help to encourage accommodation between (and within) Fiji's divided Indian and indigenous Fijian communities. These incentives for election would thus work to move Fijian politics away from the extremes towards more moderate, centrist, and multiracial competition for power.

The arguments put forward for the accommodative affects of AV by the CRC thus replicate, to a significant extent, those put forward by advocates of AV in Papua New Guinea. Interestingly, an earlier commission of inquiry into Fiji's electoral system in 1975, chaired by Professor Harry Street, also came to a similar conclusion. The Street Commission, as it was known, recommended a series of reforms, based on implicit centripetal principles, to the electoral provisions of Fiji's 1970 independence constitution. It argued that Fiji needed an electoral system 'which is fair and equitable, and which at the same time does not encourage or perpetuate communal thinking or communal politics'. Its conclusion was that the Fijian parliament should comprise a mixture of communal and open seats, with 25 members elected in open competition from 5 multi-member constituencies using STV, and 28 members elected from communal rolls in single-member constituencies using AV (Parliament of Fiji 1975, 12–16). It is instructive to note how similar these recommendations, which were never implemented, were to those put forward by the CRC over twenty years later, especially considering that the failure of democratic politics in Fiji has been attributed by some observers to the 1970 constitution's rigid communal structure (Lawson 1988; 1991).

Both the Street Commission and the CRC also specifically rejected the case for consociational solutions based on the proportional representation of ethnic parties in parliament and a 'grand coalition' government featuring power-sharing between all communities. Both commissions argued that the list PR electoral systems favoured by consociationalists gave too much power to party bosses, unnecessarily constrained voter choice and, because of the need for large national or regional districts, often failed to provide the necessary links between a voter and his or her member of parliament (CRC 1996, 307; Parliament of Fiji 1975, 13). The CRC's critique of list PR also questioned the case for proportional representation in general. Under proportional electoral rules, they argued, ethnic parties could be expected to be represented in the legislature in proportion to their numbers in the community, irrespective of whether they were inclined towards moderation or not. Hence PR, when combined with communal seats, offered 'few incentives to parties to become more multi-ethnic in their composition or more willing to take account of the interests of all communities' (CRC 1996, 312). While their major objection to list PR was its lack of geographical accountability due to the need for large multi-member electoral districts, a related concern focussed on the distinction between minority *representation* facilitated by PR electoral rules and minority *influence* under AV:

> In the circumstances of the Fiji Islands, the Commission considers that electoral incentives are necessary to reinforce accommodations reached by agreement among ethnic communities. The system in force since before independence [i.e. communal roll elections] has, in effect, focussed on the need for their adequate representation. It is evident that such representation alone has not brought about multi-ethnic governments. (CRC 1996, 312)

This is an important point, as the communal roll system used in Fiji ensured, if nothing else, that for many years the members of the respective communities were represented in the legislature in fairly close proportion to their numbers in the general community (although this was not the case under the 1990 constitution, where ethnic ratios were deliberately weighted in favour of indigenous Fijians). However, between 1970 and 1987, the more-or-less proportionate representation of ethnic groups in the legislature resulted in one group forming a more-or-less permanent government, while the other formed the opposition (see Lawson 1988, 35–47). There was little if any genuine accommodation between groups – a situation magnified, according to the CRC, by the 'artificial solidarity within communities resulting from representation through communal seats filled by voting on a communal roll' (1996, 312). Proportional ethnic representation in the Fijian parliament based on communal electorates may thus have served to reinforce divisions between the indigenous and Indian communities.[2] This conclusion is in line with most analyses of communal elections; one commentator has even claimed that

> this is one of the few matters within the range of political science in which there is complete agreement between theory and practical experience. Communal elections strengthen communal feelings because in public debate appeals are made principally to the interests of each community, and within each community the more violent and selfish spokesmen of special interests outbid the moderates and public-spirited. (Mackenzie 1958, 34–5)

For this reason, centripetalists naturally reject communal and other systems which require a formal identification of ethnicity, as such an overt identification can itself contribute to the consolidation of ethnic politics rather than its breakdown. By contrast, proponents of consociational approaches argue that, as long as communal seats are distributed proportionately, communal rolls and other devices which explicitly recognise ethnic identity are entirely consistent with consociationalism (Lijphart 1985, 25).

The CRC recommended that Fiji move 'gradually but decisively' away from communalism towards a free, open and multi-ethnic political system. Acknowledging that political parties in many ethnically divided societies tend to be based around particular ethnic groups, the CRC's stated objective was 'to find ways of encouraging all, or a sufficient number, of them to come together for the purpose of governing the country in a way that gives all communities an opportunity to take part' (1996, 308). Instead of the majority of seats being elected by communal voters only, as was the case under the 1970 constitution, the CRC recommended that most seats should enable open contests between candidates from any group. They recommended that 45 of the 70 seats in parliament be elected from 15 three-member 'open' constituencies, with boundaries drawn so as to ensure a significant degree of ethnic heterogeneity. There would be no communal qualifications for voters or candidates in these open seats. The remaining 25 seats would continue to be elected on a communal basis from single-member constituencies, with 12 seats reserved for indigenous Fijians, 10 seats for Indo-Fijians, 2 for

---

[2] According to one account, 'Fiji's highly proportional electoral rules appear to have interacted with ethnic issues to cause the coup' (Bohrer 1997, 223).

General Voters and 1 for Rotumans. The upper house would comprise 35 seats, 28 elected in open competition and 6 appointed by the president, who would be elected at a joint sitting of both houses of parliament. Elections for both parliament and the presidency would all be held under an AV-like electoral system, although with some unusual variations: all seats would be multi-member and, to avoid problems of intra-party competition in the multi-member seats, the first, second and third preferences given to each candidate would be added together before the elimination of candidates with the lowest number of votes began (CRC 1996, 329).

Following extensive public discussion and debate, the Fijian parliament adopted a new constitution in June 1997. While largely in line with the CRC's thinking, the electoral arrangements provided by the 1997 constitution differed from those advocated in several crucial respects. Most importantly, the Fijian parliament did not make the recommended decisive move away from communalism, and in fact reversed the suggested breakdown between open and communal seats recommended by the CRC. All up, 46 of the parliament's 71 seats would continue to be elected on a communal basis, with 23 reserved for Fijians, 19 for Indo-Fijians, 3 for General Electors, and 1 for Rotumans. Moreover, all bar 6 of the Fijian communal seats were to be based around rural provinces, creating a focus on local issues and a potentially unhealthy demographic skew on the parliamentary representation of the indigenous community. This left only 25 'open' seats in which genuine inter-ethnic competition could take place. Taken together, these amendments greatly changed the centripetal nature of the CRC's report and undermined future prospects for cross-ethnic behaviour.

In addition, concerns about the workability of the multi-member AV system advocated by the Commission, and its recommendation that preference votes be cumulated rather than counted separately in the new electoral system, were both discarded following interventions pointing out the unworkability of such a scheme (Reilly 1997c, 83–9), and the government ended up adopting a single-member AV system. This choice of a single-member rather than a multi-member system placed great pressure on those drawing electoral boundaries, as the type of 'preference-swapping' between different communities envisaged by the CRC assumed that constituencies would be ethnically heterogeneous, and thus that boundaries would be drawn in such a way as to create ethnically mixed electoral districts. The government also rejected a number of the Commission's other recommendations for an elected upper house, and added a significant element of consociationalism to the final constitutional package by providing that all parties achieving at least 10 per cent of the seats in parliament should be invited to join the cabinet, in proportion to their overall seat share. The final constitution thus included a combination of centripetal electoral institutions (AV in the twenty-five 'open' seats elected from multi-ethnic constituencies) with consociational power-sharing ones (the option for all significant parties to take part in a grand coalition executive) – an unusual combination of two previously divergent approaches to constitutional engineering, and not necessarily a coherent one.

Case study: the 1999 Fijian elections

How did this unusual constitutional architecture work in practice? Fiji's 1999 parliamentary election, the first held under the new dispensation, provided an opportunity to put the new system to a practical test. Early signs were encouraging for the advocates of constitutional reform. Apparently in reaction to the new incentives for cross-communal vote-pooling and cooperation in the reformed electoral system, even before campaigning began parts of Fiji's previously settled party system began to change. In a move that would have been unthinkable just a few years earlier, political parties from both sides of the ethnic divide came together to make early pre-election alliances, with the result that the election was effectively fought between two large multi-ethnic coalitions rather than the predominantly mono-ethnic parties of previous years. Parties representing the three official ethnic groups – indigenous Fijians, Indo-Fijians and 'General' electors – formed the core of both coalitions. The first, under the leadership of the former coup-master, Sitiveni Rabuka, was built around the governing *Soqosoqo ni Vakavulewa ni Taukei* (SVT), the National Federation Party (NFP), and the United General Party (UGP). Each of these parties had a clear ethnic base: the SVT with indigenous Fijians, the NFP with Indo-Fijians, and the UGP with general electors. The alternative coalition group was headed by the multi-ethnic but Indian-backed Fiji Labour Party (FLP) – whose election to government in 1987 had been the catalyst for the coup – but also included hard-line Fijian parties such as the Party of National Unity (PANU) and the Fijian Association Party (FAP). Known as the 'People's Coalition', this alliance was headed by the Indo-Fijian leader of the FLP, former trade union boss Mahendra Chaudhry. The parties in this alliance formed only a loose coalition, and stood multiple candidates in several seats, while the SVT-led group formed a more conventional binding pre-election coalition, designating an agreed first-choice candidate in each constituency. But the trend was clear: for the first time in Fiji's history, cross-ethnic politics began to emerge. Coalition possibilities created new bargaining arenas and brought together former adversaries from across the ethnic divide, encouraging 'understanding and cross-cultural friendship among candidates facing each other in the election' (Lal 1999, 6).

The election campaign was the first in Fiji's history not to be dominated by the issues of race. The campaign, according to Lal, 'was the most relaxed in living memory. Trading preferences with other parties dampened what would have been a fiery campaign. For once, race was relegated to the background because both coalitions were multiracial' (1999, 5). However, many of the preference-swapping arrangements struck between parties were motivated primarily by political expediency and rational calculations, rather than shared visions or aligned interests. In twenty-two seats, for example, the FLP directed its preferences to the traditionalist and ultra-nationalist *Veitokani Ni Lewenivanua Vakaristo* (VLV), a party whose interests ran counter to that of most Indo-Fijians. The main alternative to the FLP for most Indo-Fijians, the NFP, placed the VLV last on their preference orderings as a matter of 'principle and morality'. In the end, however, the FLP chose expediency:

> For Labour . . . the election was not about principle and morality: it was about winning. To that end, it put those parties last which posed the greatest threat. Among these parties was the NFP, its main rival in the Indian communal seats. Labour's unorthodox tactic breached the spirit and intention of the preferential system of voting, where like-minded parties trade preferences among themselves and put those they disagree most with last. Political expediency and cold-blooded ruthlessness triumphed. (Lal 1999, 20)

At the election, preferences were distributed in 50.7 per cent of the country's seventy-one constituencies – a high level by comparison with Australian and Papua New Guinean examples – although all contests in the Indian and Rotuman communal seats were won outright. Moreover, in five of the open seats and nine of the Fijian communal seats, the leader on first preferences lost as a result of preference distribution. One effect of this was to channel votes not so much across the ethnic divide, but from more extreme to more moderate ethnic parties. The militant Fijian Nationalist Party, for example, distributed most of its lower order preferences towards more moderate Fijian parties such as SVT, despite the latter's coalition arrangement with the NFP. In general, however, the fragmentation of the Fijian vote was a major cause of an unprecedented – and largely unexpected – landslide victory for the People's Coalition. The mainstay of the Coalition, the Indo-Fijian backed FLP, gained a majority in its own right, enabling Mahendra Chaudhry thus to become Fiji's first ever Indo-Fijian prime minister. The FLP was the only party to gain a good spread of votes in both rural and urban seats, and in both open and communal constituencies, although it was a poor performer in the Fijian communal seats. It fielded several indigenous Fijian candidates and ran largely on a multi-ethnic, class-based platform. Nonetheless, the People's Coalition was viewed by many indigenous Fijians as Indo-Fijian dominated, despite the new cabinet comprising representatives of the three People's Coalition partners and the VLV. In total, eight parties and three independents gained seats in parliament. The former governing party, the SVT, which could have taken up its mandated seats in cabinet under the Constitution's 'grand coalition' provisions, elected to move to the opposition benches. While the SVT lost heavily – winning just eight seats – its Indo-Fijian ally, the NFP, did even worse, not winning a single seat. The new government thus entered office with a massive and unforeseen parliamentary majority, while the opposition parties were reduced to a small rump group.

A transfer of power across not only party but also ethnic lines was a new experience for Fiji, and constituted a major test of the new institutional arrangements and of the country's political maturity. Unfortunately, it was not to last. Popular discontent on the part of many indigenous Fijians at the presence of an Indo-Fijian prime minister continued to simmer, and Prime Minister Chaudhry's sometimes outspoken advocacy of Indo-Fijian rights served to deepen mistrust over key issues such as land ownership. In May 2000, in an eerie echo of the 1987 coups and exactly one year after the 1999 election, a group of gunmen headed by a failed part-Fijian businessman, George Speight, burst into the parliament building and took the new government hostage, claiming a need to restore Fijian paramountcy to the political system. Utilising weapons apparently stolen from army depots, Speight and his supporters – some of them members of the Fijian army's Special Forces Unit – amassed an extraordinary armoury of firepower which enabled them not only to violently overthrow the elected government, but also to engineer the collapse of most of the state institutions that were central to Fiji's return to constitutional rule – including not just the parliament and the prime ministership but also the presidency and even key indigenous bodies such as the Great Council of Chiefs. Apparently robust institutions and forums fell apart at the first push. By the time the hostages were released and Speight and his supporters arrested, Fiji had returned to military rule, with the military-appointed prime minister, Laisenia Qarase, announcing yet another review of the constitution, with new elections several years away.

To most observers, the 1999 Fijian coups marked another, and possibly decisive, nail in the coffin for hopes of a multi-ethnic and democratic future for the country. As in 1987, the election of an Indo-Fijian led government, combined with the waning influence of some traditional power-holders within indigenous ranks, provided fertile ground for extremist elements within the Fijian community to arouse popular discord and fear. As in 1987, once these fears had crystallised into direct attack on the country's democratic institutions, the traditional defenders of public order such as the police and the army – both indigenous-Fijian dominated institutions – were nowhere to be seen. Indeed it is clear that significant elements of both institutions actively supported the 2000 coup and the overthrow of the elected government, just as they did in the 1987 coups. Elaborate constitutional provisions which had served to encourage the first tentative steps towards multi-ethnic politics were no match for men with guns who encountered no resistance from the security forces as they marched into parliament. History was repeating itself.

Lessons from Fiji

The familiar circumstances of the May 2000 coup, and the apparently recurring phenomenon in Fiji of extra-constitutional attacks upon demo-cratic institutions which deliver the 'wrong' result in ethnic terms, suggests the latest breakdown of democracy in Fiji was not just a failure of constitutional engineering but a broader failure of political leadership, capacity and commitment within Fiji to the idea of a multi-ethnic democracy. Nonetheless, some observers *did* see a link between the 1997 constitutional reforms and the 2000 coup. In a newspaper article published at the height of the hostage crisis, academic Jonathan Fraenkel claimed that 'Speight's attempted takeover has received considerable support amongst indigenous Fijians because many felt politically margin-alised under Chaudhry's People's Coalition Government. An important part of the reason for this was the way Fiji's Australian-style electoral system operated at the elections in May last year.' Fraenkel argued that the electoral system 'manufactured' an overly large majority for the People's Coalition, meaning that it was able to ignore the needs of its indigenous Fijian allies and thus make resort to extra-parliamentary action more likely. In addition, the preferential voting system 'gave the Fiji Labour Party key indigenous Fijian votes that it would not otherwise have been able to obtain . . . the transfer of these preference votes were, in most cases, not a genuine expression of voters' choices'. Overall, the electoral system, he argued, 'proved extraordinarily complex, the results remarkably ambiguous and its merits as a tool for promoting ethnic co-operation highly questionable' (Fraenkel 2000).

While Fraenkel's arguments were overdrawn and contested by a number of other observers,[3] he did raise some important issues that highlighted the weakness of Fiji's electoral reforms. In particular, three apparently minor changes made to the electoral system shortly prior to the poll had a significant impact on the election result, and on some of the broader phenomena that observers like Fraenkel believed encouraged Speight's coup. First, in imitation of Australian practice, both registration and voting were made compulsory for the 1999 election, meaning that those who failed to vote could in theory be fined – which presumably was something of a spur for Fiji's very high turnout of 90.2 per cent. This provision, which was not part of the CRC's recommendations, appeared to have a clear partisan impact: the FLP, for example, managed to more than double its 1994 vote. Second, and consistent with mandatory voting, the expression of preferences on the ballot paper was also made compulsory, meaning that voters had to number at least three-quarters of all names on their ballot or have their vote declared invalid. Finally, and probably as a result of the uncertain affects of compulsory preference marking, a 'ticket' voting option, as per the Australian Senate, was included on each ballot paper. This allowed voters to forgo the task of manually ranking all candidates on the ballot by instead with one tick opting to accept their favoured party's full ordering of preference distribution amongst all candidates standing, from a list which had previously been lodged with the electoral authorities.

The 'ticket vote' option was exercised by around 95 per cent of all voters, and had a marked effect on the eventual election outcome and on the capacity of the electoral system to encourage inter-ethnic accommodation. Because electors were encouraged to accept a party's pre-set preference ordering, a major impact of ticket voting was that it pushed the decision on preference marking out of the hands of voters and towards the party elites. The arenas of cross-cultural communication which the preferential system was supposed to engender became sharply attenuated and focussed predominantly at the level of party apparatchiks and strategists, as it was ultimately the party leadership, not voters, who effectively determined where lower-order preference votes would be directed. In effect, the 'ticket vote' option meant that the system acted much more like a consociational cartel of elites than a mechanism for genuine inter-ethnic accommodation. The introduction of ticket voting thus served to remove a key moderating device from the electoral machinery, as individual candidates had little incentive to interact with other parties or to address wider groups of voters once preference-swapping deals had been made by party bosses. In particular, ticket voting

---

[3] See the Letters to the Editor, *Sydney Morning Herald*, 10 June 2000.

served to undermine the incentives for preference-swapping at the candidate level, as deals struck in advance at a national level formed the basis of most vote-transfer arrangements.

The deleterious impact of ticket voting was exacerbated by the way electoral districts were drawn, which ensured that opportunities for genuine inter-ethnic cooperation at the constituency level were rare. Because only the twenty-five open electorates enabled multi-ethnic competition, and of these no more than eight were reasonably balanced in their mixture of indigenous Fijian and Indo-Fijian voters, the vast majority of electorate-level contests provided no opportunity at all for cross-ethnic campaigns, appeals or outcomes. Some estimates suggest that only six seats were genuinely competitive between ethnic groups, as the heterogeneous electoral districts required to make cross-ethnic transfers an optimal strategy for electoral success did not in fact exist in most cases (see Roberts 1999). The CRC's recommendation for a 'good' proportion of members of both major communities in all open seats was interpreted extremely loosely, to mean ethnic balances of up to 90:10 in some cases, which obviated the need for intra-communal vote swapping. In most seats, clear Indian or Fijian majorities prevailed. Given this, it is perhaps not surprising that relatively little cross-ethnic vote trading actually occurred in most seats. As one report noted, 'Fiji's new electoral system remains heavily skewed along racial lines, even after the constitutional review. It took nearly twice as many voters to elect a Member of Parliament in an open seat as in a communal seat . . . the electoral system was heavily weighted against open seats' (see Fraenkel 1999, 44).

Nonetheless, largely as a result of the inter-elite deals on the direction of preferences from ticket voting, votes *did* transfer across group lines in a surprisingly large number of cases. Preferences were distributed in a majority (thirty-six) of the seventy-one constituencies, and resulted in a candidate who was not leading on first preferences winning in sixteen of these – which, at 22 per cent of all seats, represents the highest rate of preferences changing outcomes of any AV election in any country to date. In five of these cases, seats were won on preferences by candidates from the *minority* ethnic community in the constituency – which suggests a significant degree of cross-ethnic voting. The big losers of the 1999 election, for example, the Indo-Fijian NFP and the indigenous Fijian SVT, lost most of their seats in communal districts – defeat that cannot be attributed to inter-ethnic accommodation or lack thereof, although Fraenkel (2000) claims that 'both parties were defeated because of their willingness to compromise with the other'. By contrast, the Fiji Labour Party – a consciously multi-racial party – gained more seats from AV than it lost, and in fact it was transfers from three largely Fijian-backed parties that gave Labour its absolute majority.

However, most of this vote transfer activity came as a result of the sometimes bizarre ticket voting agreements made by party leaders. In some seats, for example, a ticket vote for one party actually counted as a first preference vote for a candidate from another party (Roberts 1999, 6). In others – such as the case of FLP directing their preferences away from their main rival for Indian votes, the NFP, and towards nationalist Fijian parties like the VLV – the strategic considerations of party leaders which led to such 'deals with the devil' would clearly *not* have been replicated by most ordinary voters. Most Indo-Fijians who voted for the FLP would have probably passed their preference vote on to an allied party like the NFP if they did not have the ticket option. In fact the NFP, which won 14.8 per cent of the votes but no parliamentary seats, appeared to be a clear victim of the ticket voting system. This, and the over-representation of the victorious FLP, led to an extremely disproportional electoral outcome, with more than double the level of disproportionality of AV elections in Australia. The affect of this was not so much of under-representing minorities as of wiping out some of the majority parties. The SVT, for example, obtained the largest share of the ethnic Fijian vote, 38 per cent, but gained only eight parliamentary seats, while the NFP did even worse, winning no seats at all despite gaining 32 per cent of the Indo-Fijian vote.

Such a level of disproportionality clearly undermined prospects for an accommodative outcome in Fiji. Combined with the bizarre impacts of ticket voting, it points to some serious deficiencies in the Fijian electoral model which served to negate some of the beneficial impacts of centripetalism. First, the drawbacks of the ticket voting option in terms of moving the power of decision-making away from ordinary voters and towards more calculating party elites clearly undermined the intention of vote-pooling. Analyses of the elections featured numerous accounts of how ordinary voters did not understand the direction in which their preferences were heading under the ticket vote arrangements.[4] Overall, the way in which ticket voting served to skew the election results outweighed any benefits in terms of simplicity it may have provided. In addition, the parliament's decision to adopt single-member electorates, rather than the

---

[4] The following account is typical: 'In hindsight, many Fijian voters are wishing they had familiarised themselves more with the preferential system. More so when they voted above the line. "If I knew VLV gave first preference to the Labour candidate in my open constituency, I would have voted for the SVT," says a VLV supporter ruefully. There are many like him.' See 'How Fijians dumped Rabuka', *The Review*, June 1999, p. 40.

multi-member districts recommended by the CRC, meant that it proved almost impossible to draw electoral constituencies that were ethnically heterogeneous – a key facilitating condition for vote-pooling. And, as most seats remained communal contests anyway, the CRC's proposals were, in effect, never properly put to the test.

If the CRC's recommendations were to be reinstated in the future in Fiji, one clear conclusion is that a more proportional preferential system which enables the drawing of heterogeneous multi-member electorates, such as STV, deserves serious consideration – as some observers prior to the 1999 election were in fact suggesting (see Reilly 1997; Arms 1997). Keeping some form of preferential voting is also important – despite the drawbacks of the electoral system as implemented, it is clear that the introduction of preferential voting *did* play a modest but important role in breaking old habits of mono-ethnic politics in Fiji, facilitating cross-ethnic bargaining, and helping to build new routines of inter-ethnic bargaining and cooperation. In particular, the opportunities for inter-ethnic bargaining that the new rules provided were both eagerly exploited and adapted by elites from both communities and, in combination with the expectations of places at the power-sharing cabinet table, served to significantly cool the rhetoric of the campaign. Indeed, one of the most striking aspects of the election was how, in marked contrast to previous election campaigns which concentrated on racial issues, the 1999 campaign was strongly focussed on 'bread and butter' issues such as the economy, rather than ethnic ones (Lal 1999). Whether this marked anything more than a temporary aberration in Fiji's unfolding cycle of intermittent democratic elections followed by anti-democratic coups, however, remains to be seen.

Sri Lanka

Like Fiji, the island of Sri Lanka is one of the world's foremost examples of a 'constitutional laboratory', having experimented with several different forms of state structure, including both parliamentary and presidential systems of government and a series of different electoral arrangements, in a bid to solve its persistent ethnic conflicts. With a death toll of over 60,000 to date, Sri Lanka's recent history of bloody communal violence also stands as a stark reminder of the limits of electoral engineering strategies for deeply divided societies. A conflict which began as a relatively minor communal grievance between Sinhalese and Tamil Sri Lankans in the early 1960s has escalated into a bitter campaign for self-determination, making Sri Lanka the site of one of the world's most intractable ethnic conflicts. The separatist insurgents of the Liberation

Tigers of Tamil Eelam (LTTE) demand an independent Tamil state in the north of the country; successive national governments dominated by the majority Sinhalese community have rejected these demands and attempted to defeat the insurgents on the battlefield; and a vicious cycle of civil war, terrorism and assassinations has followed. This is despite Sri Lanka's impressive history of democracy and, at the time of its independence, high levels of education and economic development. In many ways, Sri Lanka's recent history represents a textbook example of how early political failure to accommodate ethnic differences and minority interests can, over time, lead to increasing polarisation and ethnic 'outbidding' in the political process, pushing political competition in a centrifugal direction and turning what could have been a negotiable political dispute into a national crisis.

Like most of the other cases examined in this book, Sri Lanka is a plural society comprised of several ethno-linguistic groups. The majority group, the Sinhalese, constitute approximately 74 per cent of the population. Sri Lankan Tamils make up 12 per cent, so-called 'Indian' Tamils approximately 6 per cent, and Muslims another 7 per cent of the population. Other smaller minority groups are also present. Most groups are linguistically, religiously and regionally distinct, being concentrated in different parts of the Sri Lankan landmass (see Map 3). The Sinhalese are mostly Buddhists who speak Sinhala, and predominate in the island's southwest; both Tamil groups are Hindus and speak Tamil as their mother tongue, with Sri Lankan Tamils concentrated in the northeast and Indian Tamils in the tea plantations in the centre of the island; and Muslims are found on both the east and west coasts, often speaking Arabic, in addition to other languages (Shastri 1997, 133–4). Given this structure of reinforcing religious, linguistic and regional cleavages, it is not surprising that Sri Lanka has experimented with a variety of innovative constitutional and electoral arrangements in its efforts to ensure minority groups have a meaningful stake in the political process, with varying degrees of success.

Like many other former British colonies, Sri Lanka inherited a Westminster model of parliamentary government, with the first full general election for the parliament (consisting of a House of Representatives and a Senate) held in 1947. Although independence was achieved in 1948, it was not until 1972 that Sri Lanka adopted its current name (it was previously known as Ceylon) and embarked on the process of writing its own constitution as an independent state. In 1978, a select committee under the chairmanship of the nation's most dominant political figure to date, J. R. Jayewardene, drafted a revised constitution which transformed the Sri Lankan system of government into an executive presidency, with

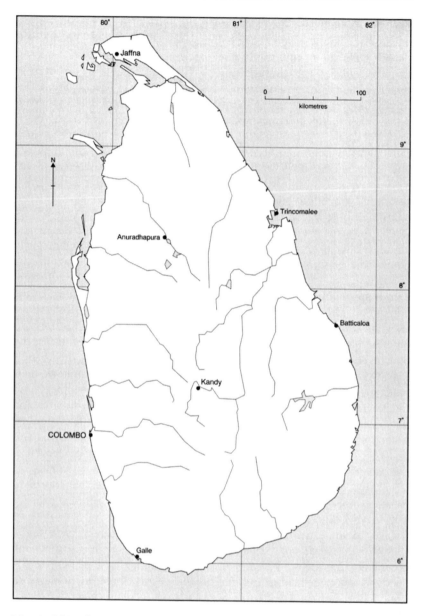

Map 3 Sri Lanka

Jayewardene vacating his position as prime minister to assume the new office of an elected executive head of state. The structure of government chosen in 1978 was similar to the French 'semi-presidential' system: a powerful executive president counterbalanced by a legislature elected by proportional representation. Like her counterpart under the French model, the Sri Lankan president has substantial executive authority, with the added power of being able to hand-pick the ministry, including the prime minister – hence the characterisation of the Sri Lankan Second Republic as 'the Gaullist system in Asia' (Wilson 1980). In terms of electoral arrangements, Sri Lanka adopted the British FPTP system for its first general elections in 1947, before experimenting with a range of unusual and sometimes conflicting electoral structures, which has confirmed its self-proclaimed reputation as one of the world's 'constitutional guinea pigs'.[5] In particular, Sri Lanka is of special interest to this study because it is the only country in the world which uses a preferential electoral system to elect an executive president.[6]

Sri Lanka's electoral arrangements

Sri Lanka has a long and impressive history of competitive elections and democratic procedures, although these have been significantly marred by the escalating ethnic conflict and political assassinations of the last two decades. Universal adult suffrage was introduced in 1931, giving Sri Lanka a record of democratic elections unequalled in Asia. In 1959 the voting age was lowered to 18 years, predating a similar move in most Western countries by at least a decade. Prior to the adoption of a new constitution in 1978, Sri Lanka's electoral arrangements had been almost purely in the Westminster mode. Election in most seats was by FPTP in single-member constituencies, although a few multi-member constituencies returning two or three members were created 'with the intent of enhancing the chances of election of candidates belonging to one of the island's ethnic minorities'

---

[5] Interview, R. K. Chandrananda de Silva, Colombo, Sri Lanka, 22 March 1996. R.K. Chandrananda de Silva was Sri Lanka's commissioner of elections between 1978 and 1994 and was responsible for a number of the electoral experiments discussed in this chapter.

[6] This statement needs some qualification due to the case of the Republic of Ireland. Ireland has a non-executive president who occupies an almost exclusively ceremonial office but who is, nonetheless, popularly elected (although half of all scheduled presidential elections to date have been uncontested). Article 12.2.3 of the Irish Constitution specifies that the electoral system for presidential elections shall be 'proportional representation by means of the single transferable vote', which is identical to AV when used for elections of one representative, such as a president.

(Wilson 1980, 80). The electoral devices intended to facilitate this outcome give a pointer to Sri Lanka's later adoption of preferential voting. In the multi-member constituencies, each voter could cast as many votes as there were candidates to be elected; all the votes could be cast for a single candidate or distributed amongst several candidates – the assumption being that ethnic minorities would be likely to deliver all their votes to their ethnic candidate, an assumption that appears to have held true with respect to Sri Lanka's Muslim population at least (Wilson 1980, 80).[7] Such multi-member seats were, however, in a minority, with most candidates elected from single-member electorates under a standard FPTP electoral formula. The party system promoted by this arrangement, however, was quite unlike the fluid and fragmented party constellation experienced under FPTP in Papua New Guinea. In Sri Lanka, the longstanding and deep-rooted cleavages of religion, ethnicity, language and ideology resulted in a well-developed party system structured largely along ethnic lines.

As in so many other cases, the ethnic divisions of Sri Lanka's society were thus largely replicated as political divisions in the emerging party system. But it was unusual throughout Sri Lankan electoral history for one party to command a monopoly of support from a particular ethnic group; the majority Sinhalese electorate, for example, tended to split its votes almost equally between two large parties. The finely balanced nature of Sri Lanka's multi-party system was increasingly characterised in the 1960s and 1970s by competition for government between two core Sinhalese parties, the United National Party (UNP) and the Sri Lankan Freedom Party (SLFP), with smaller Marxist or Tamil parties sometimes holding the balance of power. Moreover, the 'seat bonuses' provided by the FPTP electoral system to the winning party meant that small changes in vote share could and did result in major changes in the make-up of parliament. Prior to 1978, Sri Lanka experienced a change of government at almost every election, with the winning party's vote share often considerably smaller than their eventual proportion of seats. In 1970, for example, the SLFP gained 37 per cent of the vote but over 60 per cent of seats in the legislature. In 1977, this was turned around when the UNP scored 51 per cent of the vote but won 83 per cent of all seats. Such highly lopsided election results led to popular push for the introduction of proportional representation for parliamentary elections.[8] Sri Lanka thus

---

[7] This system was thus a rare example of the 'cumulative vote' in action.

[8] The system also disadvantaged geographically dispersed minorities – a problem exacerbated by the fact that, until 1978, electoral divisions were allocated on the basis of population (inclusive of non-citizens) rather than electors. This meant that voters in those areas which had substantial numbers of non-Sri Lankan citizens (including many 'Indian' Tamils and Sri Lankans who had opted for

introduced an unusual system of party-list PR for its parliamentary elections in 1978, although subsequent political wranglings meant that the first elections under these new rules were not held until almost a decade later.

This change focussed attention on the method of election for the new office of the president, and particularly on the means by which ethnic minorities could be included in the selection process rather than being overwhelmed by the Sinhalese majority. Implicit in this was the desire on the part of the governing UNP to end the endemic post-election violence 'which has been a characteristic feature in Sri Lanka at least since 1965' (de Silva 1979, 198). As both the head of government and the head of state, the president would have to represent all groups in Sri Lankan society and be seen as a figure capable of moderating between opposing interests. The method of election for such a figure would thus be crucial to the fate of the office and would require, at the very least, an absolute majority of support for the successful candidate. But, as noted earlier, only once since independence had any political party secured a majority of the vote at a national election; most governments were in fact elected with considerably less than that.

Sri Lanka's solution to this problem was to introduce a preferential vote system for presidential elections, so that the successful candidate would have to be elected (either outright or via preferences) by an absolute majority of all voters, making presidential candidates look beyond their own party or ethnic group for support so that 'the votes of minority groups would be decisive in determining the winning candidate' (Shastri 1997, 149). As much of the 1978 Constitution had its philosophic origins in the French Fifth Republic model of a strong executive presidency combined with an elected legislature, initial plans provided for a French-style run-off system of elections. However, the extra cost and security issues associated with holding two separate elections within a two-week period appears to have prompted the decision to combine the initial and run-off rounds of voting into one election via the expression of preferences.[9] To achieve this, Sri Lanka's constitutional draftsmen independently developed, by design rather than imitation, a SV electoral system that compressed both the first and second round stages of a run-off election into one. Interestingly, there is no evidence that the parliamentary committee which recommended this reform made refer-

Indian citizenship), who were not allowed to enrol and vote, were proportionately over-represented in the legislature. In practice, the effect of this provision was to give a disproportionate weighting in favour of the rural Sinhalese in many areas, to the disadvantage of minorities (de Silva 1994, 20).

[9] Interview, R. K. Chandrananda de Silva, Colombo, Sri Lanka, 22 March 1996.

ence to the experience of any other countries.[10] Instead, it appears to have started from first principles, seeking to ensure that any president would be elected by an absolute majority of voters and then devising the appropriate institutional mechanisms to achieve this. In keeping close to the French model, they decided that preferences would only be distributed to the two leading candidates in the event that neither obtained an absolute majority on first preferences. The expression of preferences beyond the first was not only made optional, but restricted so that voters could express no more than three preferences. Thus, even if thirteen candidates stood for election, as was the case in 1999, the voter is limited to marking a first, second and third choice only.[11]

As SV is structurally a cross between a run-off election and AV, Wilson's assessment of Sri Lanka's 1978 constitution as 'a hybrid, a cross between the British and the French' (1980, xiii) is right on target. But the hybrid nature of both the constitution and its specific presidential electoral provisions has not made it a popular choice in Sri Lanka, where constitutional reform is a perennial realm of dispute. Some Sri Lankan parties such as the SLFP argued in 1978 that a preferential system

---

[10] Interview, K. M. de Silva, Kandy, Sri Lanka, 26 March 1996.

[11] These rules are embedded in the Sri Lankan Constitution. Section 94(1) of the 1978 Constitution provides that:

> At the election of the President every voter casting his vote for any candidate may –
>   (a) where there are three candidates for election, specify his second preference; and
>   (b) where there are more than three candidates for election, specify his second and third preferences.
> (2) The candidate, if any, who receives more than one-half of the valid votes cast shall be declared elected as President.
> (3) Where no candidate is declared elected under paragraph (2) of this Article, the candidate or candidates, other than the candidates who received the highest and second highest number of votes, shall be eliminated from the contest, and –
>   (a) the second preference of each voter whose vote has been for a candidate eliminated from the contest, shall, if it is for one or the other of the remaining two candidates, be counted as a vote for such candidate and be added to the votes counted in his favour under paragraph (2), and
>   (b) the third preference of each voter referred to in sub-paragraph (a) whose second preference is not counted under that sub-paragraph shall, if it is for one or the other of the remaining two candidates, be counted as a vote for such candidate and be added to the votes counted in his favour under sub-paragraph (a) and paragraph (2),
> and the candidate who receives the majority of the votes so counted shall be declared elected as President.

discriminated against rural and less well-educated voters, and proposed a run-off system instead (Second National State Assembly 1978, 151). The UNP's response was that rural voters were sophisticated enough to write 1, 2 and 3 in order of their preference and that, in any event, the optional nature of the system made the SLFP's objections questionable (de Silva 1979, 199). The real reason for the SLFP's objection to the new system appeared to be their well-founded concern that the preferences of Tamil and other minorities would flow to the more moderate UNP candidate under a preferential ballot. Following this scenario, some scholars hailed the introduction of the SV system as 'even more important than PR for its implications for ethnic relations in the island', arguing that it should provide incentives for the major parties to take account of minority groups in their campaigning and in their formal arrangements for preference sharing (de Silva 1994, 22). This was contrasted with the practices of earlier elections, where there was little or no disadvantage in a subtle or even blatant anti-Tamil campaign in the Sinhalese areas; indeed previous elections were won or lost in these areas, and the major parties could ignore the north and east of the island where the Tamil population is concentrated.

In reality, however, the actual impact of preferential voting in Sri Lanka appears to have been more mixed. On the one hand, as indicated above, one of the justifications for the new system was the prospect of better recognition for minorities, so that 'no party or individual aiming at the presidency could afford to alienate minorities, or fail to campaign in the Tamil areas of the north and east, as well as among the Indian plantation workers and the Muslims and Roman Catholics' (de Silva 1994, 22–3). On the other hand, there is little evidence that appeals for preference votes have ever played a major part in determining the results of Sri Lankan elections – in part because the major presidential contenders have never seriously campaigned for secondary preferences across group lines. The strong party and personal following of political leaders in Sri Lankan politics has meant that at every presidential election so far held, the winning candidate has scored a clear majority of votes on first preferences alone. In effect, this means that elections to date have been identical to FPTP contests, obviating the need for second or third preferences to be counted. Moreover, Sri Lanka's electoral authorities have not surveyed either the extent or the nature of preference marking.[12]

This is not to suggest that the introduction of SV laws have had no impact in Sri Lanka. There is, for example, evidence of informal

[12] Interview, A. D. de Silva, deputy commissioner of elections, Colombo, Sri Lanka, 20 March 1996.

cross-ethnic vote-pooling at work. Thus at the 1994 presidential election the winning candidate, Chandrika Kumaratunga, entered into formal coalition arrangements with the major Muslim party, and her candidature was backed by parties representing Sri Lankan and Indian Tamils as well, in recognition of her more moderate approach to ethnic issues (Schaffer 1995, 423). Similar arrangements were in evidence in 1999, although minority support from Tamils, in particular, tended to go to Kumaratunga's main Sinhalese opponent, opposition leader Ranil Wickremasinghe. This supports the contention that although the real impact of preference-swapping remains uncertain due to the majority outcomes at all presidential elections to date, preferential voting 'does allow minorities to have a stake in the process'.[13] Thus, while to date it is not possible to measure the extent of preference flows from minor to major party candidates in exchange for policy concessions, we can make some more general observations about the affect of the new electoral laws on the election process, and particularly on the attitudes of major party candidates towards minority groups. Whether this has translated into identifiable changes in policies on ethnic issues or indeed in greater accommodation between ethnic groups at the non-party level, however, remains unclear.

Case study: four presidential elections in Sri Lanka

Presidential elections under preferential vote rules in Sri Lanka have been held four times to date – in 1982, 1988, 1994 and 1999. At the first presidential election in 1982, the major parties were fairly well differentiated on the key issue of their attitude to Tamils, and the more moderate candidate, J. R. Jayewardene of the UNP, scored a clear victory with 52 per cent of first preferences. However, the circumstances of the 1982 election were less than ideal: the rival SLFP candidate was not permitted to stand for election, and the major Tamil organisation did not put forward a candidate in protest at its demands being ignored. The upshot was that no formal preference-swapping arrangements were made, lower-order preference votes were not campaigned for and, because of Jayewardene's absolute majority in the polls, the new constitutional provisions were not tested. The commissioner of elections suggested in his post-election report that the preferential system 'should be re-examined' as it had caused confusion amongst voters and there was doubt as to 'whether there was any serious campaign for the marking of preferences' (1983, 61).

---

[13] Interview, K. M. de Silva, Kandy, 26 March 1996.

Following the elections, increasing inter-ethnic riots and Tamil ter-
rorist attacks in 1983 saw a sharp decline in the prospects for inter-ethnic
accommodation in Sri Lanka. By the time of the next presidential
elections in 1988, a civil war was being fought in Tamil areas. Most
Tamils again boycotted the poll, which was won by the new UNP
presidential candidate, Ranasinghe Premadasa, by a slim majority on first
preferences (50.4 per cent). Again, the vote-pooling potential of the
preferential system was not tested, although the UNP was clearly the more
conciliatory party and had the support of most of the minority groups
taking part in the poll – including Indian Tamils, Muslims, Sinhalese
Christians and a substantial minority of Sinhalese Buddhists (Horowitz
1991a, 192fn). As the 1988 campaign was the most closely fought
presidential election to date, it may be instructive to examine in detail the
process of the count. Under section 56 of the Presidential Elections Act
1981, preferences are not counted if one candidate has an absolute
majority of all votes cast. If no candidate has an absolute majority, the act
provides that the electoral commissioner must:

(a) where there are three candidates at the election –
 (i) eliminate from the contest the candidate who has received the
     lowest number of votes, and
 (ii) direct each returning officer to take such steps as may be
      necessary to count the second preferences of each voter whose
      vote has been for the candidate eliminated under sub-paragraph
      (i) of this paragraph, as a vote in favour of one or the other of the
      remaining two candidates; or
(b) where there are more than three candidates at the election –
 (i) eliminate from the contest the candidates other than the two
     candidates who received the highest number of votes, and
 (ii) direct each returning officer to take such steps as may be
      necessary –
      (aa) to count the second preference of each voter whose vote has
           been for a candidate eliminated under sub-paragraph (i) of
           this paragraph, if it is for one of the other of the remaining
           two candidates, as a vote in favour of such remaining
           candidate; and
      (bb) where the second preference of a voter is not counted under
           this sub-paragraph, to count the third preference of such
           voter if it is for one or the other of the remaining two
           candidates, as a vote in favour of such remaining candidate.

In 1988, only three candidates stood for election, and thus voters were
restricted to marking a first and second preference only. The final result
on first preferences in 1988 is set out in Table 5.1.

Table 5.1. *Result of the 1988 Sri Lankan presidential election*

Candidate	Vote	% of total
Ranasinghe Premadasa (UNP)	2,569,199	50.42
Sirimavo Bandaranaike (SLFP)	2,289,860	44.94
Oswin Abeygunasekera (SLMP)[a]	235,719	4.62
Total votes	5,094,778	100.00

[a] Sri Lanka Mahajana Pakshaya

According to this tally, Ranasinghe Premadasa received a bare majority of first preferences votes and was declared elected. A shift of less than 1 per cent of votes would have seen no candidate gain an absolute majority of votes, and second preferences would then have determined the outcome. As no provisional count of preferences is made if a candidate wins an absolute majority, it is not possible to say how preferences would have affected the outcome. What can be said with some confidence is that, with such a slim margin of victory, the 1988 result heightened the realisation amongst Sri Lanka's political actors that second preferences may well become crucial in deciding future results – particularly considering that Sri Lankan Tamils had again boycotted the 1988 poll.

The next presidential elections, in November 1994, saw the first change of executive government in Sri Lanka for seventeen years. Following its victory at the August 1994 parliamentary elections, the People's Alliance (PA) – an off-shoot of the SLFP – contested and won the presidential elections with an overwhelming victory for their candidate Chandrika Kumaratunga, who won 62.3 per cent of the first preference vote. Following such a massive win, preferences were once again irrelevant and uncounted, limiting our ability to analyse the effect that the electoral system may have had. It is significant to note, however, that the PA entered into vote-pooling arrangements with some minor parties (notably the Sri Lankan Muslim Congress), that Kumaratunga's candidature was backed by several Tamil parties, and that she gained support from almost all areas of the country. Commentators saw this as having important implications for future ethnic relations on the island:

> Kumaratunga's massive triumph in the presidential election was as impressive in scope as in size. She carried all but one of the country's 160 polling places, losing only a remote area inhabited largely by aboriginal tribespeople. She got solid support from the majority Sinhalese community, which comprises 74 per cent of Sri Lanka's population. She did even better amongst the minority Tamils (18.2 per cent) and Muslims (7.4 per

cent). The magnitude of her victory significantly consolidated the mandate of the People's Alliance as it sought to bring about major political and social reforms. (Schaffer 1995, 409)

Again, however, the lack of preference vote data and the clear decline in inter-ethnic relations during Kumaratunga's presidency mean that it is not possible to make any confident assessment of the impact of the electoral system on this outcome – except that there probably wasn't much of one. The 1994 campaign itself had been racked by ethnic violence, with the UNP's chosen candidate, Gamini Dissanayake, assassinated by a suicide bomber two weeks prior to the poll; the party then erred seriously by appointing his widow, who had no previous political experience, as its presidential candidate. Victory for Kumaratunga was largely seen as a foregone conclusion after the results of the earlier parliamentary elections, and her personal popularity (she hails from a Sri Lankan political dynasty) was also a significant factor. In addition, however, and as was the case in the 1988 election, the victor (Kumaratunga) was clearly the more moderate and accommodative candidate, and the institutional incentives for embracing ethnic minorities (in the form of preference votes) may have impacted on the nature of her overall campaign. In other words, the *possibility* that preference distribution might have decided the result may have been as potent a factor in 1994 as whether preferences ultimately needed to be counted.

The most recent elections in 1999 were almost a repeat of the 1994 contest, except that Tamil support flowed away from Kumaratunga and towards the UNP's Ranil Wickremasinghe, who had advocated direct negotiations with the LTTE to end the country's sixteen-year war with Tamil separatists. The election campaign was also dominated by the candidates' different approaches to dealing with the civil war and by the merits of various devolution and peace proposals. Kumaratunga's plan for regional autonomy, which formed the basis for her 1994 election victory, had been stalled in parliament, and military conflicts and bombings had increased. The election campaign took place in the midst of a government offensive against the LTTE, and was marred by suicide bomb attacks by the Tamil Tigers on both major Sinhala candidates, Kumaratunga and Wickremasinghe, which killed dozens of people just days before the poll. Kumaratunga, who was injured in one of the attacks, went on to win the election with a bare majority (51 per cent) of the vote, amid allegations of widespread fraud and intimidation (*Washington Post*, 22 December 1999). Despite increased information about preference voting, again the system was not tested in action. And once again a boycott by many Tamil voters marred the legitimacy of the election

contest, which represented a further chapter in the increasing cycle of
violence and retribution into which Sri Lanka's once promising democracy had fallen.

Conclusion

One of the central hypotheses examined in this book is the proposition
that preferential electoral systems can, in situations of ethnic division, be
utilised to promote co-operation between competing ethnic groups and
ensure a stake in the political process for minorities who would otherwise
be excluded. Why have centripetal strategies played, at best, a modest and
insufficient role in promoting multi-ethnic democracy in Fiji, while
having little discernible impact at all upon ethnic relations in Sri Lanka?

One explanation is the strength of incentives for inter-ethnic
accommodation presented by the various electoral models. At Fiji's 1999
election, the main political parties both calculated that their electoral
interests would be enhanced if vote-pooling deals across ethnic lines were
struck, but the eventual shape of some of those deals appeared to
undermine rather than enhance prospects for inter-ethnic accommodation. By contrast, the pre-existing institutional incentives for inter-
ethnic accommodation in the Sri Lankan system are relatively weak.[14]
While the SV presidential electoral system does indeed provide some
institutional incentives for moderation, these incentives all run in one
direction – Sinhalese presidential candidates can realistically hope to pick
up some Tamil second preferences were a Tamil to stand for president,
but Tamil candidates cannot realistically expect to achieve electoral
victory via second preferences from Sinhalese voters. In addition, what
has been dubbed the 'difficult combination' of proportional representation in the legislature with a directly elected president has resulted in
similar government instability and legislative deadlock in Sri Lanka as has
been the case in other regions like Latin America (Mainwaring 1993) –
with the inability of successive Sri Lankan governments to control the
legislature having a particularly negative impact on attempts to find a
settlement to the ongoing ethnic conflict.

[14] There are no incentives for vote-pooling at the legislative level – in fact, there is
some evidence that the 'open list' nature of the parliament's PR ballot allows
voters to reject candidates from minority ethnic backgrounds even if they have
been placed in winnable positions on the party list by their party hierarchy. This
has also resulted in candidates from the same party sometimes opposing each
other on policy issues and adopting populist stances on issues of caste, ethnicity
or region of origin in a bid to distinguish themselves from their running mates.
Interview, R. K. Chandrananda de Silva, 22 March 1996.

Both Fiji and Sri Lanka also point to a crucial but often overlooked aspect of electoral engineering: the complexity and comprehensibility of electoral reforms. Fiji's 1999 election, for example, took place at an early stage of return to democracy under a complex set of new electoral rules. Elites, for predictable reasons, displayed far greater understanding of the possibilities and consequences of the new arrangements than ordinary voters, and the implications of the new system were not widely understood by the electorate at large. Moreover, the presence of two apparently minor institutional features – the fact that the expression of preferences was a compulsory feature of a valid vote, and the consequent introduction of a 'ticket' vote option in which a complete preference ordering could be expressed simply by adopting a party's pre-arranged preference schedule – both impacted negatively upon the working of the new system in Fiji.

By contrast, some of the simplifying features of the Sri Lankan system have tended to undermine its effectiveness. As the marking of preference votes is optional and not widely understood, and as there is no requirement to express second and later preferences on the ballot, it appears that few voters do so. Initial estimates by the commissioner of elections after the 1982 presidential poll put the rate of preference marking as low as 2 per cent, and its usage does not appear to have increased appreciably in later elections (1983, 60). Nonetheless, some commentators have attributed the reduced turnout at Sri Lanka's first presidential vote in 1982 to 'the apparent complexity of the new preferential voting system' (Samarasinghe 1983, 162). Even the electoral authorities initially opposed the introduction of SV rules in 1978, arguing that preferential voting 'presupposes a sophisticated and literate community', and foreshadowing potential problems of illiteracy and confusion (Second National State Assembly 1978, 151). In reality, some of these objections are less serious than they first appear – the rate of illiteracy, for example, is considerably lower in Sri Lanka than in most other developing countries. But overall there is no hard evidence either way regarding the level of understanding of preferential voting on the part of voters or political parties, despite efforts to explain the mechanics of the system via press releases and media interviews (Commissioner of Elections 1992, 321). One of the problems to date in Sri Lanka appears to be a matter of political education: so far, political parties have not grasped the full potential of preference aggregation strategies inherent in situations where second or third preferences may determine the election result. Unlike the practice of Australian elections, parties in Sri Lanka do not distribute 'how-to-vote' cards specifying a preferred form of preference marking for voters to follow on election day, and it is doubtful whether the full implications of preference distribution is understood beyond a relatively small group of politically aware voters.

Another reason for the varying degrees of success of preferential voting in Fiji and Sri Lanka is the existence of a small but influential group of moderate voters, who will sometimes cast their ballot on issues other than ethnicity and appear prepared to respond to cross-ethnic appeals. Fijian electoral history suggests that, despite the country's deep divisions, there are sufficient 'floating' voters prepared at some level to support candidates from rival ethnic groups or multi-ethnic coalitions to make vote-pooling a viable political strategy. The 1980s and early 1990s saw an increasing fragmentation of ethnic identity, particularly within the indigenous Fijian community, and growing commoner assertiveness against chiefly rule, perceptions of regional privilege and discrimination. This, combined with an emerging class-consciousness amongst poorer indigenous Fijians, all resulted in a fragmentation of the Fijian vote prior to both the 1987 and 1999 elections. These emerging *non*-ethnic cleavages prompted the emergence of 'cross-cutting' political issues that overrode ethnicity – resulting in 1987 in at least 10 per cent of the Fijian vote going to what was seen as an Indo-Fijian dominated coalition.[15] Similarly in 1999, the Indian-backed FLP was able to win seats in constituencies where over 70 per cent of voters were ethnic Fijians. This challenges the argument made by some ethnic conflict scholars that cross-ethnic voting is unlikely in divided societies as 'members of the opposing conflict group are not likely to change their party attachments on the basis of a secondary issue' (Nordlinger 1972, 102). In Fiji, 'secondary issues' did indeed result in a change of party attachments. The outraged reaction of many indigenous Fijians to the 2000 coups, particularly those from Fiji's western regions who have traditionally felt subservient to the more traditionalist powers in the country's east, emphasise just how much room there remains for moderate voices in Fiji, even after the latest round of coups.[16]

While there is some evidence of similarly split party support and 'cross-cutting' concerns affecting voter choice in Sri Lanka, they have been much less influential in determining election outcomes, although there have been informal coalition or vote-pooling arrangements struck between major and minor parties. But the Sri Lankan example also points to the limits of constitutional engineering as a means of ethnic conflict management. Indeed, it is questionable whether Sri Lanka should really be seen as an example of deliberate engineering at all: preference voting for presidential elections was not introduced as a conflict management

---

[15] These issues are explored in depth in Lal 1988.
[16] See 'Poll Three Years Away, Says PM', *Sydney Morning Herald*, 31 July 2000.

mechanism, but primarily as a reaction to the oscillating status of Sri Lanka's government during its Westminster phase. As such, it was both too little and too late to address the deep ethnic divisions that were already clear in 1978. Moreover, while there is evidence that the more moderate Sinhalese candidate has generally triumphed at most elections, it is unclear to what extent (if any) the preferential electoral system has impacted upon electoral strategies and outcomes. The fact that Tamils have boycotted most presidential elections to date is itself an indication of the impotence of strategies based on institutional incentives which presume that aggrieved political actors will remain 'in the game' rather than choose to carry on their fight outside the electoral arena (in the Sri Lankan case, by civil war). In general, while moderates have indeed been elected to the presidency, there is little to suggest that this in itself has served to dampen the communal conflict in Sri Lanka. In fact, tensions have almost certainly escalated over the 20 years since the relevant constitutional reforms were introduced.

A final problem presented by the analysis of both the Fijian and Sri Lankan cases is their limited comparative value and utility for coming to more generalizable conclusions. In the case of Fiji, for example, while the expectation of cross-ethnic vote transfers was at least partly fulfilled, the broader impacts of the new centripetal structures are unlikely to become clear from one election. In general, it takes a minimum of several consecutive elections before we can judge the longer-term effects of any new electoral system, as successive iterations of contests under the same electoral rules are required both for political learning to occur and for the systemic effects of electoral rules to stabilize. This is shown most clearly by the longer-term examples of preferential voting such as Australia, where strategically optimum behaviour such as major-minor party preference-swapping has tended to develop over time as the deeper logic of the electoral system becomes clearer to political actors. Likewise in Sri Lanka, successive constitutional reviews, coupled with the failure of numerous reform attempts, make analysis of the effects of the electoral system in a stable institutional environment extremely difficult.

Both the Fijian and Sri Lankan cases thus point not just to the possibilities, but also the limitations, of electoral engineering. Changing electoral and constitutional rules may well be able to place a centripetal spin upon political competition, but it cannot change the basic circumstances of a conflict like Sri Lanka's, in which a geographically-segregated minority has engaged in decades of brutal civil war with a majority population. Nor can it have much impact on the willingness or otherwise of the Fijian security forces to protect their own parliament from criminal attack. Finally, and whatever their future electoral arrangements – which at the time of writing remain uncertain in both countries – the Fijian and Sri Lankan cases together point to the necessity for policymakers to think hard about the consequences of even minor technical innovations when specifying such proposals. The very real possibility that the apparent failure of the 1997 constitutional reforms in Fiji, for example, may be directly attributable to some seemingly minor technical choices over the makeup of constituencies and the method of marking preference votes, should serve as a graphic reminder not just that institutions matter, but that even small changes can have potentially highly uncertain effects. Learning the consequences of the 'rules of the game' is a challenge not only for voters and politicians, but for electoral engineers and analysts as well.

6

Electoral engineering and conflict management in divided societies (II): Northern Ireland, Estonia and beyond

So far, this book has focussed largely upon the conflict-management potential of one preferential electoral system: the alternative vote. However, as discussed in Chapter 1, there are at least three different preferential voting systems used for national elections around the world, consisting of two majority systems – AV and SV – plus the single transferable vote (STV) form of proportional representation. Interestingly, all of these system variations have been advocated, at various times, as the most appropriate electoral systems for divided societies. STV in particular has attracted legions of admirers and many advocates in both homogeneous and multi-ethnic societies, but has been introduced in relatively few countries. SV was, as we have seen, introduced as part of Sri Lanka's 1978 constitutional settlement, and subsequently recommended by scholars like Donald Horowitz as being particularly appropriate for divided societies elsewhere. And, as we have also seen, AV has attracted a considerable degree of support in countries like Papua New Guinea, and was introduced in 1997 as part of the constitutional settlement in Fiji.

These and other forms of preferential voting also have an interesting history of experimentation in other regions, particularly in Europe and North America. STV, for example, has been used for elections in several European states since the 1920s, and was once also widespread in local jurisdictions in North America – at one stage being used for Canadian provincial elections in Alberta, Manitoba and British Columbia, and for council elections in around two dozen cities in the United States. There is evidence from some of these cases that the consensual, preference-swapping strategies evidenced in places like Australia have also occurred in other contexts – particularly from the experience of elections in the

Republic of Ireland, where cooperative campaign strategies featuring reciprocal preference-swapping between candidates has been a well-documented feature of STV elections (see Cullen 1993). Irish elections also provide numerous examples of the way preferential voting can encourage pre-election vote-pooling deals and coalition arrangements between parties, such as those struck between Fine Gael and Labour prior to several elections in the 1970s (Laver 2000). Unfortunately, despite such cases, in general most European and North American examples of preferential voting provide relatively little comparative evidence for our examination of the affect of such systems in ethnically divided societies, taking place in unusually homogeneous social contexts (exemplified by the largely Catholic population of the Irish Republic) or over short time periods in the early twentieth century (in the case of most US and Canadian examples).

Nonetheless, two very different ethnically divided jurisdictions in Western Europe *have* utilised preferential voting, in the shape of STV, for recent national elections. These are Northern Ireland, which has used STV intermittently since 1973, and Estonia, which experimented with STV for its first post-Soviet election in 1990. Examination of these two cases – particularly the breakthrough 1998 'Good Friday' peace agreement and subsequent election in Northern Ireland – provides important evidence for assessing the impact of STV in divided societies, and more broadly for assessing the centripetal expectation that inter-party bargaining arenas and the possibilities of preference-swapping deals can encourage modera-tion and centrist policies. Running in parallel with these cases, there are also interesting recent trends in a number of countries towards the adoption of preferential voting for the election of single-person offices, such as city mayors in the United Kingdom and the United States, as well as for the tripartite presidency in the deeply divided Balkan state of Bosnia-Herzegovina. All of these cases deserve some examination when assessing the potential benefits and pitfalls of the centripetal model.

STV and the politics of accommodation in Estonia and Northern Ireland

Of all the preference-voting electoral systems, none has received more prominence or attracted more proponents than STV. As well as receiving widespread academic approval, a number of scholars have argued that STV is the best electoral system for ethnically divided societies, as its combination of a preferential ballot with proportional outcomes means that incentives for cross-ethnic behaviour can coexist with the fair representation of minorities and majorities alike (Lakeman 1974, 136).

The introduction in 1920 of STV for local elections in both the Irish Free State and Northern Ireland, for example, was explicitly aimed at managing minority issues and religious tensions in both jurisdictions (Farrell 1997, 113–14). However, STV's application at national parliamentary elections has been limited to a few cases – Malta (since 1921), the Republic of Ireland (since 1922), Northern Ireland (since 1973) and for one election in Estonia, in 1990 – plus the Australian Senate since 1949. (The system is also used in two Australian state and territory jurisdictions, for elections to the Tasmanian House of Assembly and the Australian Capital Territory Legislative Assembly.) This limited range of cases, all of which – bar Estonia – have occurred in countries once ruled by Britain, has made it difficult to assess empirically the frequent claims made on behalf of STV by electoral theorists.

Nonetheless, STV would probably top the poll of most political scientists' ideal electoral system. As a mechanism for choosing representatives, it is amongst the most sophisticated of all electoral systems, allowing for choice both between parties and between candidates within parties. The final results also retain a fair degree of proportionality, and the fact that in most actual examples of STV the multi-member districts are relatively small means that an important geographical link between voter and representative is retained. Furthermore, the ability for electors to spread their vote across a number of parties and candidates means that, in theory, they can influence the composition of post-election coalitions (as has been the case in Ireland), and thus encourage inter-party cooperation via the reciprocal exchange of preferences. STV also provides a better chance for the election of popular independent candidates than list PR, because voters are choosing between candidates rather than between parties (although a party-list 'ticket vote' option can be added to an STV election, as is done for the Australian Senate). However, the system is also criticised on the grounds that preference voting is unfamiliar in many societies, and demands, at the very least, a degree of literacy and numeracy. The intricacies of an STV count are themselves quite complex, which is also seen as being a drawback. STV also carries the disadvantages of all parliaments elected by PR methods, such as increasing the power of small minority parties under certain circumstances. Moreover, STV can provide pressures for political parties to fragment internally, because at election time members of the same party are effectively competing against each other, as well as the opposition, for votes. This has been a frequent source of criticism of STV in the Irish Republic, where members of the same party are competing as much against each other as against rival party representatives.

Until recently, the limited empirical record of STV in divided societies offered little opportunity for evaluating arguments that STV can encourage the same kinds of inter-ethnic vote-trading and centrist politics that has been evidenced at some AV elections. Prior to the crucial 1998 Northern Ireland Assembly election held under the terms of the British–Irish 'Good Friday' agreement, the only use of STV in ethnically divided states has been at 'one-off' national elections – once in Estonia in 1990, and twice in Northern Ireland in 1973 and 1982 (and, since 1979, for its elections to the European parliament). Only one of these cases, Estonia, offered evidence of vote-pooling or accommodation on ethnic issues at work. However, at the 1998 Northern Ireland elections, discussed below, STV *did* appear to play a modest but important vote-pooling role, allowing pro-agreement votes to transfer across party and group lines to the advantage of non-sectarian middle parties. How do we explain these different outcomes?

Estonia

One important factor appears to be the need for successive elections to be held under the same system, to enable a period of political learning so that the full utility of the electoral rules becomes clear to political actors. This was one clear lesson from the only use of preferential voting in the post-Soviet Baltic state of Estonia, which used STV for local elections in 1989 and for its first post-Soviet national elections in 1990, before discarding it in favour of a list PR system for the next elections in 1992. The story of the hasty adoption and even quicker discarding of STV for elections in transitional Estonia provides a good example of the essentially accidental nature of many electoral system choices.

Estonia was an independent state with a largely homogeneous population prior to its annexation by the Soviet Union during the Second World War. One of the many results of this action was the development in Estonia, as in the other Baltic states of Latvia and Lithuania, of a large Russian-origin and Russian-speaking minority, as well as smaller groups of Ukrainians and Belorussians. As the Soviet Union began to disintegrate in the late 1980s, pro-independence movements, including both the anti-communist Popular Front as well as reformists within the Estonian Communist Party, gained the ascendancy in Estonian politics. By the time of the re-emergence of a free society in 1990, fifty years of Soviet occupation had resulted in an ethnically diverse and divided society, split between the majority national Estonian (60 per cent) community and the minority (35 per cent) immigrant Russian one. In early 1990, the first free national elections in 50 years for the Estonian Supreme Council were held. The Council functioned as the parliament of the Soviet Estonian republic and had, since the fall of the Berlin Wall, become a focal point for pro-independence reformers, who looked to reform and democratise existing representative institutions from within (Lieven 1993).

As part of this process of internal democratisation came the choice of new electoral laws. STV was adopted as a compromise choice between the Communists and Popular Front, which satisfied the Communist desire to avoid party lists and focus on individual candidates while still leading to generally proportional outcomes, as required by the reformists. Following its successful use for local government elections in December 1989, STV was used for the country's first free elections in March 1990. Estonian politics at this stage was in a transition from *de facto* to *de jure* home rule and independence, which was not achieved until 1991. At the time of the elections, Soviet army units remained garrisoned in the country's north-east, and the emerging political system reflected this somewhat schizo-phrenic situation. Communists were evenly split between pro-Kremlin and pro-independence camps, the Popular Front was itself breaking up into several smaller parties, and issues of ideology were largely absent from the campaign. In keeping with the nature of transitions from authoritarian rule, the structure of the party system at this time was amorphous and fluid, and the political knowledge of the newly enfran-chised electorate – and of politicians – was relatively low. The election was thus held in a political environment of some confusion about optimum electoral strategies – a confusion which was reflected in the election itself, where personalities appeared to be more important than parties in determining voter choice (Taagepera 1990).

Because party labels did not even appear on the ballot papers, with some candidates endorsed by multiple parties, it is difficult to assess the extent of inter-party vote transfers, but overall there is little evidence of centripetal activity on either side of the ethnic divide. In fact, the available evidence suggests the contrary – ethnic identity, as a proxy for pro-independence Estonians versus (partly) anti-independence Russians, ap-peared to be the dominant factor in voter choice. Russian electors, for example, voted predominantly for liberal democratic 'Russian' parties, but their second preferences 'went overwhelmingly to reactionary imperialist Russian candidates rather than liberal but ethnically Estonian ones. Likewise, voters with Estonian first preferences continued with Estonian names' (Taagepera 1996, 31). While there was some evidence of cross-ethnic voting, particularly in support for Estonian candidates by non-Estonian voters, this did not appear to have much influence on political outcomes. The elected parliament, with a three-quarters majority of ethnic Estonians, quickly passed a declaration of independence, from which most Russian members abstained. Unsurprisingly, given the heated atmosphere of transitional politics, the parliament itself also exhibited little in the way of inter-ethnic accommodation, passing legislation that disenfranchised non-citizens and required Estonian language competence as the basis of citizenship and employment rights.

However, there is some evidence from Estonia that the short-lived application of STV in the transition process did help to encourage the early development of an aggregative multi-ethnic party system, itself a crucial agent of conflict management in divided societies. Analysis of party formation and nomination strategies at the 1990 election by Ishiyama (1994), for example, found that STV's combination of proportional outcomes with individual (rather than group-based) candidacy and voting promoted a relatively structured multi-ethnic party system, and restricted incentives for parties to form purely around ethnic lines. Later comparative studies of ethnic conflict have added weight to this finding. Looking at the choice of institutions in post-Communist Europe, one such study concluded that an optimal strategy of electoral system design should attempt to 'represent groups proportionally to diffuse protest actions, while promoting systems of representation that accentuate individualism' – and hence that STV may be 'just the trick' for preventing ethnopolitical conflicts (Ishiyama 2000, 65).

Had STV been maintained on an ongoing basis for future elections, it is probable that electoral strategies would have become more sophisticated as political actors grew more knowledgeable about the system and its effects. However, this was not to be: in 1992 the new parliament abandoned STV and changed the electoral system to a variant of list PR, after several leading parties calculated that a change of voting system could be to their benefit. The political effect of STV upon Estonian politics is thus extremely difficult to evaluate, given the quickly changing conditions, and the way it was adopted in conditions of limited information as a political compromise and then discarded for similar reasons. Taagepera points to two general lessons: first, that even a country with as limited a recent experience of free elections as Estonia had no problems with the relatively complex STV ballot, and second, that 'whichever electoral rules one adopts, keep them for at least two elections before getting into the revamping game' (1996, 36).

Northern Ireland

In contrast to the Estonian experience, Northern Ireland's erratic but ongoing use of STV across three decades appears to have enabled a much greater degree of political learning to occur. This gradual process of increasing understanding of the electoral system and its strategic possibilities by both voters and political elites has had important consequences for the development of centripetal political strategies in Northern Ireland. However, as demonstrated all too clearly by its tortured modern history, accommodative outcomes from Northern Irish elections have, for the most part, been conspicuous by their absence. The 1998 'Good Frioday' elections, however, appeared to mark a break with this sorry history.

Northern Ireland was established following the partition of Ireland in 1921 between the six Protestant-majority counties of Ulster and the twenty-six counties of the Irish Free State to the south. It was, from the beginning, a jurisdiction deeply divided along multiple overlapping cleavages of religion, class and nationhood. Like Estonia, Northern Ireland's basic ethnic cleavage is a bi-polar one, between nationalist (pro-Irish) Catholics and unionist (i.e. pro-British) Protestants. For over four decades, the province was governed by an uneasy combination of the Westminster parliament – under whose ultimate sovereignty Northern Ireland, as part of the United Kingdom, existed – and, intermittently, a regional assembly in Belfast. The latter, elected since the mid-1920s by FPTP by an electorate that numbered two Protestants to every one Catholic for most of this period, effectively operated under permanent unionist control, with Protestants forming a permanent governing majority and Catholics a permanent opposition. Such an imbalance in representation, itself inherently unstable, was greatly compounded by the decades of discrimination practised by the Northern Ireland administration against Catholics in employment, education, housing and other areas. A highly segregated and politically stagnant society developed, with two almost totally separate communities living parallel lives in a patchwork of small, segregated urban neighbourhoods and rural areas. The stagnation ended in the 1960s when 'The Troubles', which began as a conflict between Catholics and the state over civil rights, escalated into an increasingly deep-seated and violent conflict between unionists and nationalists over the ultimate status and sovereignty of Northern Ireland as a continuing part of the United Kingdom or of an ultimately united Ireland. By 1972 the Northern Ireland government was in complete disarray. What began as a civil rights protest by the Catholic community towards the unionist government was transformed into a war of liberation waged by the Irish Republican Army against the British government and army, and against the local police (see Bloomfield 1998).

In their belated attempts to deal with the crisis, the British government's initial prescription for devolution and power-sharing under the so-called Sunningdale Agreement of 1972 introduced a new Northern Ireland Assembly, elected by STV, in which a power-sharing executive including both Protestant and Catholic interests would govern the province.[1] But at the first elections to the abortive Assembly in 1973, most parties were formed along ethno-religious lines and neither campaigned for nor received votes across the Protestant–Catholic divide. One reason for this was that, given the deeply hostile relations between the two communities, 'the chances of winning an extra seat by adding a few votes from the other community were much less than the chances of losing votes by appearing "soft"' on key sectarian issues (Rose 1976, 78). The results of the 1973 election represented a decisive rebuff to moderation, and it was estimated that less than 0.25 per cent of vote transfers crossed the sectarian divide (see Dixon 1997, 5). Not surprisingly, the power-sharing executive envisaged in the Sunningdale Agreement fell apart within a matter of months amid increasing inter-communal violence and the dearth of any apparent middle ground.

Such sectarian voting patterns were again in evidence at the next election in 1982, following a brief revival in plans for a new power-sharing assembly. As was the case in 1973, parties contesting the 1982 election showed little interest in campaigning for preference votes across the communal divide, little in the way of vote-pooling, and even less inter-ethnic accommodation. The short-lived assembly was boycotted by a number of key parties from both sides of the divide. In both 1973 and 1982, attempts to elect a centrist legislature actually pushed the locus of politics away from the centre and towards the extremes, as the dearth of middle ground between the unionist and nationalist representatives saw the power-sharing experiment collapse almost before it had begun. In perspective, the period from the early 1970s to the mid-1990s in Northern Ireland can be characterised as a history of failed political initiatives, with both communities growing more polarised than ever. More than 3,000 people died over this period as the conflict simmered amidst intermittent peace talks, occasional short-lived cease-fires, and the ebb and flow of an increasingly predictable cycle of violence.

In 1998, however, it looked as though this pattern might finally be changing. After years of negotiation, the so-called 'Good Friday' British–Irish agreement of April 1998 provided for a host of new local, regional and international cross-border institutions aimed at managing the conflict between unionist and nationalist interests – among them power-sharing elections to a new Northern Ireland assembly held, once again, under STV rules. In contrast to the dearth of moderation evident at previous elections, by 1998 there clearly *was* a core group of moderates,

---

[1] Northern Ireland has also used STV for local elections (since 1973), for the 1975 Constitutional Convention election, and for European Parliament elections since 1979.

from both sides of the communal divide, who perceived peace as an optimal strategy for achieving their political aims and who were prepared to take substantial risks to see the peace deal implemented – indeed, the agreement would scarcely have been possible without them. This factor, which enabled the establishment of the power-sharing executive formed under the British–Irish agreement, is absolutely crucial to the long-term success of centripetalism in Northern Ireland. As the previous case study of Sri Lanka and Fiji made clear, political institutions themselves cannot create the moderate sentiment that is the prerequisite for successful constitutional engineering.

Case study: The 1998 Northern Ireland Assembly election

Under the Good Friday agreement, the new Northern Ireland Assembly consists of 108 parliamentarians elected by STV from 17 multi-member districts. Despite the overt similarity of these electoral arrangements to the abortive agreements of the early 1970s and 1980s, and the failure of the 1973 and 1982 elections held under similar STV rules, the 1998 Northern Ireland Assembly election succeeded in producing a 'pro-peace' power-sharing government. In contrast to previous elections, analysis of the 1998 results strongly suggests that the vote transfer element of STV had a beneficial influence both upon the types of political alliances that could be formed and on the eventual composition of the new Assembly, in which over 70 per cent of those elected belonged to 'pro-agreement' parties. Preliminary studies of these elections, discussed below, have found striking evidence that the representation of moderate sentiment in the Assembly was greatly assisted by Northern Ireland's STV electoral system.

The main attribute of STV at the 1998 elections was that it allowed votes to transfer between pro-agreement parties, not just across the ethnic divide, but also (and more significantly) *from ethnic sectarian parties to non-ethnic centrist ones*. It appears that this single factor – made possible because of preference voting – significantly assisted the peace process in a number of ways. First, it provided direct incentives to the major parties to moderate their position in the hope of attracting preference votes from moderate voters. Brendan O'Leary (1999), for example, argues that the possibility of picking up lower-order preference transfers was instrumental in moving the hardline republican party, Sinn Féin, away from its commitment to armed struggle towards less extreme policy positions, and that this movement was increasingly rewarded by moderation-inclined voters, as indicated by the increasing flow of lower-order preferences to Sinn Féin from more centrist nationalist parties such as the Social Democratic and Labour Party (SDLP). Second, on the unionist side, STV enabled those voting for anti-agreement unionist parties to transfer their lower-order votes to other unionist parties and candidates, many of whom were 'pro-agreement'. Pro-agreement parties on both sides of the sectarian divide benefited from such vote transfers, which – among other things – were ultimately crucial in converting a bare 'anti-agreement' unionist voter majority into a bare 'pro-agreement' unionist parliamentary majority. Evans and O'Leary, for example, conclude that the principal reason that a workable assembly emerged from the 1998 elections 'was the adoption, or re-adoption, of the single transferable vote . . . voters' lower-order preferences kept the Assembly on-track by reducing the numbers of seats that the anti-Agreement unionist parties won in the election' (1999, 3–4).

One of the most interesting aspects of this process in Northern Ireland compared to other cases was that it appears to have occurred largely independent of specific instructions from party leaders. Although a number of prominent parties and civic leaders, particularly on the nationalist side, publicly suggested that voters should transfer their lower-order preferences to pro-agreement parties, there was no evidence of the kind of formal pre-election vote-pooling agreements between party leaders that has been present in other countries. Those vote transfers that did occur appear to have originated predominantly with voters themselves. Perhaps because of this, lower-order vote transfers particularly benefited the political centre, allowing pro-agreement communal parties, such as the (Protestant) Ulster Unionists (UUP) and Progressive Unionists (PUP), or the (Catholic) SDLP, to gain lower-order vote transfers from other pro-agreement forces. This process also benefited other non-sectarian 'middle' parties such as the Alliance and the Women's Coalition (which received lower-order preference votes from both sides of the political divide) as well.

As a consequence, while the overall election results themselves were fairly proportional, there was a 'seat bonus' for the major centrist parties, who were proportionately over-represented in the legislature. Pro-agreement parties such as the UUP and the SDLP gained additional seats on the back of vote transfers – most clearly in the case of the UUP, which gained 26 per cent of the parliamentary seats with 21 per cent of the first-preference vote. In short, 'some of the SDLP's and Sinn Féin's voters found it rational to reward David Trimble's UUP for making the agreement by giving its candidates their lower-order preferences . . . likewise, some of the UUP's and PUP's voters transferred their lower-order preferences to pro-agreement candidates within their own bloc, amongst the others, and amongst nationalists . . . Within-block rewards for moderation also occurred' (O'Leary 1999, 10).

The first session of the resulting power-sharing executive was troubled, with the Assembly being suspended at one point by the British government following a dispute over weapons decommissioning, before being reinstated. At the time of writing it is unclear where the process will go next. But while it is too early to assess whether the latest agreement has been a success or a failure, there are a number of lessons for electoral engineers to be gleaned from the 1998 elections. The first is that, as with previous cases examined, there is evidence that vote-transfer systems can encourage accommodative outcomes by advantaging the 'moderate middle'. Clearly, this is not the full story in Northern Ireland or elsewhere, and it is not enough to guarantee accommodative outcomes by itself. But it can occur. The second lesson is best framed as a question: why did vote-transfers assist the process of moderation in Northern Ireland in 1998, but not in 1982 or 1973, or, for that matter, in Estonia in 1990? There are three possible answers. One is that the existence of a core group of moderates, both in the political process and in the wider electorate, represented a crucial facilitating condition that was not present in all cases. Centripetalism depends in part on assumptions that there is sufficient moderate sentiment within a divided community for cross-voting deals to be possible. In some circumstances, the presence of vote-pooling institutions may even encourage the development of this type of moderate core, via repeated inter-elite interaction within bargaining arenas. But it cannot invent moderation where none exists. This suggests that the lack of such a core group of moderates in Northern Ireland's earlier elections, and their clear presence in 1998, was a major factor in centripetalism's past failures as well as its more recent success. This is reflected in part by the fact that, at the 1998 election, there were far more vote transfers from sectarian to non-sectarian 'middle' parties than there were across the ethnic divide *per se* (Sinnott 1998).

A second conclusion to be drawn from the experience of both Northern Ireland and Estonia, is the way successive *iterations* of the electoral game can produce political learning and political change. Both cases suggest that early elections under vote-transfer electoral systems may not produce optimal outcomes until the full strategic potential of the electoral system becomes clear to politicians and voters alike. This appears to be one explanation for the difference in Northern Ireland between the results of the 1998 election and previous attempts at establishing a power-sharing assembly in the early 1970s and 1980s. It is vital that structural incentives are kept constant over several elections before attempting to judge the effects of any electoral package, but this is particularly the case for vote-transfer systems, where the routines of deal-making and pre-ference-swapping by politicians, and the understanding of these devices by voters, takes time to emerge. The Estonians, for example, discarded STV after one election on the mistaken understanding that it does not allow parties to coalesce – and ended up with a new system containing fewer incentives towards coalescence than STV. One reason that few of the expected reactions to the preferential system were evident in Estonia may have been due to the fact that the routines of interaction between the new political parties and the electoral rules had not had time to become institutionalised. Hence Taagepera's (1998) sage advice that several elections under the same rules need to take place before their systematic effects stabilise and both parties and voters learn to use them to their best advantage.

Finally, what do these cases tell us about the relative merits of STV compared to other preferential systems, particularly its ability to aggregate moderate interests? Prior to the 1998 Northern Ireland poll, it would have been hard to dispute negative assessments that claimed there was no evidence of STV encouraging the development of 'moderate coalitions' or 'limited multiparty systems', and that rather 'the effect of STV has been just the reverse, allowing each pole to fragment into numerous and mutually antagonistic splinters . . . STV removes disincentives to frag- mentation' (Katz 1984, 141). Indeed, some scholars such as Lijphart have argued that STV should only be used in socially homogenous contexts (1990, 11), while others like Horowitz speculate that the threshold for winning a seat in a multi-member STV district may be too low to ensure that incentives for preference-swapping influence party campaign strate- gies in divided societies (1991a, 191). The 1998 Northern Ireland election, however, suggests otherwise: vote transfers across party and sometimes group lines in a deeply divided society *did* occur, and for the most part they advantaged moderate forces. The results were also reasonably proportional, and clearly contributed to the creation of Northern Ireland's first power-sharing executive government.

The social context in which such elections are held appears all important. The major ethnic groups in both Northern Ireland and Estonia, each of which feature 'bi-polar' splits between two large and relatively cohesive ethnic groups, were both guaranteed representation under STV's proportional election rules. In both cases, there were few districts where the relative size of the groups did not exceed the required quota for election under STV. But in 1998 in Northern Ireland, there was also a third force: the middle, non-sectarian parties which were not clearly bound to either community. By advantaging the representation of this group, STV promoted outcomes which would not have been likely under AV or other majority systems, or under the more common party list versions of PR either. In other cases, however, where there is greater ethnic heterogeneity or a much smaller non-ethnic centre, STV may work less well – indeed, did work less well in previous Northern Ireland elections. All of which suggests that a key element of any electoral engineering prescription must be a careful understanding of the prevailing social and demographic conditions – an issue I will return to in the final chapter of this book.

Other experiments: preferential voting in Europe and North America

In addition to its use in Northern Ireland and Estonia, preferential voting has also become increasingly scrutinised as a possible electoral reform in a number of well-established democracies in Europe and North America, particularly in jurisdictions seeking to mitigate some of the more perverse impacts of first-past-the-post, or in deeply divided states such as Bosnia-Herzegovina. In addition, both AV and SV systems have been seriously investigated as potential new electoral systems by the United Kingdom's Labour government (in the form of 'AV plus', i.e. AV in combination with some form of proportional representation), and by a number of state-level governments, both Democrat and Republican, in the United States of America (where AV is commonly referred to as 'instant run-off voting'). In contrast to its steady spread and acceptance in Australia, in both the United Kingdom and the United States interest in preferential voting has waxed and waned over the years. While the electoral reform debate in both countries seldom focuses on the conflict management potential of preferential voting, issues of interest aggregation and centrist politics – both key elements of centripetalism – are prominent issues of concern in almost all cases.

AV in the United Kingdom

An interesting aspect of the near-introduction of AV in the United Kingdom in 1918, and of subsequent attempts to introduce the system since then, is how closely the progress of the debate matches the Australian experience, both chronologically and in substance. As in Australia, the original motivator for electoral reform in the United Kingdom was the perceived danger of vote splitting under FPTP. In 1903, the Liberal government came to an agreement with the new Labour Party not to encroach upon the other's electoral territory. While this pact, known as the Gladstone–MacDonald agreement, worked reasonably well, it soon became clear that it was not an arrangement that could last indefinitely, and that the Liberals would have to consider AV 'if they were not to hand a number of seats to the unionists on a split vote' (Bogdanor 1981, 121). Like their counterparts in Australia, the British Liberals established a Royal Commission on Electoral Systems; its report released in 1910 recommended the adoption of AV but made little impact, and was not debated in either house of parliament. Support for AV, however, remained widespread if not constant: in 1912 the first draft of the Liberal government's abortive franchise bill provided for its adoption, and only a shortage of parliamentary time saw it omitted from the final bill introduced to the Commons. The bipartisan Speaker's Conference of 1916–17, which grappled with numerous issues of electoral reform, made a majority recommendation that AV be adopted in all non-borough constituencies, about two-thirds of all electorates. The government refused to accept this recommendation and moved a free vote on the choice of electoral system, with the majority of the Commons in favour of AV but the House of Lords committed to STV. The end result was a stalemate between the two houses and the maintenance of FPTP – to the historical cost of both the Labour and Liberal parties.

Since the emergence of a disciplined party system around the 1920s, a calculation of the likely partisan impacts of change has been the dominant criterion by which political parties have assessed proposals for electoral reform. In 1931, another attempt by the minority Labour government (with Liberal support) to introduce AV met with a similar lack of success to previous attempts. When a Commons vote to adopt AV was again blocked in the Lords, it appeared that Conservative opponents of reform had won the day: Winston Churchill famously derided the system as 'the worst of all possible plans' which guaranteed an outcome 'determined by the most worthless votes given to the most worthless candidates' (*Hansard*, 2 June 1931). In 1958, by contrast, concern that a rise in the number of Liberal candidates would split the anti-Labour vote prompted a flurry of interest in the system from Conservatives, who saw it as 'a mechanism by which the Tory-preferring middle vote would not be "wasted"' (Steed 1975, 50). In 1998 the latest incarnation of the debate, a proposal for 'AV plus' – a mixed system with 80 per cent of seats elected by AV, and the remaining 20 per cent elected from a PR list to balance proportionality – was unveiled by the governing Labour Party's Independent Commission on the Voting System.[2]

---

[2] Prime Minister Tony Blair was reported to favour AV over FPTP, despite opposition from colleagues in favour of the status quo (*The Guardian*, 4 June 1996). Blair has not revealed his favoured choice openly, but is on record as stating that an electoral system must 'aggregate opinion without giving disproportionate influence to splinter groups' – a succinct description of one benefit of AV (*The Economist*, 14 September 1996).

While it is quite possible that the United Kingdom will adopt AV, or a variant of it, as a new electoral system in the future, the historical failure to do so reflects more than anything a mutual antipathy between supporters of the status quo on the one hand and the proponents of PR on the other. The result for most of this century has been a proliferation of vote splitting, both accidental and deliberate. The impact of this phenomenon on electoral results should not be underestimated. Research from British elections in the 1990s, for example, suggests that the selected *withdrawal* by one of the main opposition parties (at that time, Labour and Liberal Democrat) of their nominated candidate in selected constituencies would have allowed the remaining candidate to beat the Conservative; and that the effective use of such strategies could be enough to change government. In other words, a party could theoretically increase its likelihood of participating in government by selectively withdrawing some of its candidates – a fact which surely represents 'one of the more bizarre properties of the first-past-the-post voting system' (Sharp 1994, 129). Given this state of affairs, it is not surprising that electoral reform is back on the political agenda. The only prediction on the future of Britain's electoral arrangements that can be made with confidence, however, is that partisan interest – as ever – will be the determining factor behind any change.

AV in Bosnia-Herzegovina

AV has also been recommended – but not, at the time of writing, implemented – as an electoral reform in Europe's most deeply divided state, Bosnia–Herzegovina. The very existence of a Bosnian state is the result of four and a half years of warfare within the former Yugoslavia which left more than 100,000 people dead and about half of Bosnia's 4.3 million population expelled from their homes in a process of so-called 'ethnic cleansing'. Under its 1995 Constitution – which forms an integral part of the Dayton Peace Accord which ended the war – Bosnia's political institutions are split along ethnic lines, emphasising a representational balance between the Croatian, Serbian and Bosniac (i.e. Muslim) communities in the country's three-person presidency, its bi-cameral national legislature, and in the governing structures of its two sub-entities, the Federation of Bosnia and Herzegovina and Republika Srpska, as well. This has led to the political representation of ethnic groups, but very little in the way of inter-ethnic moderation or accommodation. In fact, the electoral incentives have, if anything, pushed in the other direction. The outcomes of nationwide elections in 1996 and 1998, which resulted in the election of hard-line nationalists over moderate extremists, both emphasised the need for cross-ethnic electoral incentives to encourage more peaceful and democratic politics. Because Bosnia's three major ethnic parties have been able to rely virtually exclusively on the votes of their own community for their electoral success, they have had little incentive to act accommodatively on ethnic issues. The result at the 1996 and 1998 elections was effectively an ethnic census, with electors voting along ethnic lines and each of the major nationalist parties gaining support almost exclusively from their own ethnic group (see Reilly 1998).

In 1999, after criticism both within Bosnia and internationally, and following a lengthy inquiry into electoral reform options, the United Nation's High Representative in Bosnia recommended a package of electoral reforms aimed at encouraging more open, multi-ethnic politics – including the introduction of an AV system for Bosnia's future presidential elections. Under the proposal, voters for Bosnia's tripartite presidency (which, under the Bosnia–Herzegovina constitution, consists of one Bosniac, one Croat and one Serb, each of whom are effectively elected only by their co-ethnics) would be allowed to rank-order candidates from their ethnic group running for one of the three seats. However, under the UN proposal, voters would not be allowed to indicate preferences for candidates from other ethnic groups, thus greatly weakening any centripetal incentives engendered by the system (the same rules, it is proposed, would also apply to the presidency and vice-presidency of Bosnia's 'constituent entity', Republika Srpska).[3] While, at the time of writing, debate on the strengths and weaknesses of this reform was continuing, with no guarantees that the proposed electoral reforms would succeed, the international community's interest in implementing AV in such a crucial test case of political engineering does suggest a growing acceptance of centripetalism as a conflict management mechanism.

Preferential voting in the United States and Canada

By comparison with these cases, and despite the fact that AV was, as detailed in Chapter 2, 'invented' in the United States, it has historically attracted little interest in North America. Maryland used the system briefly in the early years of the twentieth century for its party primaries, but for the election of single-person offices such as mayors, run-off procedures are much more common. STV, by contrast, became a key

---

[3] See Permanent Election Law Working Group 1999. A version of AV was used for presidential elections in Republika Srpska in November 2000 but, as the environment in which the elections took place was almost entirely mono-ethnic, it not surprisingly had no impact on ethnic accommodation.

element of the municipal reform movement of the 1920s, and eventually twenty-three US cities adopted proportional representation for council and school board elections. But reform movements led by the party machines saw to the replacement, in almost all cases, of STV with non-preferential majoritarian systems – with the notable exception of Cambridge, Massachusetts, which continues to use STV for its local elections. Several Canadian provinces also experimented with a combination of AV and STV for their provincial elections earlier this century. In 1924, provincial governments in Alberta and Manitoba both introduced STV, using the system for almost three decades before replacing it with FPTP in 1957. British Columbia also used a combination of AV and STV briefly in the 1950s.

Preference voting using the *supplementary vote*, by contrast, has a long but little-known history of use at the state and local government level in the United States. SV election laws were first adopted in 1912. Four states – Florida, Indiana, Alabama and Minnesota – used versions of SV, with a batch elimination of all but the top two candidates, for party primaries early last century. Seven other states used a modified version of the supplementary vote, known in the United States as the 'Bucklin' system. But the Bucklin system was found to be defective, as it allowed a voter's second-choice vote to help defeat a voter's first-choice candidate. Under these circumstances, most voters refrained from giving second choices, and the intent of discovering which candidate was favoured by a majority of voters was thwarted. After a series of primary elections in which alternate preference votes played no role in determining the winner, this voting procedure was eclipsed in all four states. By the 1930s all of these preference voting systems had been replaced by other reforms, such as the use of a run-off primary in the event of a non-majority outcome.

However, the supplementary vote reappeared in 1975 in Ann Arbor, Michigan for mayoral and council elections. The presence at that time in Michigan of a third party, the Human Rights Party, created a genuine three-way contest which saw the first ever black Democrat mayor elected on the strength of second preferences transferred from the eliminated Human Rights Party. This victory prompted Republicans, the beneficiaries of vote splitting under FPTP rules, to lead a repeal effort, which was ultimately successful. More recently, preferential voting has again become a live issue in several US states such as Vermont, New Mexico and Alaska, particularly where the emergence of viable third parties are creating splintered-vote situations for the major political parties (Vermont Commission 1999).

Conclusion

The arguments for the moderation-inducing effects of preferential election rules are premised on the assumption that politicians are rational actors who will do what needs to be done to gain election. Under different types of preferential voting rules, however, 'what needs to be done' varies considerably, depending on the electoral formula in place and the social makeup of the electorate. For example, where a candidate is confident of achieving an absolute majority or winning the required quota of first preferences, they need only focus on maximising votes from their own supporters in order to win the seat. In cases where no candidate has outright majority support, however, the role of second and later preferences becomes crucial to attracting an overall majority. For this reason, some scholars such as Horowitz favour the SV and AV forms of preferential voting – both majority systems – rather than the proportional form of preference voting, STV. Horowitz does not reject proportional alternatives out of hand, noting that if the choice is between PR and FPTP, then proportional systems are to be preferred. In general, however, he argues that proportional preferential systems like STV will produce weaker incentives for cross-ethnic accommodation than majority systems because of their lack of a majority threshold (1991, 191).

The evidence of this chapter suggests, on the basis of close examination of real-world experience, some important modifications to Horowitz's specific prescriptions for electoral engineering. For one thing, the Northern Ireland case indicates that Horowitz's critique of STV as a mechanism for conflict management deserves reconsideration. This system clearly had a beneficial impact on the representation of moderate sentiment at the 1998 'Good Friday' election at least. In addition, Horowitz's case for 'vote pooling' is based on the purported benefits of cross-ethnic voting – that is, the assumption that even in deeply divided societies, some electors will be prepared to give some votes, even if only lower order ones, to members of another ethnic group. In Northern Ireland, however, where vote transfers played an important role in promoting accommodation, these transfers ran predominantly from anti- to pro-agreement parties on the same side of the sectarian divide, or from sectarian to non-sectarian 'middle' parties, rather than genuinely across the communal cleavage from a unionist candidate to a nationalist one or vice versa (Sinnott 1998). While truly cross-communal vote transfers along these lines *did* occur (see Wilder 1998 for one example), they were much less common than sectarian to non-sectarian transfers. This is an important distinction, as it points to both what is *likely* in divided societies – that is, vote transfers between extremists and moderates within communal groups, or to non-sectarian groups, but not necessarily across a deep ethnic cleavage – but also to what is *desirable* – that is, the creation of broad, multi-ethnic but non-sectarian centre parties that can help to surmount the pivotal position of ethnic issues as a primary focus of politics. As I have argued in previous chapters, systems that encourage the development of a multi-ethnic or non-ethnic 'centre' are absolutely crucial to centripetal strategies for electoral engineering.

The account of the workings of STV in divided societies like Northern Ireland suggest that it can, under certain circumstances, provide strong incentives towards moderation, and may well be preferable to AV in situations where proportionality of outcomes and minority representation is of primary importance. One key variable appears to be the number and distribution of various groups. The evidence from Northern Ireland suggests that STV may be particularly apposite for societies in which there are two evenly balanced groups separated by a core group of moderates. In such a situation, STV can ensure not just the proportional representation of this 'moderate minority', but also bolster their influence via vote transfers from the flanks. In the past, when evaluating the recommendations of the Fiji Constitution Review Commission, I have argued that STV and AV should be seen as variations on the same basic theme, not either/or choices (see Reilly 1997c). AV is simply the application of STV to single-member districts, while STV becomes more AV-like the smaller the number of members to be elected in each district becomes. The effect of each system is mediated by the social structure in which it is applied. For example, STV in three-member districts has a quota for election of just over 25 per cent – considerably lower than the 50 per cent majority threshold required for election under AV. But this only tells half the story, because the application of STV with three seats per district in a bipolar society (assuming district heterogeneity and core political parties on both sides) would usually guarantee one seat each for each group, but make the third seat dependent on vote-pooling and eminently winnable by a non-ethnic centre party. In other words, such a system design could, under the right social conditions, have the advantage of not just *encouraging* but often *requiring* vote-pooling to take place, at least for the third seat in each district. This suggests that in some circumstances a mixture of AV and STV rules may well represent an optimal centripetal model.[4] Both systems have their specific advantages – AV is simpler and maintains

---

[4] A mixture of single-member seats elected by AV and multi-member seats elected by STV was recommended by the Street Commission (1975) as the most appropriate electoral arrangements for Fiji, but never implemented. Estonia's 1990 STV election did include some single-member seats in the (Russian-dominated) northern electorates, but was mostly STV.

single-member representation, STV is more complex but also more
proportional – but their similarities outweigh their differences and, in
fact, one is a variant of the other.

The theoretical claims of using SV elimination procedures are, by
contrast, much less clear. The types of examples of third placed 'middle
candidates' coming through a divided pack to gain election, as will sometimes be the case at AV elections, is not possible under SV rules. Because of
this, SV forces voters to vote strategically, as it is not possible for third or
lower-placed candidates to win. This provides another point of contrast
with Horowitz's recommendations. In most of his writings to date,
Horowitz has concentrated on the Sri Lankan supplementary vote system
when discussing the accommodative potential of preferential voting. As
the above discussion of the relative properties of AV and SV makes clear,
however, on most comparative indicators AV is a superior system. Because
its counting rules ensure the progressive elimination of lower-placed
candidates one-by-one rather than simultaneously eliminating all but the
top two, AV potentially offers much greater minority involvement in an
election than SV. Under AV, any candidate bar the lowest placed has a
chance to win the seat; under SV only the two top-placed candidates have
this opportunity. Some see this as an advantage: while under AV it is
possible for a candidate leading on first preferences to be knocked out by a
third or fourth-placed candidate who receives an influx of preference
votes, only the top two place-getters on first preferences can win a SV
ballot. Critics argue that these lower-order preferences, transferred from
eliminated candidates under AV rules, will not always reflect voters' 'real'
preferences (Dunleavy *et al.* 1997). But from the standpoint of encouraging
moderation in divided societies, this also suggests that SV will not be as
effective an instrument as AV, as it effectively limits the choices and
prospects of success for candidates who are unlikely to come first or second
on first preferences alone, and consequently reduces the impact that
minorities may have on the overall result.

All of which suggests that institutions matter not just at the macro level
but at the micro level as well. The long-term impacts of apparently minor
variations in electoral rules is a key aspect of electoral engineering that
deserves greater recognition when making suggestions for system design.
As we have seen, even what appear to be trivial mechanical differences,
such as the method of elimination for lower-placed candidates, can have a
major impact upon electoral outcomes. This point will be emphasised in
the following chapter, which looks at the theoretical pros and cons of
preference voting and the type of micro-level institutional choices which
can often mean the difference between the success or failure of centripetal
strategies for democracy in divided societies.

7

Technical variations and the theory of preference voting

Introduction

As the discussion in Chapter 6 shows, minor variations in the technical specifications of different voting systems can have a major impact on their relative performance. In the same way, 'second tier' electoral system design choices, such as the number of members elected from each district or the layout and structure of the ballot, can significantly affect the efficacy of different systems as instruments of constitutional engineering. Two particularly important alternatives when implementing preferential voting systems are the choice between single-member versus multi-member electoral districts, and the alternatives of making the marking of preferences a legal requirement for a valid ballot or leaving the decision to mark preferences in the hands of the voter. I will argue in this chapter that such apparently trivial decisions can have major implications for the success or failure of centripetal strategies.

In his seminal work on the political consequences of electoral laws, Douglas Rae (1967, 16–39) argued that there are three crucial sources of variation between different electoral systems:

1. Electoral formula – that is, the method by which votes cast are translated into seats won, e.g. choices between majoritarian formulae such as FPTP, AV, SV and run-off systems; semi-proportional formulae such as parallel systems or the single non-transferable vote; and forms of proportional representation such as list PR or STV.
2. Districting and 'district magnitude' – that is, the question of whether electoral districts are single-member or multi-member, and the con-

      sequences of these institutional variations for wider issues of political
      geography and representation.

3. Ballot structure – that is, whether the layout of the ballot paper and
      the instructions given for marking a valid vote serve to structure a
      voter's choice so that only one discrete option is available (as in FPTP
      and list PR systems); or whether a degree of choice amongst or
      between parties or candidates is able to be expressed (as in AV, SV,
      STV and, by virtue of a second round of voting, run-off systems). Rae
      called the former 'categorical' ballots and the latter 'ordinal' ballots.

So far this book has focussed on Rae's first variable, the choice of
electoral formula. However, the two other variables – district magnitude
and ballot structure – also have a major impact on the performance of
different electoral choices for conflict management – and, in practice, all
three factors are so intertwined that it is not usually possible to discuss
one in isolation from the other. In some circumstances, the choice of
electoral formula determines these in advance: STV, for example, *always*
utilises multi-member electoral districts. By contrast, both AV and SV
elections can be held in either single or multi-member districts, although
the single-member version is much more common. Multi-member AV
has been used in the past in Nauru and some Canadian provinces, and in
the Australian Senate between 1919 and 1948. A version was originally
recommended, although not implemented, by the Fiji Constitution
Review Commission in 1996. When the Australian state of Queensland
used SV, some two-member electorates were used alongside the more
familiar single-member districts, although other applications of the
system appear to have occurred exclusively in single-member seats.

    All preferential systems can themselves be further broken down into
'compulsory preferential' and 'optional preferential' versions, depending
upon whether the decision to mark preferences beyond the first choice is
left to the voter (as in most cases) or whether it is a legislative requirement
for a valid ballot that a complete rank-ordering of preferences for all candidates be expressed. Compulsory preferential AV is used in Australia for
federal elections to the House of Representatives, and for state government
elections in Victoria, South Australia, Western Australia and the Northern
Territory. The only national-level application of optional preferential AV
was in Papua New Guinea between 1964 and 1975.[1] However, it was also
used for elections to state and provincial parliaments in Australia and
Canada in the early years of the twentieth century, and has more recently
been adopted in the Australian states of New South Wales and Queens-

---

[1] It was, however, also used as the electoral system for the twenty 'white' seats in
   Zimbabwe's 1980 and 1985 elections.

land. All examples of SV to date have featured optional preference marking. Finally, for elections held under STV, only the Australian Senate makes a complete expression of all preferences compulsory.[2]

At first glance, this combination of optional versus compulsory preference marking and single versus multi-member electoral districts presents a potentially confusing range of preferential voting alternatives. In practice, however, most jurisdictions make preference marking optional rather than compulsory, while almost all contemporary systems of preferential voting, with the exception of STV, utilise single-member rather than multi-member electoral districts. A full typology of these variations, at both the national and the state or provincial level, in the application of preferential electoral systems around the world is presented in Table 7.1.

Single-member versus multi-member districts

The number of members elected per district has long been recognised as a key variable influencing factors like proportionality and accountability. But this variable also has major implications for those designing preferential systems. Some system designs which work well under one district structure will create bizarre and anomalous results when used in other circumstances. For example, when AV is used in multi-member districts, the majoritarian features of the system become overwhelming. This is amply illustrated by the experience of multi-member AV in the Australian Senate between the First and Second World Wars. In these elections, in order to utilise AV in multi-member districts, each Senate seat was effectively filled by a separate election, but with the same electorate voting at each. Under this system, three members were elected from each of the six states at regular 'half-Senate' elections held every three years, but because of the way preferences were aggregated and counted, preference transfers flowed overwhelmingly from a party's first-listed candidate to the next on their list, meaning that one party tended to dominate at each election. Due to the stability of party support in the electorate, this procedure displayed a strong tendency to produce an outcome under which the same party grouping won every seat in a state. Of the sixty occasions on which a state-based Senate election was held under multi-member AV, fifty-five produced such an outcome. This experience graphically illustrated the dangers of using a majority electoral system in a situation of 'at large' multi-member electorates which demanded a proportional system to work effectively.

---

[2] In Tasmania, voters must express as many preferences as there are candidates to be elected (five per electorate).

Table 7.1. *A typology of preferential electoral systems*

Type of election	Single transferable vote	Supplementary vote	Alternative vote (optional preferences)	Alternative vote (compulsory preferences)	Alternative vote (multi-member districts)
National legislative elections (lower house)	Denmark 1855–64 Ireland 1922– Malta 1921– Northern Ireland 1973– Estonia 1990	–	Papua New Guinea 1964–75 Zimbabwe 1979, 1985 (white seats only)	Australia 1918– Fiji 1997–	Nauru 1951–71
National legislative elections (upper house)	Australia (Senate 1949–) Ireland 1922	–	–	–	Australia (Senate 1919–48)
National presidential elections	–	Sri Lanka 1978–	Ireland 1937–	–	–
State and provincial elections	Tasmania 1907– Australian Capital Territory 1993– New South Wales 1918–26 New South Wales (upper house) 1978– South Australia (upper house) 1982– Western Australia (upper house) 1989–	London mayoral 2000– New South Wales 1926–8 Queensland 1892–42	Queensland 1992– New South Wales 1981– Northern Territory 1980 Victoria 1911–15 Western Australia 1907–11[a] Alberta 1926–55 British Columbia 1952–4 Manitoba 1927–36	Victoria 1916– Queensland 1962–92 Western Australia 1912– South Australia 1936– New South Wales 1929–80 Victoria (upper house) 1916– Tasmania (upper house) 1909–	South Australia 1929–35

Sources: Wright 1980; Crisp 1983, 137; Goot 1985; Jaensch 1995; Farrell, Mackerras and McAllister 1996; Corry and Hodgetts 1960.
[a] Note that Wright 1980 and Crisp 1983 both incorrectly classify Western Australia 1907–11 as using the contingent (i.e. supplementary) vote.

The system's configuration also meant that it gave virtually no encouragement to minor parties to participate in Senate elections. At single-member AV elections held for the House of Representatives elections during the same period, it was possible for party dissidents to win election as independents or as representatives of new parties, particularly if they had a geographically concentrated base of support, and thirty-three such candidates were elected at general elections from 1919 to 1946. Because Senate elections, by contrast, used an entire state as one multi-member district, these pockets of support were swamped and minor party representation was effectively impossible. This created periods of such sustained and nationwide dominance by one party that on a number of occasions the Senate was scarcely workable as a legislative body, let alone as a house of review: in the period from 1947 to 1950, for example, there were only three opposition Senators – a leader, a deputy leader, and a whip – facing thirty-three government Senators. Such a level of system dysfunction and extreme disproportionality meant that the electoral system itself was primarily responsible for the erosion of public confidence in, and the legitimacy of, half the federal parliament; some have argued that it increased popular opposition to any strengthening of the federal government's powers (see Goot 1985, 226). Multi-member AV was replaced with STV in 1948 which, having been designed for multi-member constituencies, has operated in a far more logical way. The inappropriateness of multi-member AV evidenced by the case of the Australian Senate was such that no serious proposal for multi-member AV has ever again been forthcoming in Australia (Reilly and Maley 2000).

Given the extremely lop-sided and disproportional election results that multi-member AV can deliver, it is highly likely that such a system would be even more damaging if applied in an ethnically divided society, as it could result in large sections of the population being excluded completely from parliamentary representation. In fact, the extreme disproportionality and unpredictability of multi-member AV makes it an inappropriate system for any society, not just a divided one. Nonetheless, in recent years several proposals featuring multi-member AV have been advanced by constitutional engineers as part of an institutional package for democracy in divided societies. In 1991, in his work on constitutional engineering in South Africa, Horowitz proposed that multi-member AV might have to be used to ensure sufficient electorate-level heterogeneity there (1991a, 195) – a proposal that attracted considerable criticism from electoral systems scholars, most of whom focussed on the unworkability of multi-member AV as a major point of concern (see Lijphart 1991a; Reynolds 1995; Lijphart 1997). Similarly, the Fiji Constitution Review

Commission's original recommendation that forty-five seats in the Fijian parliament be elected from fifteen three-member constituencies was widely criticised by electoral experts, who pointed to the inequitable results delivered at Australian Senate elections under precisely this configuration. As noted earlier, the multi-member AV recommendations were dropped from the final draft of the 1997 Constitution, and replaced with single-member electorates.

Elsewhere, multi-member AV was also used in the tiny Micronesian state of Nauru, before being replaced with an even more unusual structure that is unique amongst the world's electoral systems. In 1971, Nauru retained their multi-member electorates and preferential ballot, but changed the way votes are tallied by counting voters' preferences as fractional votes – a first preference being worth one vote, a second preference being half a vote, a third preference worth a third of a vote, and so on. This ensures that lower-order preferences are not counted at the same weight as higher order ones, but are 'weighted' to reflect their lower ranking in a voter's preference order. The way these preference scores are tallied is also different to AV. Instead of the cycle of elimination of lowest placed candidates and transfer of preferences that occurs if no candidate has an outright majority on first preferences under AV, in Nauru there are no eliminations. Instead, each candidate's total preference 'score' is cumulated by simple addition of all preference rankings. After all votes are tallied, the leading candidates in each district, depending on the number of members to be chosen, are declared elected. This method thus represents the only national-level application of a Borda count that I am aware of anywhere in the world. This system was introduced in 1971 as an adaptation of the AV counting rules which Nauru had inherited at independence in 1968 – which was itself a direct transfer of the system used in Australia, which had administered Nauru as a United Nations Trust Territory since 1947 on behalf of its fellow trust powers, Britain and New Zealand. With only 9,000 people, no political parties and little in the way of political campaigns, it is difficult to generalise about the impact of these procedures upon politics and ethnic relations in Nauru, although the limited evidence available suggests that identity factors such as family links and religion are major influences upon voter choice (Crocombe and Giese 1988, 46). Preference-swapping strategies are thus virtually inevitable due to the combination of divided and intermixed ethnic groups with centripetal electoral institutions.

Optional versus compulsory preference marking

The relative merits of optional versus compulsory marking of preferences has also been the subject of disagreement and debate amongst the various proponents of different systems (see, for example, Laponce 1957, Punnett 1987, CRC 1996). Under optional preferential voting, electors are not required to express a preference for every candidate; if they wish, they can express a preference for only one. In the words of former Australian Prime Minister Gough Whitlam, optional preferential voting is 'perhaps the only electoral procedure in the world which allows electors to express their indifference to candidates' (1985, 679).[3] Optional preferential voting has the major advantage of not forcing electors to make choices between candidates about whom they are unfamiliar uncaring: not surprisingly, a national survey in 1979 showed a majority of Australian electors in favour of preference marking being optional rather than compulsory, with 72 per cent preferring the optional version and only 26 per cent favoring compulsory preference marking (Hughes 1990, 141).[4] A further clear advantage of leaving the decision to mark preferences in the hands of the voter is that problems of spoilt or invalid ballots due to numbering errors, a common problem associated with full preferential systems, are largely removed. For this reason, the optional version is probably the only form of preferential voting suited to conditions of low literacy or numeracy.

---

[3] Whitlam was presumably unaware of approval voting, in which voters mark their ballots only for those candidates they 'approve' of.

[4] At the federal level in Australia, the major political parties have been divided on this issue because of its partisan impacts. Until 1974, the Labor Party traditionally opposed preferential voting of any sort, seeing it (correctly) as a means by which the non-Labor forces were able to aggregate their vote shares to defeat Labor candidates. The Liberal–National Coalition, for the same reason, has tended to support compulsory preferential AV. Following the election of a Labor government in 1983, a parliamentary committee recommended the introduction of optional preferential AV for all future federal elections in Australia. This recommendation was not accepted by the government, principally because without a majority in the Senate, the government knew that it had little hope of forcing through any change. This proved to be a fortunate outcome for Labor: as discussed in Chapter 3, by 1990 the rise of new issues on the left of the political spectrum such as environmentalism saw the second and later preferences of voters supporting minor parties drift increasingly to Labor. This trend would undoubtedly have been less pronounced if the expression of such preferences had been optional. Labor consequently changed its official policy in 1991 to support 'full preferential voting for all elections for lower houses of Parliament' (Australian Labor Party 1991). Recent electoral history has thus emphasised the truth of Rose's (1983) dictum that, once chosen, electoral rules tend to persist by their own inertia: legislatures are almost always the product of the existing system and tend to be wary of the uncertain ramifications of change.

A major problem of optional preferential voting, however, is the tendency for voters to 'plump' for one candidate rather than express lower preferences, thus effectively turning many elections into FPTP contests. This was a recurring problem when optional preferential AV was used early last century for elections to Australian state lower houses in Western Australia and Victoria, and in the Canadian provinces of Alberta, Manitoba and British Columbia. In all of these cases optional preferential voting was abandoned – for full preferential AV in Australia, and for FPTP in Canada – because of the system's increasing approximation to a FPTP contest (Corry and Hodgetts 1960, 272). 'Plumping' has also been a problem in Northern Ireland at some elections – although less so at the 1998 elections, where one survey found that only 8 per cent of the electorate were 'plumpers', and that most expressed an average of four preferences, with about 10 per cent of voters marking a vote transfer from unionist to nationalist candidates, or vice versa, at one or more points in their preference ordering (Evans and O'Leary 1999). But the special conditions in evidence at Northern Ireland's 'Good Friday agreement' election, which featured highly motivated voters and a clear delineation between pro- and anti-peace agreement forces, may not apply more generally. Following the introduction of optional preferential AV for Australian state elections in New South Wales in 1981 and Queensland in 1992, for example, the rate of 'plumping' in both cases has increased over time. The extent to which voters express preferences also appears to be closely related to the recommendations made by parties on their 'how-to-vote' cards. In a survey conducted at two Australian by-elections in 1992, fully 75 per cent of electors followed party voting directions, resulting in plumping rates of 43 per cent in one district and 63 per cent in another.[5]

All of this suggests that making preference marking optional rather than compulsory may well undermine incentives for vote-pooling in divided societies. In Sri Lanka, for example, surveys suggest that only a small minority of voters usually express any preferences after the first. Similar trends are in evidence in other optional preferential elections: in

---

[5] Personal communication, State Electoral Office of New South Wales, 12 July 1996. In Queensland, plumping rates stood at 23 per cent at the first optional preferential AV election in 1992, but were significantly higher in those seats where how-to-vote material from one of the major parties did not suggest marking preferences (Electoral Commission Queensland 1995, 14). There is also a clear partisan component to plumping rates which reflects the long-standing coalition arrangements between the Liberal and National parties: in both New South Wales and Queensland, Labor voters are considerably more likely to 'plump' than supporters of the coalition parties (Lucy 1982, 105).

Malta only 1 per cent of votes for major-party candidates are transferred across party lines (Hirczy and Lane 1997, 23), while at Estonia's 1990 STV election ethnicity overrode other concerns in the ranking of candidates, with most voters restricting preference transfers to members of their own ethnic group (Taagepera 1996, 31). This confirms Laponce's theoretical speculation that under optional preference marking, voters in divided societies are more likely to fail to indicate any secondary choices than to give their preference vote to members of another community:

> it is very doubtful that the different choices of an elector will go from the candidates of one community to that of another. If the elector runs short of candidates he likes within his own community he will usually, rather than give a second, third or fourth choice to a candidate of a community other than his own, fail to indicate such subsidiary choices. (Laponce 1957, 327)

Similarly, in a comparison of optional and compulsory preferential AV, Punnett found that optional preference marking undermines 'at least two of the supposed merits of the Alternative Vote: the efficient mutual delivery of second preferences between allied parties, and the election of "legitimate" MPs who can claim to have the support of an overall majority of electors' (1987, 43). On the other hand, the experience of Papua New Guinea's optional preferential AV elections and Northern Ireland's 1998 'Good Friday' poll suggests that, where incentives are strong and the institutional possibility to do so is understood, voters will sometimes be prepared to pass their lower-order votes across the ethnic divide. Nonetheless, making preference marking compulsory to some degree, as is the case in both Fiji and Nauru, clearly increases the chances of intercommunity vote transfers taking place. For this reason, proposals to reintroduce AV in Papua New Guinea have focussed on the possibilities of a 'limited preferential vote' in which a minimum number of preferences (e.g., three) must be marked to ensure a valid vote (Papua New Guinea Electoral Commission 1995, 1).

One problem of making preference marking compulsory is that it creates difficulties of intelligibility for some voters, particularly in developing countries or in communities with low literacy levels. One way around this problem is to include a 'ticket vote' option, as in Fiji, so that with one mark voters can adopt their favoured party's entire preference ordering – although, as we have seen, this can give rise to a range of other unanticipated side-effects. Another is to adopt the ballot structure proposed for the supplementary vote in Britain, where a second choice vote is marked with cross in a separate column rather than with a number (Dunleavy et al. 1997). A third option is for electoral officials to assist voters, as occurred in Papua New Guinea's early elections. Interestingly, even under conditions of weak political development and low literacy or formal education, research indicates that most voters find the *concept* of rank-ordering makes sense. Assuming basic voter education is forthcoming, comparative experience suggests that voters usually understand the logic, if not the mechanics, of preferential voting. Examination of election results in both pre-independence Papua New Guinea and outback Australian Aboriginal communities, for example, has found that the concept of rank-ordering potential representatives is intelligible to voters, and that they have little difficulty marking their ballots, particularly following several electoral iterations. As one Aboriginal educator in Australia's Northern Territory put it, even at his remote settlement, voters 'clearly knew how to mark "1" for the good bloke and "3" for the bad bloke' (quoted in Loveday and May 1981, 154). The results from four remote Aboriginal settlements at the 1987 Northern Territory election showed that rates of informal voting were equivalent to the average figure for rural polling places elsewhere in the Territory, at around 7.8 per cent (Loveday 1987). Similarly, Papua New Guinea's electors appeared to have little difficulty with the system by the time of the third AV election in 1972, and even initially sceptical observers have been persuaded of the intelligibility of the system in places like the Enga province of highlands Papua New Guinea (see Gordon and Meggitt 1985, 142).

Theoretical pros and cons

The question of optional versus compulsory expression of preferences also has important theoretical consequences. Most preferential systems are vulnerable to the effects of 'preference truncation', giving strategic voters an incentive not to rank all candidates in certain situations (Brams and Taylor 1996, 211). This needs to be tempered somewhat: a voting system which *requires* electors to express preferences they may not in fact possess, such as a full preferential system, is susceptible to random effects such as the 'donkey vote' phenomenon observed at federal elections in Australia, in which some electors simply number sequentially from 1 onwards down the ballot paper. In such cases, a system in which electors rank only as many preferences as they actually possess is clearly superior to one that forces them to invent preferences. As noted above, however, if all electors only expressed one preference, then the resultant contest would effectively become a FPTP contest, which has some serious theoretical limitations of its own.

Nonetheless, it is hard to find anyone interested in electoral systems who opposes the rank-ordering of candidates *per se* – indeed, many argue that a fundamental test of any electoral system is whether it enables a voter to formally express their personal rankings of parties and candidates on the ballot. McLean claims that some facility for preference ordering is one of three basic requirements of a good voting system: as most voters can normally rank at least some of the candidates for election against each other, the more information a voting procedure can use, the better (1987, 154). Similarly, Blais and Massicotte write that 'the more information the ballots reveal about voters' preferences, the more accurate the representation of preferences is likely to be' (1996, 76). Lijphart concurs, arguing that the facility for transferring and accumulating votes – possible only with some form of preferential ranking – are two innovations 'that appear to work particularly well and that deserve to be recommended as models for electoral engineers elsewhere' (1994a, 145).

Of course, the actual manner in which transferability, accumulation and rank-ordering of preferences is achieved depends primarily on the way an electoral system permits the expression of preference information via its ballot structure. Rae's distinction between *categorical* and *ordinal* ballots, enumerated at the start of this chapter, is again important here. A ballot is categorical if it forces voters to say they prefer one party or candidate as opposed to all others, as is the case in FPTP systems, 'closed' list PR systems and those 'open' party lists which enable voters to choose between candidates but not between parties. An ordinal ballot structure allows a more complex expression of choice via a rank-ordering of parties or candidates, as under AV, SV and STV elections (Rae 1967, 17–18). Rae also defined as ordinal those systems that enable 'cumulation' (the ability to give more than one vote to the same candidate) or 'panachage' (the ability to vote for several candidates from different party lists), as exists in Switzerland and Luxembourg.

The distinction between ordinal and categorical ballots exists on a different dimension to the standard typology of electoral systems, which seeks to classify different systems into examples of majoritarian formulae on the one hand and proportional representation formulae on the other (Lijphart 1984, 150–68). In contrast to this way of classifying electoral systems, ordinal balloting is found across both PR and non-PR systems. It are also a feature of run-off systems, which effectively force voters to make choices about their preferred candidates in two separate contests. By contrast, most versions of PR do not enable electors to vote for more than one party or to express the strength of their choice. All of the continental European democracies except France use some form of party list PR, for example, and most of these give the voter some choice as to the ordering of candidates within a party list.[6] But in all of these cases (bar the exceptions of Switzerland and Luxembourg noted above), voters can only choose between candidates *within* a chosen party list, not between candidates from rival parties. The defining feature of preferential voting, and the factor that makes preference-swapping such an effective political tool – the ability to rank candidates from different parties – is not present.

While most political scientists would argue that the greater choice available under an ordinal ballot makes it unequivocally a good thing, there are also more subtle difficulties in forcing voters to make an ordinal choice when they register their vote. Most famous is the 'voters' paradox': that for any three given voters (A, B, C) and options (p, q, r) it is possible that voter A ranks the options pqr, voter B ranks the options qrp and voter C ranks the options rpq. On any choice, p beats q, q beats r and r beats p. In such a case the options are said to 'cycle', meaning that there is no 'Condorcet winner'. A Condorcet winner is any option that can beat all others in a pairwise contest. In 1785, the Marquis de Condorcet first observed that in many voting systems, results were not necessarily fair if each option (or, in the case of an election, each candidate) could compete individually with each other candidate. If there are only two options, one of them must always be a Condorcet winner; but if there are more than two, then it is possible that none of them are. A good illustration of this paradox is the following example based on British parliamentary elections in which three candidates from the Conservative (C), Labour (L) and Liberal-Democrat (D) parties are competing for election. A hypothetical but plausible preference ordering of voters might be as follows:

Table 7.2. *A hypothetical preference ordering for British parliamentary elections*

Conservative voters (45%)	Labour voters (35%)	Liberal-Democrat voters (20%)
C	L	D
D	D	L
L	C	C

[6] For a detailed discussion see Katz 1986.

In a pairwise contest, it can be seen that 45 per cent of voters prefer C to L; 35 per cent prefer L to D; and 55 per cent prefer D to C (the other combinations are the obverse of these, i.e. 55 per cent prefer L to C; 65 per cent prefer D to L; and 45 per cent prefer C to D). The Condorcet winner is clearly D, who can beat both L and C in a pairwise contest (by 65 per cent and 55 per cent respectively). However, if this was a real British election held under FPTP then candidate C would have won the seat and candidate D would have come last. This is not a fanciful scenario: some reports have found that in 70 per cent of three-candidate elections, the outcome is affected by the voting procedure used.[7]

This example helps to explain the conviction of many electoral theorists that an ideal electoral system design should pick the Condorcet victor. McLean, for example, argues that any good voting system should pick a Condorcet winner if it exists (1987, 154). The problem is that all preferential systems can be shown to be capable of failing this condition. If we examine again the results from the seat of Richmond at the 1990 Australian election (Table 3.2), it is clear that candidate Blunt of the National Party is, *on first preferences*, the most popular candidate. His first-preference vote (28,257) is clearly superior to his two main rivals, candidates Newell (18,423) and Caldicott (16,072), and to all other candidates. However, as the distribution of preferences shows, it is equally clear that Blunt was not the most-favoured candidate of a majority of all voters: more people wanted someone other than Blunt to win the seat than wanted Blunt himself to win. As we are not privy to the preference orderings of those who voted for the non-eliminated candidates (Blunt and Newell), it is impossible to know whether there was a Condorcet winner; it may be that there wasn't one. Assuming that Downs' median voter theorem applies, and that issues are uni-dimensional, there should always be a Condorcet winner (see Downs 1957, ch. 8). Where issues are multi-dimensional – that is, are not capable of being placed on a linear continuum, such as left–right – then all bets are off: there are no guarantees that a Condorcet winner exists.

When a Condorcet winner does exist, preferential voting systems will sometimes fail to pick the Condorcet winner, but they can never pick the Condorcet *loser* – that is, the least-favoured party or candidate. By contrast, any system which does not take account of a complete ordering of preferences (such as FPTP), and even sometimes those that do, are open to the possibility of the Condorcet loser being chosen. Under a categorical ballot, a voter is often faced with a dilemma: is it better to support the most favoured candidate even though that candidate is

---

[7] See 'The Mathematics of Voting', *The Economist*, 4 March 2000.

unlikely to win, or to support a less preferred but more widely popular candidate who may have a better chance of victory? The dilemma of such 'strategic voting' – voting for a candidate who is not one's first choice – is one of the most basic problems with all ordinal ballot voting systems, particularly those that use a FPTP formula. One of the great advantages of preferential voting systems is that they are much less susceptible to the effects of strategic voting – partly because the requirement to rank candidates makes some kinds of strategic activity unnecessary (see Lijphart 1994a, 189), and partly because the information requirements to successfully effect strategic voting at mass elections are so onerous (see Bartholdi 1991, 341–54). Lijphart has found a 'virtual absence of strategic voting' (1994a, 98) in Australia, and there is no evidence that strategic voting of the type that regularly occurs at British elections has ever been a factor under any preferential voting system anywhere. Nonetheless, under certain theoretical scenarios, all non-dictatorial voting systems can be subject to manipulation and strategic voting, and preferential systems are no exception.[8]

If the two major theoretical advantages of preferential voting systems are that they enable both the expression and aggregation of voters' preferences amongst candidates, and that they are not (except in extremely unlikely circumstances) susceptible to strategic voting, then what about the theoretical *disadvantages* of preferential voting? One disadvantage has already been identified: *compulsory* marking of preferences, such as in Australia, compels voters to express preferences which they may not in fact possess, while *optional* preferential systems are susceptible to becoming straight FPTP contests if nobody expresses more than a first preference. These are potentially serious problems, but relatively minor when compared to the more fundamental theoretical objection that preferential voting is not always *monotonic*. A voting system is monotonic if gaining more votes can never hurt a candidate. While it is true that simply gaining more first preference votes will not harm a candidate's chances under preferential voting, it does not follow that a change in the number of first preferences taken from one candidate and given to another will always help the beneficiary of those votes. It is easily proven that, as a result of altering the sequence in which lower-placed candidates are eliminated, gaining more first preference votes can see a candidate lose an election he would otherwise have won. The following example is

---

[8] This is the essence of the Gibbard–Satterthwaite theorem on the manipulability of electoral systems (see Gibbard 1973; Satterthwaite 1975). For a discussion of strategic voting applied to preferential systems, see Dummett 1984, 210–30.

taken from Brams and Fishburn's analysis of the vagaries of STV, but it applies equally to other forms of preferential voting such as AV or SV:

> Assume there are four classes of voters, with the indicated numbers of voters in each class ranking four candidates (a, b, c, d) as follows:
>
> | I. | 7: *abcd* |
> | II. | 6: *bacd* |
> | III. | 5: *cbad* |
> | IV. | 3: *dcba* |
>
> Since no candidate has a majority (i.e. 11 votes out of the total number of 21), the lowest scoring candidate, *d*, with 3 votes, is eliminated and his second preferences passed on to candidate *c*, giving *c* 8 votes. Because none of the remaining candidates still has a majority, the (new) lowest placed candidate, *b*, is eliminated next, and his six second preferences go to candidate *a*, who is elected with 13 votes.
>
> Now examine the situation where the three class IV voters raised candidate *a* from fourth to first in their rankings, so that their new ordering would be *adcb*. Now *a* has ten votes (one short of a majority), *b* has six votes and *c* has five votes. As the new lowest placed candidate, *c* is eliminated and his five second preferences passed on to *b*, who is elected with an absolute majority of 11 votes (Brams and Fishburn 1984, 150–1).

This remarkable result is illustrative of one of the fundamental paradoxes of all voting systems: they are all open to manipulation in some manner, and almost all can be proven to fail relatively undemanding tests of fairness and rationality. The explanation for the apparently capricious scenario outlined above is in the sequence by which preferential voting systems eliminate lower-ranked candidates if no-one has an absolute majority of first preferences. When the candidate with the lowest number of first preference votes is eliminated, his or her second and later preferences are then transferred to the continuing candidates as required. However, the *order* of this transfer of preferences is essentially arbitrary: the secondary preferences of voters who chose a relatively unpopular candidate are counted before the secondary preferences of those who chose a more popular candidate (who will still be in the running). There is no logical reason for privileging one preference ordering over any other, but this is precisely what happens under preferential voting. Indeed, in many cases the latter preferences of the leading candidate(s) will not be counted at all. In enabling all voters to express their preferences, elimination-based systems like AV and STV inadvertently makes some preference orderings count more than others.

The question of monotonicity may seem theoretical and remote from the real world, but it isn't. Lack of monotonicity was crucial to the Labour

Party Plant Commission's rejection of STV (and, by implication, AV) as a desirable electoral system for Britain in 1992 (see Plant Commission 1992, Appendix 1). The commissioners, influenced by Oxford professor of logic Michael Dummett, were apparently sufficiently concerned at the theoretical possibilities of extra preference votes harming an individual candidate to reject STV as a viable electoral system for Britain – although curiously their favoured system, the supplementary vote, has this same weakness. A more likely explanation for the Labour Party's unexpected interest in the theory of voting paradoxes was that the stated concerns about monotonicity were in fact a convenient justification for ruling out a PR system which would not necessarily have assisted the party's electoral prospects. As one Labour campaigner explained: 'Dummett's criticism concerning the lack of monotonicity . . . was the excuse Labour was looking for because, with the press we have and the internal variety which goes to make up the Labour coalition, there was no way that Labour would, on its own, embrace a system where its candidates fight each other' (Georghiou 1993, 82). Nonetheless, the question of monotonicity has introduced a significant theoretical argument against the use of any preferential electoral system into the ongoing debate on electoral reform in the United Kingdom. While the non-monotonicity of preferential voting is a serious theoretical flaw, it would appear that the likelihood of Brams and Fishburn's scenario taking place in a real-world contest is remote (see Dummett 1984, 222). The chief electoral officer for Northern Ireland, for example, has found no evidence in twenty-two years for a non-monotonic election result (Bradley 1995), while one estimate has put the likely incidence of a non-monotonic election outcome under STV in the United Kingdom at less than one case every century (Allard 1995).

Conclusion

The message of this chapter is a simple one: all preferential systems are not equal, and apparently minor technical differences between the various electoral systems, such as the number of preferences to be marked or the number of seats to be elected in each district, can have major consequences in terms of electoral outcomes. For example, optional preferential voting appears to be less effective at ensuring cross-ethnic vote transfers than a full preferential version which makes marking of all preferences on the ballot compulsory. In addition, a number of systems which have been advocated as being particularly good choices for ethnically divided societies are found, upon closer examination, to have a range of undesirable consequences. For example, as the experience of elections to the Australian Senate between 1919 and 1948 made clear, multi-member AV

suffers from some major technical flaws which deliver highly disproportional election results, making it a particularly *unsuitable* system for
multi-ethnic societies, where it could quite likely lead to the complete
exclusion of even large minorities from representation. Horowitz's 1991
recommendation for the use of multi-member AV in South Africa thus
represented a serious flaw in his overall prescription for constitutional
engineering there. It also served to some extent to overshadow the merits
of his basic proposal for electoral engineering, and may well have retarded
more serious investigation of the benefits of single-member AV. A similar
criticism can be applied to his proposal that Fiji should, if it was unable to
ensure ethnic heterogeneity in single-member districts, instead utilise

> larger constituencies, in which two or three separately elected seats would
> be located. These would not be multi-member seats; two or three
> members would have to be elected by the same electorate to fulfil the
> requirement of constituency scale for heterogeneity, but candidates
> competing for one seat would compete only with candidates competing
> for that same seat, and preferences would be transferred only within single
> seats. (Horowitz 1997, 31)

Unfortunately, this would have mirrored, in practice, the way multi-
member AV worked in Australia: because each vacancy would have
effectively been filled by a different election, stable party identification in
the electorate could easily have resulted in every seat being won by the
same party. Also, it would most likely have created serious headaches in
terms of party nomination strategies. It was therefore not surprising that
this proposal was not adopted in Fiji.

In sum, and contrary to much of the existing literature, a comparison
of the relative performance of the various preferential electoral systems
suggests that either (single-member) AV or (multi-member) STV, pre-
ferably with compulsory marking of preferences but without ticket voting,
is likely to offer the most powerful incentives for encouraging centripetal
outcomes. This raises the question of what socio-structural conditions
facilitate the use of such systems, as centripetal methods can only work to
encourage inter-ethnic accommodation when constituency boundaries
can be drawn in such a way as to create ethnically heterogeneous districts.
We have already seen one way of dealing with this problem: elections to a
single office, such as a president or mayor, necessarily make use of the
whole population as one large single-member electorate, and thus
maximise prospects for heterogeneity. In other situations, such as parliamentary elections in Papua New Guinea, for example, there are *so many*
ethnic groups, numbering in the thousands, that even relatively small
single-member districts tend to include, in most cases, a number of

different ethnic groups all competing for election. Thus the key facilitating conditions for centripetal electoral methods to succeed – ethnic heterogeneity and a corresponding multiplicity of candidates – are both present. But what about other situations of ethnic group structure and demography? The final chapter of this book will examine the social conditions necessary for centripetal strategies to work effectively.

8

Conclusion: assessing the evidence

Let us briefly recall the core arguments for centripetal theories of electoral system design put forward in the first chapter. Drawing on theories of bargaining and cooperation, centripetalism advocates institutional designs which encourage opportunities for dialogue and negotiation between opposing political forces in the context of electoral competition. By privileging cooperative campaign strategies with increased prospects of electoral success, candidates representing competing (and sometimes violently opposed) interests are presented with incentives to negotiate for reciprocal support, creating an 'arena of bargaining' where vote-trading arrangements can be discussed. Under a preferential voting system, depending on the makeup of the electorate and the relative strengths of the parties, the result of an election may turn on the secondary preference votes received from supporters of rival parties. Parties that succeed in negotiating preference-trading agreements for reciprocal support with other parties will be rewarded, thus presenting them with an *a priori* motivation to moderate their policy positions on key ethnic issues so as to broaden their appeal. This gives them strong institutional incentives both to engage in face-to-face dialogue with their opponents, and to negotiate on broader policy issues than purely vote-seeking ones. The overall effect is thus to reorient electoral politics away from a rigid zero-sum game to a more fluid, complex and potentially positive-sum contest. The theory of centripetalism postulated in this book is therefore primarily based upon the importance of the incentive structures and payoffs that particular electoral rules can offer.

Critics of centripetalism have in the past rejected these claims as unproven and unsustainable. Arend Lijphart, for example, described proposals for vote-pooling as a 'courageous challenge' to the scholarly consensus on democracy in divided societies which 'however courageous . . . does not deserve to succeed' (1991a, 99). He argued that consociational forms of democracy based around proportional representation of ethnic interests and constraints on majority rule are 'the *only* workable type of democracy in deeply divided societies' (1994b, 222). By contrast, centripetal prescriptions featuring majoritarian electoral rules like AV are 'deeply flawed and dangerous' models for multi-ethnic states (1994b, 224), while STV is suitable 'only for reasonably homogenous societies' (1990, 11).

The experience of AV and STV forms of preferential voting in at least four of the deeply divided societies examined in this book – Papua New Guinea, Fiji, Estonia and Northern Ireland – together call these conclusions into question, and suggest a need to look at preferential voting in a more expansive way than many commentators have attempted. As detailed in previous chapters, there is clear evidence in all three cases of inter-ethnic cooperation and centrist electoral outcomes being encouraged by the provision of the electoral law. This has clear implications for many other multi-ethnic societies searching for appropriate electoral institutions. As Esman has noted of ethnic politics in general,

> Electoral systems in which politicians depend on votes only from coethnics tend to reward ethnic extremists who assert maximal demands. Systems in which politicians seeking election must appeal to members of more than a single ethnic community and depend on their electoral support generally produce more moderate politics and reward accommodative politicians with cross-ethnic appeals. (1994, 258)

The evidence from this book lends support to Esman: in most of the cases examined, vote-pooling systems *did* indeed appear to produce more moderate politics, in terms of campaigning behaviour at least, and rewarded those politicians who made cross-ethnic appeals. In addition, the history of centripetal institutions in a non-divided society, Australia, suggests that the use of preference voting can encourage a search for the political 'middle ground' by the major parties, as well as promoting coalition arrangements and preference-swapping deals. The evidence from Australia also suggests that the long-term application of preferential electoral arrangements has contributed to the development of a stable, aggregative and centrist political party system – an important finding, as it is precisely this type of party system that has been identified by political scientists as providing the best prospects of democratic consolidation in transitional or divided societies (see Diamond, Linz and Lipset 1995, 35; Diamond 1996, 239).

As noted at the beginning of this book, a perceived dearth of supporting examples has long been the Achilles heel of centripetal theories. Sisk (1996), for example, argues that centripetalism is theoretically convincing but suffers from a lack of empirical examples which policymakers can examine. Most critiques of centripetal theories have similarly focussed on this lack of empirical evidence as a key weakness (see, for example, Sisk 1996, 44, 62; Diamond and Plattner 1994, xxiv; Lijphart 1995b, 863). In addition, the scholar most closely associated with the centripetal model, Donald Horowitz, provided few real-world examples of centripetalism in action. For this reason, the clear evidence for centripetal outcomes in Papua New Guinea, Fiji and Northern Ireland, apparently in response to the incentives presented by the electoral system, is itself an important finding for political scientists and political engineers. In particular, as a result of the detailed observations and electoral studies of Papua New Guinea's three AV elections, there is considerable empirical support for the claim that preference voting procedures can encourage ethnic accommodation. The Papua New Guinea case also illustrates the clear differences between the effects of preferential (AV) and non-preferential (FPTP) electoral laws in an ethnically fragmented society.

Vote-pooling in Papua New Guinea took place in three primary ways, all of which were predicated on the assumption that most voters would invariably give their first preference vote to their own clan or 'home' candidate. The most common and successful method of vote-pooling was for a candidate who had a limited 'home' support base to campaign widely for second-level support amongst rival groups. This required a range of techniques, such as translating campaign speeches and travelling widely throughout an electorate, with the essential request being not for a first-preference vote but for a second or third preference. For this strategy to succeed, candidates needed to be able to sell themselves as the 'second-best' choice – which meant, in general, someone who would look after all groups fairly – and to campaign as much for second preference votes as for first preferences. A second strategy was for candidates with significant existing support bases to reach out to selected allies for secondary support. Traditional tribal contacts and allegiances could be utilised to create majority victors, as was the case in the Dei Open electorate at the 1972 elections, where the winning candidate forged close connections with a rival tribe and urged his supporters to cast their preferences for a member of that tribe as well as for himself. A third strategy, and increasingly common by the time of Papua New Guinea's third AV election in 1972, was for groups and candidates to form mutual alliances, sometimes campaigning together and urging voters to cast reciprocal preferences for one or the other. These alliances were a response to the incentives presented by AV for campaigning on a common platform, whereby the sharing of preferences between aligned candidates was perceived as a rational activity which maximised prospects of electoral victory. They also appear to have given some impetus to the need to organise politically, and can thus be seen as the forerunners to the establishment of political parties in Papua New Guinea. In general, the Papua New Guinea case offers powerful evidence in favour of what Lijphart (1991a, 95) called 'the dubious claim that AV induces moderation'.

Additional evidence for centripetal approaches to conflict management comes from Australia, Fiji, Sri Lanka, Estonia and Northern Ireland. The combined evidence from these cases is mixed but does suggest that, under certain conditions, preferential voting systems can indeed encourage cooperative political behaviour and accommodative outcomes. The evidence from Fiji, for example, suggests that the new opportunities for inter-elite negotiation and reciprocal preference deals provided by the application of AV electoral rules encouraged both multi-ethnic coalitions and cross-ethnic bargaining at the 1999 election. In particular, the new rules opened up avenues for inter-elite negotiations and strategies that simply were not present under previous, non-preferential, electoral systems. A similar conclusion applies to Northern Ireland's crucial 1998 elections which ushered in the power-sharing executive under the 'Good Friday' agreement. Analysis of this election suggests that preference-vote transfers served to give voice and representation to the 'moderate middle' sentiment for peace that existed within the community, and to translate this sentiment into an electoral majority for 'pro-agreement' parties. The evidence from Estonia suggested that STV may have encouraged the early development of multi-ethnic politics. In addition to such cases there is the instructive example of Australia, discussed in Chapter 3. While not a divided society, the Australian case shows the way preference voting has, over time, encouraged the aggregation of political interests and provided the centrist major parties with the opportunity to cooperate to expunge a rising extremist movement from legislative representation. Only Sri Lanka, which has used a preference voting system to elect its president since 1978, appears to present ambiguous or negative evidence for the combination of vote-pooling and inter-ethnic accommodation.

The evidence from Papua New Guinea, and to a lesser extent from Fiji and Northern Ireland as well, also quells two of the other concerns frequently raised by critics of centripetal theories: the 'questionable assumptions' that politicians in ethnically divided societies will respond to electoral incentives for moderation, and the issue of whether voters in divided societies would be willing to give second-preference support to candidates from outside their own ethnic group (Sisk 1992, 43). In most of the cases examined, then, there is empirical evidence to support the hypothesis that vote-pooling electoral laws can encourage centripetal political behaviour. The evidence also suggests that the effect of preferential electoral rules can be clearly distinguished from non-preferential rules in at least ten discrete areas: incentives for moderation; the impact of iteration; fairness of outcomes; mass versus elite activity; impact on party system development; incentives for coalition promotion; centralism versus extremism; bargaining and cooperation; the psychological impact on the electoral process; and facilitating socio-structural and demographic conditions. In the remainder of this conclusion I will briefly discuss and summarise each of these issues in turn.

Incentives for moderation

Different electoral systems offer different types of incentives for cooperation. In Papua New Guinea, comparison of an electoral system which acts as a zero-sum game (FPTP) compared to an electoral system which, under certain circumstances, acted as a positive-sum game (AV) illustrates this point quite well. Just as there is evidence that AV served to encourage cooperative and accommodative political strategies and behaviour, there is also evidence for the obverse: that is, when incentives for cooperation were removed by a change of electoral system in 1975, ethnic groups reverted to their traditional hostilities. This return to conflict was encouraged by incentives for non-accommodative behaviour inherent in FPTP rules when applied in a fragmented society, which reward vote-splitting and encourage zero-sum campaign tactics. Attempts in Papua New Guinea in recent years to constrain these activities have generally proved unsuccessful: candidates have reacted to the incentives for victory under FPTP by focusing their energies on maximising their clan-based vote, and in many cases restricting the campaigning of opposition candidates to their own home areas. This has led to politicians being elected on increasingly small pluralities, and to ever-increasing numbers of candidates standing for election, as under FPTP the higher the number of candidates, the smaller the total vote needed to gain a plurality and hence win the seat.

This distinction between two apparently similar electoral systems on the basis of their zero-sum versus positive-sum characteristics is particularly important, as a recurring criticism of the case for AV in ethnically divided societies has been that AV is no more likely to reward moderation than FPTP. Lijphart in particular has argued that there is no more incentive towards moderate behaviour inherent in AV than there is in FPTP. He characterised centripetal arguments by citing three imaginary candidates A, B and C supported by 45 per cent, 40 per cent and 15 per cent of the voters respectively. Under a vote-pooling scenario, A and B will have to bid for the second preferences of C's supporters in order to win – which should, according to centripetal theories, reward moderation. According to Lijphart, exactly the same argument can be made for FPTP:

> In the same example under FPTP rules, many of C's supporters will not want to waste their votes on C's hopeless candidacy, or may not even be able to vote for C at all because C wisely decides not to pursue a hopeless candidacy. Hence here too, A and B will have to appeal to C's supporters in order to win . . . the votes instead of the second preferences of C's supporters would be traded. AV and FPTP provide exactly the same incentives. (1991a, 94)

This argument assumes that voters will be prepared to cast their primary vote for an ethnic rival, or that minor candidates will pull out of an electoral race when their low support levels become clear. While this may be a defensible premise in some (usually Western) scenarios, in situations of ethnically based voting it is simply not realistic, 'especially given the emotional politics of divided societies' (Sisk 1993, 84). In Papua New Guinea, for example, many clans will put forward and support their own candidate for election, regardless of that candidate's chances of winning. Under FPTP this may indeed be a hopeless strategy, but it is justified in terms of the prestige and opportunity for social advancement associated with standing for political office. Under AV, by contrast, candidates from smaller clans (or those with a small base vote, such as expatriate candidates) were able to campaign outside their home area for other voters' second preferences, in the full knowledge that first preferences would mostly go to the local clan candidate, but that electoral victory on the back of secondary preferences was still possible. Similarly, in Australia, the introduction of AV in place of FPTP for federal elections in 1918 led to immediate changes in political behaviour. The vote splitting that had previously been widespread on the conservative side of politics was quickly replaced by moves to aggregate political interests via preference-swapping arrangements, which then developed into a long-term coalition deal between the major conservative parties.

Iteration

The sequence of increasingly sophisticated responses to the institutional incentives of the electoral game that is evident at successive Papua New

Guinean and Australian elections also illustrates the importance of the *iteration* of events – repeating the game under a stable set of rules over and over again – in forging new norms of behaviour. Because of their regularly repeated nature, electoral contests can be interpreted as a version of the infamous 'Prisoner's Dilemma' game well known to social choice theorists, in which rational players have a simultaneous incentive to adopt non-cooperative strategies but also, when the game is viewed as a regular and indefinitely repeated exercise, to reach cooperative arrangements between themselves. Under 'Prisoner's Dilemma' situations, the theoretical literature on game theory and on the evolution of cooperation highlights the rationality of 'tit-for-tat' cooperative strategies between competing participants (Axelrod 1984; Taylor 1987) – the only proviso being that games are iterated and that information is incomplete, a basic assumption of much rational choice literature in political science (see Tsebelis 1990).

The empirical evidence collected in previous chapters suggests, in line with these findings, that reciprocally cooperative strategies can develop even in markedly unpromising environments given sufficient uncertainty about the duration and outcome of the game. The evidence also suggests that political actors presented with institutional incentives for cooperation undergo a process of *political learning*, and come to view cooperation as an increasingly rational strategy as successive iterations of the game are played out. Three case studies examined in this book lend empirical support to this theoretical assumption: in the three longest-running vote-pooling systems – Australia, Papua New Guinea and Northern Ireland – the degree of cooperative behaviour tended to increase over time, as successive iterations of the electoral game provided the opportunity for optimal strategies to be discovered and refined. In Australia, the extent and influence of preference distribution has increased steadily over the past thirty years. In Papua New Guinea, each preferential voting election featured a greater degree of preferences changing electoral outcomes than its predecessor. And in Northern Ireland, the 1998 election clearly evidenced a greater degree of both usage and sophistication in utilising vote transfers than any previous election. Centripetal behaviour, it appears, can be learned over time by parties, candidates and voters alike.

Just as this temporal element of institutional design is an important element in establishing new behavioral routines, so the *timing* of cross-ethnic appeals for vote transfers is also of great significance: the earlier these begin, the greater their chances of success. A process whereby groups are given incentives to behave accommodatively towards one another *before* an election is vastly preferable to expecting the representative of one particular ethnic interest to behave accommodatively *after* an election. Under conditions of electoral uncertainty, vote-transfer systems provide incentives for groups to cooperate and compromise before an election, and reward those candidates who make early and sustained appeals beyond their own group. In so doing, they help establish patterns of reciprocal activity that increase the credibility of cross-ethnic appeals and the perceived likelihood of such behaviour becoming a recurring pattern of reliable positive-sum exchanges. Early introduction and stable application of such rules, as in many other areas of constitutional engineering, is extremely important for longer-term prospects of behavioral modification.

Fairness

A frequent criticism of vote-pooling electoral systems in general, and of majoritarian systems like AV in particular, is that they are defective in terms of the proportionality of outcomes they deliver. As discussed in Chapter 1, 'proportionality' refers specifically to the seats–votes relationship: an electoral system is proportional to the extent that a party's share of the vote is matched by its share of the seats in parliament. For many, this has become the pre-eminent criterion against which electoral systems should be assessed. As Lijphart has put it, 'there is wellnigh universal agreement that electoral proportionality is a major goal of electoral systems and a major criterion by which they should be judged'; particularly for supporters of PR it is 'virtually synonymous with electoral justice' (1994, 140). Under such arguments, proportionality between votes and seats is often considered to be something of a *sine qua non* of electoral systems: the case for PR can be summed up as a 'feeling that disproportional electoral results are inherently unfair and undemocratic' (Lijphart 1996, 176). Proportional election results are often considered to be particularly important for ethnically divided societies because they enable minorities to be represented in the legislature and (through power-sharing arrangements) to take part in governing coalitions. The argument that minorities are fairly represented is thus the cornerstone of the case for PR in divided societies, although critics counter that PR can induce the formation of narrow ethnic parties that promote ethnic cleavages (Tsebelis 1990).

There are several aspects of the debate about proportionality that deserve our attention. First, there is no doubt that preferential rules like AV and SV, as majority systems, are clearly less proportional than most forms of PR, and have often been criticised by electoral reformists for this very reason. Enid Lakeman, for example, argued that AV results could be 'nearly as unrepresentative as those of a British general election', giving the example of the 1948 AV election in the Canadian province of Alberta, at which the Social Credit party won a clean sweep of all seats with 58 per cent of the total vote (1974, 63–4). On the other hand, by most indicators preferential systems are as, or more, proportional than their non-preferential counterparts, comparing like with like. For example, STV has generally been assessed as one of the most proportional PR systems (Blondel 1969, Lijphart 1986), although its actual proportionality in real-world elections has often suffered because of the relatively small districts in which it is usually applied. Similarly, comparisons of Australian elections with those of other countries have found that AV sits around mid-way on an index of disproportionality of electoral systems, being as or more proportional than all non-PR systems such as FPTP or the double ballot, but less proportional than PR systems (Lijphart 1984, 160). Taagepera and Shugart, for example, found that Australia, as their only AV example, had one-half to one-third the deviation from proportionality of most FPTP systems, and was actually more proportional than PR systems in Spain, South Korea and elsewhere (1989, 106–7). More recently, Lijphart (1997) found that over a longer time period, Australian AV elections evidenced roughly the same levels of proportionality as FPTP systems in Britain, Canada and New Zealand.

However, measurements of proportionality in any 'candidate-centered' electoral system (as all preferential systems are) are fundamentally problematic, as voters are choosing not between parties but between individuals (Carey and Shugart 1995). In most cases, therefore, we simply do not know to what extent voters choose a candidate on the basis of his or her party affiliation, nor do we know to what extent a party vote was garnered on the basis of individual factors such as the presence of a popular candidate. This greatly complicates genuine measures of proportionality. In cases such as Papua New Guinea, for example, in the pre-independence period examined in Chapter 4 there were no political parties of which to speak; even today most of the parliament are elected as independents. This makes the traditional calculation of the relationship between a party's vote share and its seat share – a mainstay of discussions of a 'party vote' and the proportionality of electoral outcomes – extremely difficult in practice and largely meaningless as a measure of electoral support. Similar concerns, to a greater or lesser extent, could be raised about all of our other cases.

A more subtle problem when discussing the proportionality of preferential electoral systems is the way preferences after the first-preference vote are measured. Critics often contend that a major factor in the disproportionality of majority systems is their high number of 'wasted' votes – that is, votes which do not go towards the election of any candidate. However, such arguments run into serious problems when attempting to evaluate preferential systems. If a preferential voter sees his or her second-preference candidate elected, then it makes little sense to declare that such a vote is 'wasted' and the voter 'unrepresented'.[1] On the contrary, we could expect most voters to be reasonably happy with such an outcome, as the structure of a preferential ballot is specifically designed to elicit information about which candidate a voter would choose if his or her first (or second, or third etc.) choice is defeated. Nonetheless, that is precisely how most electoral scholars attempt to evaluate preferential vote rules, leading to a situation where the measurements of both disproportionality and the numbers of 'wasted' votes tend to appear higher than they really are. For this reason, assessments of preferential voting systems on the basis of their proportionality which do not consider the impact of lower-order preferences – which means most of the academic literature on this issue – offer a misconceived and sometimes misleading interpretation of the true relationship between seats and votes.[2]

Mass versus elite activity

A particular characteristic of the centripetal approach is its reliance on mass rather than elite activity as the driving force for moderation: while vote-pooling deals are made between candidates, the ultimate success of such strategies is dependent on the behaviour of their supporters 'on the ground'. By providing sufficient incentives for groups to cooperate and compromise before an election, and by providing an electoral system which rewards those candidates who reach beyond their own group for second and later preferences, centripetalism provides an impetus for conflicts to be managed at the popular rather than the elite level, before an election rather than after. Although most vote-pooling deals will be negotiated by leaders, in all cases they must be enacted by voters freely choosing between different candidates. Centripetalism posits the electorate as the engine of moderation in divided societies, and is thus particularly suitable for societies in which the focus of political competition is at the local rather than the national level. Sisk has argued that because centripetalism encourages political leaders to appeal to the moderate forces in an electorate in order to maximise their electoral

---

[1] My thanks to Donald Horowitz for suggesting this point.

[2] Some scholars therefore advocate using final count votes, rather than first preferences, to calculate disproportionality, which tends to have the effect of lowering the levels of disproportionality recorded in preferential systems. See Gallagher 1986.

prospects, it also promotes 'the kind of compromises they must make at the centre if the divided society is to be truly democratic and stable' (1995, 36). For this reason, centripetal strategies may work best when the focus of political competition is at the local level – as, for example, in Papua New Guinea.

Because of this, centripetalism also presumes much closer links between elite negotiations and the actions of voters at the mass level than consociationalism, as vote-pooling deals struck by party leaders ultimately depend upon the willingness of ordinary voters to carry them through. If vote transfers are to be sustainable, then party leaders must be able to communicate their vote-pooling intentions and vote transfer schemes to their supporters. The existence of robust elite-mass linkages is thus of great importance if centripetal strategies are to work well, as indeed they are for many broader issues of democratic development and consolidation (see Diamond 1998, 171–4). Conversely, centripetal strategies can be undermined by institutional rules which shift the locus of decision-making away from voters and towards party elites. The longer-term effects of ticket voting at the 1999 Fijian elections and on subsequent events there provide a graphic example of this.

This again illustrates a key difference between consociational and centripetal approaches to electoral system design. While in many ways both approaches use divergent means to achieve largely common ends, there is a fundamental difference in the relative weight each approach ascribes to mass versus elite activity. Consociationalism has been accurately described as government by a 'cartel of elites' (Lijphart 1969), in which there is little or no place for mass publics and mass action as agents of change. Decision-making power tends to be centralised in the hands of a small group of elites. Party leaders are of particular importance due to their power to influence which candidates are placed in winnable positions on a party list, and because of their subsequent role as representatives of distinct social and political groups during inter-elite negotiations. This means that consociational bargains can be struck even when linkages between masses and elites are relatively weak. There is little need for most voters to engage in cross-ethnic activity themselves; indeed, most consociational prescriptions presume that such behaviour is both unlikely and unnecessary – whatever deals between different groups are possible will be struck between the enlightened leaders of ethnic parties, not between voters. Consociational prescriptions for conflict management thus rely on assumptions of elite moderation and good faith, and are undermined by the increasing evidence from many regions of 'elite-initiated conflict': the clear pattern in many deeply divided societies of party leaders themselves being the ones who initiate and fuel inter-ethnic conflicts.[3] This stands in contrast to centripetal approaches, which posit ordinary electors as key actors in the process of conflict management who, by virtue of their decisions on preference allocation, are the ultimate arbiters of centripetalism's success or failure. Because of this reliance on the electorate, not elites, as the engine of moderation in divided societies, centripetal strategies may be particularly suitable for societies in which a core moderate voice exists, such as that in evidence at Northern Ireland's 1998 Good Friday agreement election.

Party system development

By facilitating alliances and aggregating common interests, in some of the cases examined in this book preferential voting appears to have also encouraged the development of broad multi-ethnic or non-ethnic political parties or coalitions of parties – itself an extremely important facilitating factor for democracy in divided societies. Scholars of ethnic conflict argue that weak and fragmented party systems are typical of ethnically divided societies, which are characterised both by the presence of many groups and the inability of any of them to dominate the political process. In post-colonial situations, where the rewards of political success become a valuable prize, parties proliferate but multi-party coalitions are difficult to hold together: 'effective party politics . . . does not usually emerge in the fragmented setting; no party is large enough to rule and the multiplicity of culture groups frustrates any attempts to form long-run multi-ethnic coalitions' (Rabushka and Shepsle 1972, 178). Many political scientists therefore view a meaningful party system as an essential element of effective representative government, sometimes identifying a functioning party system with democracy itself (Strom 1995, 924). Strong party systems, some contend, are both reflections of and indispensable pre-requisites for 'good democratic performance' (Powell 1982, 74). Diamond sums up the prevailing view of many scholars, arguing that 'political parties remain important if not essential instruments for representing political constituencies and interests, aggregating demands and prefer-ences, recruiting and socialising new candidates for office, organising the electoral competition for power, crafting policy alternatives, setting the policy-making agenda, forming effective governments, and integrating groups and individuals into the democratic process' (1997, xxiii).

In at least three of the cases discussed in this book – Australia, Papua New Guinea and Estonia – the introduction of preferential voting appears

---

[3] For a survey of the substantial evidence collected on elite-initiated conflict, see Horowitz 1991a, 140–1.

to have encouraged the development of political parties by facilitating formal alliances and encouraging the aggregation of like-minded interests into more coherent and programmatic party formations. This has important longer-term implications for democracy. Samuel Huntington, for example, argues that a key function of political parties is to present clear choices to voters and to link them closely to the political process; fragmented and personalised systems which fail to do this are extremely damaging for democratic prospects and are, consequently, found widely in the failed democracies of the developing world (see Huntington 1968, ch. 7). If it is true that the optimum political institutions for the consolidation of democracy include 'settled and aggregative' party systems in which 'one or two broadly-based, centrist parties fight for the middle ground' (Diamond 1996, 239), then the apparent spur towards aggregative party formation that preferential electoral systems appear to have provided in a number of the cases discussed in this book represent an extremely important instrumental benefit for vote-pooling electoral laws.

Coalitions

This foreshadows my next point: by presenting parties with incentives to strike pre-election vote-pooling deals in the expectation that they will work together in government, preferential voting appears to encourage political coalitions. These have typically been sustained at the electoral level by preference exchanges (the best contemporary example of which is the long-standing and apparently permanent coalition arrangement between the Liberal and National parties in Australia). In addition, most of our cases suggest that preferential electoral rules can encourage a coalition formation phase *before* elections rather than after them, 'a matter that has an absolutely fundamental impact upon the politics of coalition' (Laver and Schofield 1991, 206). This 'intertwining' of both parties and candidates in mutual alliances is central to the conflict management potential of centripetal electoral systems, which therefore act as a direct counterweight to the fragmentary and centrifugal tendencies of many other electoral systems, particularly multi-member majority or party-list PR systems (see Cox 1990). As we have seen, under a left–right policy spectrum AV in particular creates powerful centrist forces, and advantages the middle-placed candidate or party where one exists. In ethnically divided societies, the 'moderate middle', if it exists at all, tends to be composed of putatively non-ethnic or multi-ethnic parties, such as Northern Ireland's SDLP, which can be expected to reap the benefit of these centrist sentiments.

This has important implications for the argument over electoral systems in divided societies, as one of the major points in favour of proportional electoral rules is their empirical association with multi-partism and hence with multi-party coalition governments. Multi-ethnic governments are favoured by both consociationalists and centripetalists as desirable institutions for divided societies. Lewis, for example, argues that 'one of the advantages of proportional representation is that it tends to promote coalition government' (1965, 79), while Lijphart also sees the formation of inclusive multi-ethnic coalition governments as a crucial factor in sustaining democracy in plural societies (1991c, 505). On the centripetal side, Horowitz (1985, 365–95) argues that multi-ethnic coalitions are a near-essential element of conflict management for divided societies, while Arturo Valenzuela writes that fragile new states need above all 'an institutional context that encourages the formation of coalitions among parties and groups [and] the search for a majoritarian consensus that is so essential for governability in a highly variegated political society' (1993, 14). The evidence from this book suggests that, in a number of cases, preferential electoral rules did encourage such coalition agreements and, over time, also stimulated more permanent alliances that have encouraged the development of institutionalised and aggregative party formations, as has been the case in Australia.

Centralism

This advantaging of coalitions occurs in part because the electoral effect of vote transfers in deeply divided societies tends to work to the advantage of the non-sectarian 'moderate middle' more than towards true cross-ethnic voting. While cross-ethnic vote transfers do occur, even in deeply divided societies, the overall incidence of voters from ethnic group A independently voting for a candidate from ethnic group B in a society deeply divided between As and Bs is not high in any of the cases examined in this book. Rather, the evidence suggests that cross-ethnic vote transfers, when they do occur, are more likely to take place between ethnic and non-ethnic parties, rather than between two rival ethnic camps. A case in point is the 1998 elections in Northern Ireland, in which vote transfers overwhelmingly flowed from sectarian parties on both sides towards the pro-agreement but non-sectarian middle (Sinnott 1998). The obverse of this is that when extremist parties who attempt to turn up the rhetorical heat do appear – as with the sudden growth of the extremist One Nation party in Australia prior to the 1996 election – the denial of bargaining and opportunities for preference-swapping becomes a weapon that can be used by more moderate and centre-based forces to isolate and defeat such threats from the flanks (see Chapter 3).

This is not to argue that preferential voting will, in and of itself, encourage centrist political behaviour. The accommodation-inducing appeals of AV, for example, are based on the assumption that moderation on the part of political leaders will see them gain more secondary preference votes from other communities than the first preference votes they may lose from their own group by appearing 'soft' on communal interests. This assumes that there is a portion of the electorate in which sufficient sentiment for moderation exists to make such strategies electorally appealing (Sisk 1995, 38). But in very deeply divided societies which have experienced extremely bitter ethnic antagonisms, this assumption may not hold. In cases involving genocidal inter-ethnic relations, such as the 'ethnic cleansing' strategies employed in Bosnia or Rwanda, for example, relations between the major ethnic groups are so deeply hostile that it may be difficult to create or even envisage conditions under which electors of one group would be prepared to vote for candidates from another.

Another weakness of AV in particular is the way it can discriminate against third-placed parties or candidates. To give a simple example: in a situation where there are three major parties supported by three main ethnic groups, a candidate with 32 per cent of the vote will be eliminated before other candidates with 33 and 35 per cent. Tiny differences in vote share can result in major differences in the order of elimination of lower-placed candidates and thus in determining which (non-eliminated) candidates will benefit from their preference votes. While it could be argued that the preferences of the eliminated candidate will at least determine which of the remaining major candidates wins the seat, this may be completely unsatisfactory in situations of ethnic division: in an extreme case, one party or group may be left with no representation at all. AV can also be as capricious as FPTP when dealing with a situation where one party is in a permanent minority, as Johnston has argued:

> If one party has, say, forty per cent of the first preference votes, but those who do not rank the party first rank it last, then it may fail to win any seats. This would only occur if it won forty per cent of the votes in each constituency, of course, but the greater the number of constituencies in which it fell below fifty per cent in the first preferences, the greater the probability of it being underrepresented in the allocation of seats. (1984, 63–64)

While this scenario does indeed highlight one of the disadvantages of AV, it also serves to illustrate precisely why preferential voting can exert a centripetal force on politics in divided societies. By providing incentives for parties to moderate their policies in the search for second preferences, preference voting can encourage parties seeking to govern outright to move away from extreme positions and towards the policy centre. If a party has a solid support base of 40 per cent but is ranked last by all other voters, then clearly it needs to examine the reasons it so polarises the electorate – why, for example, is it not picking up at least some second preferences? Such soul-searching may well lead to a recognition that a move towards the middle ground on some important issue is required to attract preferences if the party is to be electorally viable – as Sinn Féin found in the process leading up to the British–Irish Accord in Northern Ireland, for example (O'Leary 1999). Preferential voting also enables minority interests to swap lower-order preferences for policy influence. The Labor Party victory at the 1990 Australian federal election detailed in Chapter 3 was dependent to a significant extent on the preferences it received from green and minor party voters in precisely this manner.

Bargaining and cooperation

Overall, the evidence presented in this book suggests that, provided negotiation-inducing electoral rules and certain facilitating socio-structural factors are present, cooperation can come to be viewed by political actors as a rational strategy for electoral success, even in situations of deep social division, as successive iterations of the electoral game are played out. By allowing electors to move away from static, non-negotiable positions on issues when casting their vote, and enabling them to reflect a more sophisticated and meaningful range of choices on the ballot, preferential electoral rules encourage the expression of diverse, multiplex preference orderings. In so doing, they can help move electoral politics away from being a rigid, zero-sum game towards a more fluid and nuanced contest. This has implications for all types of democracies, but particularly for those attempting to deal with deep ethnic, religious, linguistic or other types of social cleavages. However, seemingly minor technical considerations – such as the number of preferences to be marked to ensure a valid vote – can have major political implications for the broader design of political institutions, particularly the extent to which those institutions make cooperation both possible and rational for the agents involved (see Rothstein 1996). Examples of this process in action – of how the locus of political competition around basic issues such as ethnicity can be moved backwards or forwards between rigidity and fluidity and between conflict and cooperation, depending on the choice of apparently trivial electoral rules – are evident in most of the cases examined in this book.

This is not to say that the mere presence of such institutional incentives will inevitably lead to greater cooperation: communication and flexibility can serve to underline differences and room for manoeuvre as well, moving parties further away from each other rather than converging. As every politician in even the most benign society knows, not all actors will bargain in good faith, and not all negotiations will be successful. And there is doubt as to how far the 'contact theory' of ethnic relations – that increased contact between individuals will of itself increase mutual understanding – translates to group action as well (Forbes 1997). But while a willingness to engage in political bargaining and reciprocity will not of itself solve ongoing collective conflict, it does allow the focus of such conflicts to be shifted from rhetorical extravagance onto negotiable issues such as resource allocation and the distribution of political patronage (see Rothchild 1997, 44–5). The result is that as practices of political bargaining become increasingly regularised and internalised by political actors, so democracy progresses towards becoming a self-enforcing system, creating the conditions for its own persistence (Przeworski 1991, 26).

As influential works by both Elinor Ostrom (1990) and Robert Putnam (1993) have shown, the provision of forums of discussion and interaction can also transform events by building mutual trust and by changing individuals' own assessments of precisely where their self-interest lies. But much depends on the underlying patterns of political culture and the willingness to engage in cross-cultural communication. Especially in deeply divided societies, it can be extremely difficult for such communication to take place; in some circumstances it will not. But in most of the country cases analysed in previous chapters, the opportunity to increase their prospects for electoral success led to at least some political leaders sitting down and exploring the possibility of making deals with their rivals – a process of negotiation that in some cases led to other, weightier issues being discussed and even to formal coalition arrangements being established. In certain circumstances this process of negotiation also led to a 'virtuous cycle' of stable, cooperative relationships, in which coalitions initially formed to pool votes themselves acted as institutional channels for cross-cultural communication, creating further tendencies towards reciprocal stances.

Psychological versus mechanical factors

Electoral rules are generally understood to have both 'psychological' and 'mechanical' effects (Duverger 1954). Because arguments in favour of preferential voting have previously focussed more on the mechanics of preference-swapping than the psychological impacts of induced inter-ethnic cooperation, neither proponents nor critics of centripetalism have provided a cogent discussion of what I think is a core normative argument in favour of preference voting: its capacity to engineer 'arenas of bargaining' for inter-elite negotiation and cooperation. In a number of the cases analysed in this book, the simple presence of such bargaining arenas appears to have led to a more moderate style of political competition and rhetoric – as was the case, for example, at Fiji's 1999 elections. In Fiji, the new electoral rules encouraged some of the major parties to adopt election campaign strategies which relied, in part, on inter-ethnic negotiations, a tactic which had formerly been eschewed in favour of segregation and distance. As a result, increasing inter-ethnic contact – at the elite level at least – created opportunities for communication and dialogue that had not previously existed in electoral politics or indeed in wider social institutions, which tend to be segregated along ethnic lines. The psycho-social impacts of such talking forums may therefore be especially important in societies where opportunities for dialogue outside the political arena are absent, as is the case in Fiji and many other ethnically divided states where rigid social segregation is the rule rather than the exception.

A second recurring psychological effect of centripetal systems is that increased inter-ethnic contact, not surprisingly, itself appears to open avenues for increased cooperation. To put it very simply, politicians appear to act with more civility towards each other when the possibility of making vote-swapping deals are present. This is in keeping with theoretical expectations that where institutional avenues for communication exist, the cooperative and solidaristic behaviour of actors should increase accordingly (Rothstein 1996, 150). In the context of elections in divided societies, the presence of these bargaining arenas can lower the heat of the electoral game and have significant implications for the broader political culture, which will often be strongly influenced by the behaviour of elites. Institutional incentives for direct meetings also offer opportunities to build trust and explore shared attitudes: 'the effect . . . is to channel social conflict along predetermined paths, thus lending a sense of regularity and predictability to the rules and routines of the political system' (Rothchild 1997, 45).

The electoral effects of these interactions may often be more psychological than mechanical, because in most cases the extent of possible gain or loss due to preference distribution remains unknown, and its consequences unpredictable. When such calculations are possible, however, then the mechanical role of intra-party preference-swapping becomes predominant. Either way, however, *uncertainty of future electoral outcomes* is key to norms of cooperation and negotiation becoming routinised and consolidated. Uncertainty of outcomes in divided societies presumes something other than a permanent and monolithic majority for one group or another, as under such circumstances there is little incentive to engage in vote-pooling because electoral outcomes, under situations of ethnic voting, are effectively pre-determined. This is why demographic issues are ultimately of crucial importance for the success or failure of centripetalism, a theme to which I will now turn.

The significance of group demographics

Divided societies, like Tolstoy's unhappy families, tend to be divided in different ways. This may seem a simple or even simplistic statement, but it is surprising how many 'one size fits all' conflict-management packages have been recommended for divided societies without sufficient understanding of the structure of the society itself. Ethnically divided societies can be 'fragmented' into many contending groups (such as Papua New Guinea) or 'balanced' between a few similarly sized configurations, which can then be broken down into 'bipolar' (e.g. Fiji, Cyprus) or 'multipolar' (e.g. Bosnia) structures. They can feature 'dominant majorities' (e.g. Sri Lanka) or 'dominant minorities' (e.g. Rwanda). Minorities can be based on indigenous or other 'homeland' societies, or on settler diasporas (see Esman 1994, 6–9). Ethnic groups can be divided by international boundaries between several states or entirely encapsulated by them (May 1996). Groups can be territorially concentrated or widely dispersed (Gurr 1993). In short, demographic conditions can have a significant influence on the way ethnic conflicts are manifested, and consequently on the possible strategies for dealing with them.

The single most important demographic precondition for centripetal strategies to work effectively is that electoral districts be *ethnically heterogeneous*. The more heterogeneous a constituency, the more likely it is that meaningful vote pooling will take place. Vote-pooling formulae will only provide incentives for inter-ethnic accommodation if constituencies are sufficiently heterogeneous for preference-swapping between groups to be an attractive political strategy for electoral success. The best conditions for this is if the members of different ethnic groups are widely dispersed and intermingled. The worst conditions are where groups are geographically concentrated or segregated into particular areas. Under such conditions, electoral districts are much more likely to be ethnically homogenous rather than heterogeneous, meaning that there will be little possibility of inter-ethnic preference-swapping occurring. In many ethnically divided countries, however, members of the same ethnic group tend to cluster together, which means that the single-member electoral districts which are a requirement of most preferential voting systems (such as AV and SV, but not STV) will tend to result in units that are ethnically homogeneous rather than heterogeneous. By contrast, in situations where ethnic groups are fragmented and/or highly dispersed and intermixed, electoral districts which are sufficiently heterogeneous for vote-pooling to take place are much more likely. In instances of extreme ethnic fragmentation, such as Papua New Guinea, vote-pooling becomes a virtual necessity: in these cases, where it is extremely unlikely that there will be an outright majority victor, second and later preferences will almost always be counted to determine the winner. Given such conditions, under AV rules there is an in-built incentive for candidates to seek the second and later preferences of other groups to give them a chance of victory.

The demographic conditions which appear to facilitate vote-pooling strategies illustrate once again the contextual difference between the consociational and centripetal approaches to ethnic conflict management. According to Lijphart, the optimal number of segments for a consociationalist approach to work is three or four, and conditions become progressively less favourable as more segments (i.e. groups) are added (1977, 56). For the centripetal approach to succeed, the situation is reversed: assuming parties are ethnically based, three parties or groups would be the *minimum* number necessary for vote-pooling to work, and prospects for successful vote-pooling would increase as the number of groups increases. Under conditions of ethnic 'census' voting patterns, where electors overwhelmingly cast their vote for their ascriptive candidate or party, the territorial distribution of ethnic groups is therefore an all-important variable for electoral system design.

One way to create ethnically heterogeneous constituencies is via a presidential system, for then an entire country forms one massive and (in multi-ethnic societies at least) heterogeneous constituency. But this approach can create other problems. Consider the ethnic group distribution in Sri Lanka, whose 12 per cent Tamil minority are geographically concentrated in the north-east of the country. As discussed in Chapter 5, the Sri Lankan presidential electoral system utilises a SV formula which takes voters' second and third preferences into account if no candidate gains an absolute majority of first preferences. Because presidential elections treat the whole island as one giant constituency, a heterogeneous single-member electoral district is effectively created. In theory, because of this, the possibility that preferences may one day determine the outcome of a presidential election gives the major Sinhalese parties in Sri Lanka an incentive to moderate their policy positions and to take account of minority ethnic and religious groups when campaigning – incentives conspicuously lacking under other systems, such as FPTP. In practice, however, the global record of presidentialism as a conflict management mechanism is questionable to say the least (Linz 1990), and the Sri Lankan case offers little evidence of moderation or vote-pooling at work. Until we have more evidence for the inter-relationship between centripetal electoral rules and presidentialism in a divided society – perhaps Bosnia will provide such an example in the future – the case for such a combination remains unproven.

For this reason, most prescriptions focus on the application of centripetalism at parliamentary elections, with ethnically heterogeneous electoral districts. Heterogeneous districts assume one of two situations: a considerable *multiplicity* of ethnic groups, so that even relatively small single-member districts will include several ethnic groups, or a small number of ethnic groups but a high degree of group *dispersion* and *geographic inter-mixing*. Two cases examined in this book provide good examples of the different types of structure: the case of Papua New Guinea is the best illustration of group multiplicity, while the case of Fiji is a clear example of group dispersion. If either of these factors is present, then it should be possible to draw electoral boundaries in such a way as to create ethnically heterogeneous electoral districts, and thus to facilitate meaningful vote-pooling. In either case, the presence of a number of roughly equivalent-sized ethnic groups in most constituencies virtually ensures that no group will have anything like enough support to win an outright majority. If a majority threshold is in place, successful candidates *must* receive secondary support from outside their own group.

An additional, although less important, favourable condition for vote-pooling is a situation in which the major ethnic groups are themselves internally fragmented – either by divided responses towards ethnic issues (e.g. conciliatory versus non-conciliatory positions) or by non-ethnic cleavages (e.g. class) – for vote-pooling to still be required to achieve the majority threshold. This is actually the rule rather than the exception: in most ethnically divided countries it is rare for a single ideology or party to represent an entire ethnic group (Horowitz 1985, 574). As discussed in Chapter 5, in Sri Lanka, where the overwhelming majority of the population is Sinhalese, there is some evidence from presidential elections that the dominant parties have, in the past, sought the support of the minority Tamil and Muslim population in order to surpass the majority threshold. Similarly in Fiji, both the indigenous Fijian and Indo-Fijian communities are themselves politically divided between several parties, making meaningful vote-pooling strategies much more likely than if both groups were united behind dominant ethnic parties on each side.

The two distinct facilitating demographic and broader sociostructural conditions which favour the use of centripetalism as a mechanism for encouraging inter-ethnic accommodation in a divided society are thus:

(a)   an extremely high number of ethnic groups; or
(b)   a low number of ethnic groups, but a high degree of ethnic group dispersion and geographical inter-mixing.

There are two broad categories of countries which satisfy one or other of these criteria. The first case represents an unusual type of ethnic group structure: a situation in which groups are so large in number and so small in size that none has the capacity to dominate other groups at the national level. In this scenario, ethnic conflict can be deadly, but it is usually concentrated at the local, rather than national, level. Institutions which build in incentives for inter-group accommodation are thus of most utility for moderating the behaviour of various groups 'on the ground' – for example, in the course of election campaigning. And, because there are so many ethnic groups, even relatively small single-member electoral districts will be sufficiently heterogeneous to encourage accommodative electoral strategies under systems like AV. Such a structure is typified by Papua New Guinea and other Melanesian cases such as the Indonesian province of West Papua (Irian Jaya) and small island states like the Solomon Islands and Vanuatu. In all of these countries there are hundreds – or in the Papua New Guinea case, thousands – of competing ethnic micro-polities, due to the extreme linguistic diversity and the tribal or clan-based nature of ethnic identity. But while characteristic of Melanesia, this degree of micro-fragmentation appears to be rare in other regions. Even the most ethnically fragmented regions of sub-Saharan Africa, which many analysts erroneously believe to be the world's most fractionalised tribal states, exhibit considerably lower levels of ethno-linguistic fragmentation than Melanesia.

In the other type of facilitating social structure, featuring a high degree of ethnic group dispersion, the sheer number of ethnic groups tells us only half the story. We also need to know something about the *geographic concentration* of those groups. Those countries which have a dispersed and inter-mixed structure of ethnic demography are likely to produce a high degree of electorate-level *heterogeneity*, even when there are only two or three ethnic groups. As Lijphart himself has noted, this type of plural society tends to be based upon 'geographical mixture but mutual social avoidance' (1977, 17) – a good description of the basis of ethnic relations in highly inter-mixed but antagonistic 'bi-communal' societies such as Fiji, Malaysia and Guyana (see Milne 1988). Such mutual social avoidance does, of course, involve some degree of residential segregation – similar communities are likely to live in the same street or suburb. But barring ethnic gerrymandering, when overlaid by the much larger boundaries of constituency electoral districts, the result will tend towards *ethnic hetero-geneity* in most cases.

Such a demographic structure is relatively uncommon in some regions, such as Latin America and much of Africa. But it is a common feature of regions in which large immigrant populations have been imported or immigrated during times of colonial rule, and then stayed and integrated into the society while retaining their own ethnic identity, as Table 8.1 shows. The table, adapted from Ted Robert Gurr's *Minorities at Risk* (1993), lists those ethnically divided countries in the developing world in which at least 10 per cent of the population is classified as minorities, ranked in order of the aggregate proportion of minority groups which see themselves and act as a politicised community (and can therefore be expected to vote along ethnic lines). One of the most useful aspects of Gurr's study for our purposes is that it examines not only the size of minority groups, but also their type, ideological coherence and, most importantly, their *level of geographical concentration or dispersion*. When this is factored in, it is possible to identify those cases in which groups are 'widely dispersed in most urban and rural areas' (which gain the highest ranking of 1) down to those which are 'concentrated mainly in one or several adjoining regions' (which gets a lowest ranking of 6), with other levels on a sliding scale between these extremes. Where most groups are coded at a high level of geographic dispersion, many electorates will necessarily be ethnically *heterogeneous*, and should thus present the necessary preconditions for vote-pooling approaches to succeed. Cases in which all or most groups are classified as geographically concentrated, by contrast, will usually feature ethnically *homogenous* electorates and thus limited prospects of vote-pooling as a solution to ethnic conflicts.

At face value, Table 8.1 would appear to indicate that the most favourable cases for utilising centripetal methods to encourage inter-group accommodation are mostly located in Africa, as the degree of ethnic heterogeneity is so much higher in Africa than other regions. However, when we take into account the *geographical concentration* of threatened minorities, this situation changes markedly, and the Asia-Pacific region appears to have the most interspersed ethnic populations. As the table indicates, Gurr's study found that countries in the Asia-Pacific region had the lowest degree of ethnic group concentration of any region in the world, while the countries of sub-Saharan Africa had the highest degree of concentration. (The Asia-Pacific region is defined as those countries coded by Gurr as 'Asian', with the addition of the three nations of the region coded as 'Western': Australia, New Zealand and Japan.) On Gurr's scale of group concentration from 1 (dispersed) to 6 (concentrated), the average ethnic group concentration is 4.00 for the

Table 8.1. *Minority group proportions and geographic concentration*

Country	Main minority groups	Aggregated proportion of minority groups	Index of group concentration
Lebanon	Druze (4%); Maronites (33%); Palestinians (11%); Shi'is (28%); Sunis (20%)	0.960	3.6
Guinea	Fulani (30%); Malinke (30%); Susu (16%)	0.760	5.6
Niger	Djerema/Songhai (19%); Hausa (46%); Tuareg (11%)	0.760	5.0
Cameroon	Kirdi (22%); Westerners (20%); Bamileke (27%)	0.690	6.0
Ethiopia	Afars (5%); Eritreans (7.5%); Nilo-Saharans (1.6%); Oromo (40%); Somali (5%); Tigreans (9%)	0.670	5.6
Bolivia	Native highland peoples (61%); native lowland peoples (2%)	0.630	6.0
Zambia	Bemba (37%); Lozi (Barotse) (7%); Tonga (19%)	0.630	5.3
Zaire	Bakongo (10.3%); Luba (Kasai Province) (6.1%); Lingala (20%); Lunda, Yeke (5.6%); Kivu Region (13%)	0.550	5.6
Uganda	Ankole (8%); Baganda (16%); Kakwa (3%); Karamojong (2%); Konjo, Amba (3%); Langi (6%); Lugbara, Madi (4.9%); Nyarwanda (Rwandans) (5.9%)	0.528	6.0
Malaysia	Chinese (34%); Dayaks (3.95%); East Indians (8.3%); Kadazans (3.9%);	0.502	4.0
Mali	Tuareg (4.7%); Mande (43%)	0.477	6.0
Angola	Bakongo (14%); Ovimbundu (33%)	0.470	6.0
Nigeria	Hausa/Fulani (29%); Ibo (11%)	0.460	5.0
Iran	Azerbaijanis (26%); Baha'is (.08%); Bakthiaris (1.6%); Baluchis (1.7%); Kurds (9%); Turkmens (1.4%); Arabs (1.7%)	0.424	5.4
Peru	Afro-Americans (0.5%); native highland peoples (40%); native lowland peoples (1.2%)	0.417	5.7
Ghana	Ashanti (28%); Ewe (13%); Mossi, Dagomba (16%)	0.410	6.0
Kenya	Kikuyu (21%); Luo (13%); Masai (1.6%); Somali (2%); Turkana, Pokot (3%); Redille, Borana (1%)	0.410	5.7
Sierra Leone	Creoles (1.9%); Limba (8%); Mende (31%)	0.410	4.6
South Africa	Zulus (15%); Coloureds (8%); Afrikaners (8%); other Whites (6%); Indians (2.4%)	0.394	4.0
Morocco	Berbers (37%); Saharawis (0.6%);	0.376	6.0
Togo	Ewe (22.2%); Kabre (14%)	0.362	5.0
Ecuador	Afro-Americans (8%); native highland peoples (26%); native lowland peoples (1%)	0.350	6.0
Pakistan	Ahmadis (3.5%); Baluchis (4.1%); Hindus (1.6%); Pashtuns (13%); Sindhis (10.2%)	0.324	4.8

Burma	Arakanese Muslims (3.7%); Zomis (Chins) (2.4%); Kachins (1.1%); Karens (10.2%); Mons (2.5%); Shans (7.7%); Hill tribes (2.5%)	0.301	5.3
Brunei[c]	Chinese (17%); Dusun (8%); Indians (4%)	0.290	3.25[b]
Singapore[a]	Malays (15%); Indians (7%); Europeans (2%)	0.240	2.0[b]
India	Kashmiris (3.4%); Muslims (11.6%); Nagas (0.01%); Santals (0.066%); Scheduled tribes (6.1%); Sikhs (1.88%); Mizos (Lushais) (0.07%); Tripuras (0.07%)	0.208	4.6
Turkey	Kurds (18%); Roma (1.1%)	0.191	3.5
Sri Lanka	Indian Tamils (5.5%); Sri Lankan Tamils (12.6%)	0.181	4.0
Thailand	Chinese (10%); Malay Muslims (2.5%); Northern Hill Tribes (1.5%)	0.140	4.0
Bangladesh	Chittagong Hills peoples (0.49%); Hindus (12.2%)	0.127	3.5
Laos	Hmong (11%)	0.110	4.0

[a] Data from Minority Rights Group International 1997.
[b] Author's estimate.
[c] Data from Asian-Pacific Cultural Center 1995.

Source: Gurr 1993, 326–64.

Asia-Pacific, compared to 4.25 for Western Europe, 4.58 for North Africa and the Middle East, 4.78 for Eastern Europe and the former Soviet Union, 5.06 for the Americas and 5.09 for Africa South of the Sahara. Significantly, in most Asia-Pacific countries the largest minority groups were all coded at the highest level of group dispersion: Hindus in Bangladesh, Muslims in India, Chinese and Indians in Malaysia, and Malays and Indians in Singapore all fell into this category.

Put simply, what this means is that differences in demography and the patterns of ethnic settlement need to be balanced by differences in constitutional designs across different regions. In many countries, for example, indigenous and/or tribal groups tend to display a particularly strong tendency towards geographical concentration. African minorities, for example, have been found to be more highly concentrated in single contiguous geographical areas than minorities in other regions, which means that many electoral constituencies and informal local power bases will be controlled by a single ethno-political group (Scarritt 1993). This situation holds true for most of the multi-ethnic states of sub-Saharan Africa. It is therefore likely that only the most highly ethnically fragmented states in this region – Tanzania, for example – would be appropriate candidates for vote-pooling techniques, and even then much would depend upon the degree of politicisation of this ethnic fractionalisation. Contrast this with the highly intermixed patterns of ethnic settlement found as a result of colonial settlement or labour importation and the vast Chinese and Indian diasporas found in many parts of the Asia-Pacific (e.g. Singapore, Fiji, Malaysia) and the Caribbean (e.g. Guyana, Trinidad and Tobago), in which members of various ethnic groups tend to be much more widely inter-mixed and, consequently, have more day-to-day contact. Here, electoral districts are likely to be ethnically heterogeneous, and ethnic identities will often be mitigated by other cross-cutting cleavages, so that centripetal designs which encourage parties to seek the support of various ethnic groups may well work to break down inter-ethnic antagonisms and promote the development of broad, multi-ethnic parties. On such prosaic details rest much weightier prescriptions for the success or failure of consociational and centripetal approaches to the management of ethnic conflict.

Conclusion

Centripetalism has not yet received the prominence it deserves as an alternative model of democracy and inter-ethnic accommodation in divided societies. Partly this is because of the relative obscurity of the best empirical case for the model in action, Papua New Guinea; partly it is due to a misunderstanding, even by some of the major scholars in the field, of the importance of political geography when making prescriptions for institutional designs in ethnically divided societies. For example, Donald Horowitz, who pioneered the academic description of the centripetal approach to ethnic conflict management, chose South Africa as his major case study to demonstrate the utility of the model (Horowitz 1991a). However, the ethnic demography of sub-Saharan Africa in general and South Africa in particular is likely to be unfavourable to the application of centripetal techniques, due to the geographic concentration of ethnic groups and, in South Africa, the demographic legacy of apartheid which deliberately segregated different races. For his part, Arend Lijphart has argued that 'in ethnically divided societies, groups tend to be territorially concentrated, and single-member districts are therefore likely to be ethnically homogenous' (1997, 13). While this statement is probably true for much of Latin America and Africa, it is untrue as a general proposition, and particularly untrue for the Asia-Pacific region. A more accurate description of the nature of this region was given by Furnivall (back in the 1940s), who described the plural societies of South-East Asia as ones in which different sections of the same community live side-by-side but separately in a medley within the same polity, so that 'they mix but do not combine' (1948, 304).

This is not to suggest that centripetalism is exclusively an Asia-Pacific model of conflict management. Indeed, as a strategy for managing ethnic conflicts it may well be applicable to ethnically divided states in a range of regions around the globe. Cases in which members of various ethnic groups are geographically interspersed and intermixed, and where ethnic tensions appear to be the result of such intermixture, are present in many regions of the world, especially Europe – for example, the Baltics (Estonia, Latvia, Lithuania), Eastern Europe and the former Yugoslavia (where 'ethnic cleansing' has, however, dramatically increased ethnic homo-geneity in many regions) – as well as the Caribbean (Guyana, Suriname, Jamaica, Trinidad and Tobago), the Middle East (Lebanon, Israel), Central Asia (Kyrgyzstan, Kazhakstan) and the Indian Ocean (Mauritius, Seychelles), to name a few.[4] All of these states are genuinely multi-ethnic, and all feature a high degree of ethnic intermixing and, to varying degrees, ethnic tension. Depending upon the level of geographical disper-sion of ethnic groups, the centripetal approach may well be the most fruitful method of encouraging cooperative, multi-ethnic politics in cases like these. It is worth noting that in virtually all of these countries, the nature of the multi-ethnic society is a result of immigration (e.g. Russians in the Baltics) or colonial labour importation (e.g. Africans in the Caribbean) – which suggests that centripetal solutions may be particularly appropriate for the multi-ethnic sociostructural conditions found in many post-colonial polities.

But beyond such cases, the centripetal model of inter-ethnic accommo-dation is also likely to attract attention in many regions in the future due to the increasingly inter-mixed nature of ethnic group distribution around the world. According to the United Nations, over three-fifths of the world's population will be urban by 2030 (UN 1997). This worldwide trend of rural–urban migration towards multi-ethnic 'world cities' appears to be leading inexorably towards the development of massive, ethnically heterogeneous urban metropolises as models of human settle-ment in the twenty-first century. As these patterns of inter-mixed urban settlement become increasingly common, so the nature of ethnic conflict will necessarily change: tensions will be based on proximity rather than distance, and identities will likely become more fluid as other cleavages are added to ascriptive ones. But this does not imply that the salience of ethnic identity will itself necessarily break down. As ethnic groups increasingly find themselves in close physical proximity but separated by growing distinctions between rich and poor, and as both education levels and voter sophistication continue to rise, so the centripetal model of inter-ethnic accommodation is likely to become an increasingly attractive option for constitutional engineers worldwide.

---

[4] Unfortunately, none of these countries was included in Gurr's study.

References

Aitkin, D. 1982, *Stability and Change in Australian Politics*, 2nd edn, Australian National University Press, Canberra.

Aitkin, D., Jinks, B. and Warhurst, J. 1989, *Australian Political Institutions*, Longman Cheshire, Melbourne.

Allard, C. 1995, 'Lack of Monotonicity – Revisited', *Representation*, 33(2):48–50.

Allen, B. 1976, 'Pangu or Peli: Dreikikir Open Electorate', in D. Stone (ed.), *Prelude to Self-Government: Electoral Politics in Papua New Guinea 1972*, Research School of Pacific Studies, Australian National University and University of Papua New Guinea, Canberra and Port Moresby.

Amorim Neto, O. and Cox, G. W. 1997, 'Electoral Institutions, Cleavage Structures and the Number of Parties', *American Journal of Political Science*, 41:149–74.

Arms, D. G. 1997, 'Fiji's Proposed New Voting System: a Critique with Counter-proposals', in B.V. Lal and P. Larmour (eds.), *Electoral Systems in Divided Societies: the Fiji Constitution Review*, National Centre for Development Studies, Canberra.

Australian Electoral Commission 1990, *1990 Election Statistics*, Australian Government Publishing Service, Canberra.

Australian Labor Party 1991, *Australian Labor Party Platform, Resolutions and Rules as Approved by the 39th National Conference, Hobart 1991*, ALP National Secretariat, Barton.

Axelrod, R. 1984, *The Evolution of Cooperation*, New York, Basic Books.

Ballard, J. A. 1978, 'Ethnicity and Access in Papua New Guinea', mimeo, Department of Political Science, The Faculties, Australian National University, Canberra.

— 1983, 'Shaping the Political Arena: the Elections in the Southern

Highlands', in D. Hegarty (ed.), *Electoral Politics in Papua New Guinea: Studies in the 1977 National Elections*, University of Papua New Guinea Press, Port Moresby.

Bartholdi, J. J. and Orlin, J. B. 1991, 'Single Transferable Vote Resists Strategic Voting', *Social Choice and Welfare*, 8:341–54.

Bean, C. 1986, 'Electoral Law, Electoral Behaviour and Electoral Outcomes: Australia and New Zealand Compared', *The Journal of Commonwealth and Comparative Politics*, 24(1):57–73.

1997, 'Australia's Experience with the Alternative Vote', *Representation*, 34(2):103–10.

Bellamy, R. 1997, *Liberalism and Populism: Towards a Politics of Compromise*, Routledge, London and New York.

Best, K. 1993, 'Plant: A Conservative View', *Representation*, 31(116):80–1.

Bettison, D. G., Hughes, C. A. and van der Veur, P. W. (eds.), 1965, *The Papua-New Guinea Elections 1964*, Australian National University, Canberra.

Birch, A. H. 1964, *Representative and Responsible Government*, George Allen and Unwin, London.

Black, D. 1958, *The Theory of Committees and Elections*, Cambridge University Press, Cambridge.

Blais, A. and Massicotte, L. 1996, 'Electoral Systems', in L. LeDuc, R. G. Niemi and P. Norris (eds.), *Comparing Democracies: Elections and Voting in Global Perspective*, Sage, Thousand Oaks, CA.

Blondel, J. 1969, *An Introduction to Comparative Government*, Weidenfeld and Nicholson, London.

Bloomfield, D. 1998, 'Case Study: Northern Ireland', in Peter Harris and Ben Reilly (eds.), *Democracy and Deep-Rooted Conflict: Options for Negotiators*, International Institute for Democracy and Electoral Assistance, Stockholm.

Bogdanor, V. 1981, *The People and the Party System: The Referendum and Electoral Reform in British Politics*, Cambridge University Press, Cambridge.

1984, *What is Proportional Representation?*, Martin Robertson, Oxford.

Bohrer, R. E. 1997, 'Deviations from Proportionality and Survival in New Parliamentary Democracies', *Electoral Studies*, 16(2):217–26.

Bowler, S. and Grofman, B. 2000, 'STV's Place in the Family of Electoral Systems: Theoretical Comparisons and Contrasts', in S. Bowler and B. Grofman (eds.), *Elections in Australia, Ireland and Malta Under the Single Transferable Vote: Reflections on an Embedded Institution*, University of Michigan Press, Ann Arbor, MI.

Bowler, S., Farrell, D. and McAllister, I. 1996, 'Constituency Campaigning in Parliamentary Systems with Preferential Voting: Is There a Paradox?', *Electoral Studies*, 15(4):461–76.

Bradley, P. 1995, 'STV and Monotonicity: A Hands-On Assessment', *Representation*, 33(2):46–7.

Brams, S. J. and Fishburn, P. 1984, 'Some Logical Defects of the Single Transferable Vote', in A. Lijphart and B. Grofman (eds.), *Choosing an Electoral System: Issues and Alternatives*, Praeger, New York.

Brams, S. J. and Taylor, A. D. 1996, *Fair Division: From Cake-Cutting to Dispute Resolution*, Cambridge University Press, Cambridge.

Brass, P. (ed.) 1985, *Ethnic Groups and the State*, Croom Helm, London.

Bullock, C. S. and Johnson, C. K. 1992, *Run-off Elections in the United States*, University of North Carolina Press, Chapel Hill, NC.

Bulmer, M. 1986, 'Race and Ethnicity', in Robert G. Burgess (ed.), *Key Variables in Social Investigation*, Routledge & Kegan Paul, London.

Burton, J. 1989, 'Tribal Structure and Rural Ballot Box Counts in Hagen Open', in M. Oliver (ed.), *Eleksin: The 1987 National Election in Papua New Guinea*, University of Papua New Guinea, Port Moresby.

Butler, D. 1973, *The Canberra Model*, Cheshire, Melbourne.

Carey, J. and Shugart, M. S. 1995, 'Incentives to Cultivate a Personal Vote: a Rank Ordering of Electoral Formulas', *Electoral Studies* 14(4):441–60.

Chief Electoral Officer 1964a, *Report of the Chief Electoral Officer on the House of Assembly Election 1964*, Government Printer, Port Moresby.

1964b, *Statistical Returns Showing the Voting Within Each Open and Special Electorate in Relation to the General Election for the House of Assembly, 1964*, Government Printer, Port Moresby.

1968, *Report of the Chief Electoral Officer on the House of Assembly Election 1968*, Government Printer, Port Moresby.

1973, *Report of the Chief Electoral Officer on the 1972 House of Assembly Election*, Government Printer, Port Moresby.

Clifford, W., Morauta, L. and Stuart, B. 1984, *Law and Order in Papua New Guinea*, vols I and II, Institute of National Affairs and Institute of Applied Social and Economic Research, Port Moresby.

Colebatch, H. K., Colebatch, P., Reay, M. and Strathern, A. J. 1971, 'Free Elections in a Guided Democracy', in A. L. Epstein, R. S. Parker and M. Reay (eds.), *The Politics of Dependence: Papua New Guinea 1968*, Australian National University Press, Canberra.

Commissioner of Elections 1983, *Report on the First Presidential Election in Sri Lanka Held on 20th October, 1982*, Government Printer, Colombo.

1992, *Report of the Commissioner of Elections on the Second Presidential Election of Sri Lanka Held on 19.12.1988*, Government Printer, Colombo.

Constitution Review Commission 1996, *The Fiji Islands: Towards a United Future*, Parliamentary Paper No. 34 of 1996, Parliament of Fiji, Suva.

Constitutional Planning Commission 1974, *Final Report*, Government Printer, Port Moresby.

Corry, J. A. and Hodgetts, J. E. 1960, *Democratic Government and Politics*, University of Toronto Press, Toronto.

Cox, G. 1990, 'Centripetal and Centrifugal Incentives in Electoral Systems', *American Journal of Political Science*, 34(4): 903–35.

1997, *Making Votes Count: Strategic Coordination in the World's Electoral Systems*, Cambridge University Press, Cambridge.

Crisp, L. F. 1983, *Australian National Government*, Longman Cheshire, Melbourne.

Crocombe, R. and Giese, C. 1988, 'Nauru: The Politics of Phosphate', in A. Ali and R. Crocombe (eds.), *Micronesian Politics*, Institute of Pacific Studies, University of the South Pacific, Suva.

Cullen, M. 1993, 'On the Campaign Trail', in Michael Gallagher and Michael Laver (eds.), *How Ireland Voted 1992*, Folens Press, Dublin.

Dahl, R. A. 1971, *Polyarchy: Participation and Opposition*, Yale University Press, New Haven, CT.

de Garis, B. 1977, 'Western Australia', in P. Loveday, A. W. Martin and R. S. Parker (eds.), *The Emergence of the Australian Party System*, Hale and Iremonger, Sydney.

de Lepervanche, M. 1973, 'Social Structure', in P. Ryan (ed.), *The Encyclopedia of Papua and New Guinea*, Melbourne University Press in association with the University of Papua New Guinea, Clayton.

de Nevers, R. 1993, 'Democratization and Ethnic Conflict', in Michael Brown (ed.), *Ethnic Conflict and International Security*, Princeton University Press, Princeton, NJ.

de Silva, C. R. 1979, 'The Constitution of the Second Republic of Sri Lanka 1978 and its Significance', *Journal of Commonwealth and Comparative Politics*, 17(2):192–209.

de Silva, K. M. 1994, *Ethnic Diversity and Public Policies: Electoral Systems*, United Nations Research Institute for Social Development, Geneva.

Dean, E. and Ritova, S. 1988, *Rabuka: No Other Way*, Doubleday, Morebank.

Diamond, L. 1996, 'Toward Democratic Consolidation', in L. Diamond and M. F. Plattner (eds.), *The Global Resurgence of Democracy*, Johns Hopkins University Press, Baltimore, MD and London.

1997, 'Introduction: In Search of Consolidation', in L. Diamond, M. F. Plattner, Y. Chu and H. Tien (eds.), *Consolidating the Third Wave Democracies*, Johns Hopkins University Press, Baltimore, MD and London.

1998, *Developing Democracy: Towards Consolidation*, Johns Hopkins University Press, Baltimore, MD and London.

Diamond, L. and Plattner, M. F. 1994, 'Introduction', in L. Diamond and M. F. Plattner (eds.) 1994, *Nationalism, Ethnic Conflict and Democracy*, Johns Hopkins University Press, Baltimore, MD and London.

Diamond, L. and Plattner, M. F. (eds.) 1996, *The Global Resurgence of Democracy*, Johns Hopkins University Press, Baltimore, MD and London.

Diamond, L., Linz, J. and Lipset, S. M. 1995, 'Introduction: What Makes for Democracy?', in L. Diamond, J. Linz, and S. M. Lipset (eds.), *Politics in Developing Countries: Comparing Experiences with Democracy*, 2nd edn, Lynne Rienner Publishers, Boulder, CO.

Diamond, L., Linz, J. and Lipset, S. M. (eds.) 1988 and 1989, *Democracy in Developing Countries* (vol. II, *Africa*; vol. III, *Asia*; vol. IV, *Latin America*), Lynne Rienner Publishers, Boulder, CO.

Dinnen, S. 1996, 'Violence, Security and the 1992 Election', in Y. Saffu (ed.), *The 1992 PNG Election: Change and Continuity in Electoral Politics*, Department of Political and Social Change, Research School of Pacific and Asian Studies, Australian National University, Canberra.

Dixon, P. 1997, 'Paths to Peace in Northern Ireland (II): The Peace Processes 1973–74 and 1994–96', *Democratization*, 4(3):1–25.

Dorney, S. 1990, *Papua New Guinea: People, Politics and History Since 1975*, Random House, Sydney.

Downs, A. 1957, *An Economic Theory of Democracy*, Harper and Row, New York.

Dummett, M. 1984, *Voting Procedures*, Clarendon Press, Oxford.

Dunleavy, P., Margetts, H., O'Duffy, B. and Weir, S. 1997, *Making Votes Count: Replaying the 1990s General Elections Under Alternative Electoral Systems*, Democratic Audit of the United Kingdom, Human Rights Centre, University of Essex, Essex.

Duverger, M. 1954, *Political Parties: Their Organisation and Activity in the Modern State*, Wiley, New York.

1984, 'Which is the Best Electoral System?', in A. Lijphart and B. Grofman (eds.), *Choosing an Electoral System: Issues and Alternatives*, Praeger, New York.

Eckstein, H. 1992, 'Case Study and Theory in Political Science', in H. Eckstein, *Regarding Politics: Essays on Political Theory, Stability and Change*, University of California Press, Berkeley, CA.

Edelman, M. 1988, *Constructing the Political Spectacle*, University of Chicago Press, Chicago, IL.

Electoral Commission of Inquiry into Electoral Procedures 1970, *Report of the Electoral Commission of Inquiry into Electoral Procedures*, Government Printer, Port Moresby.

Electoral Commission Queensland 1995, *Mirani By-election 1994 Ballot Paper Survey: Report on Informal and Optional Preferential Voting*, Research Report 1/1995, Electoral Commission Queensland, Brisbane.

Electoral Commissioner 1987, *Report by the Electoral Commissioner on the 1987 National Elections*, Papua New Guinea Electoral Commission, Boroko.

1997, *Report to the Sixth Parliament on the 1997 National Election*, Papua New Guinea Electoral Commission, Boroko.

Epstein, A. L., Parker, R. S. and Reay, M. (eds.) 1971, *The Politics of Dependence: Papua New Guinea 1968*, Australian National University Press, Canberra.

Esman, M. 1994, *Ethnic Politics*, Cornell University Press, New York.

Evans, G. and O'Leary, B. 1999, 'Northern Irish Voters and the British–Irish

Agreement: Foundations of a Stable Consociational Settlement?', paper presented at the American Political Science Association annual meeting, Atlanta, GA, September.

Ewins, R. 1992, *Colour, Class and Custom: The Literature of the 1987 Fiji Coup*, Department of Political and Social Change, Research School of Pacific and Asian Studies, Australian National University, Canberra.

Farrell, D. M. 1997, *Comparing Electoral Systems*, Prentice Hall/Harvester Wheatsheaf, London.

Farrell, D. M., Mackerras, M. and McAllister, I. 1996, 'Designing Electoral Institutions: STV Systems and their Consequences', *Political Studies*, 19:24–43.

Fearon, J. and Laitin, D. 1996, 'Explaining Interethnic Cooperation', *American Political Science Review*, 90(4):715–35.

Finer, S. E. (ed.) 1975, *Adversary Politics and Electoral Reform*, Anthony Wigram, London.

Fisichella, D. 1984, 'The Double-Ballot System as a Weapon against Anti-System Parties', in A. Lijphart and B. Grofman (eds.), *Choosing an Electoral System: Issues and Alternatives*, Praeger, New York.

Forbes, H. D. 1997, *Ethnic Conflict: Commerce, Culture, and the Contact Hypothesis*, Yale University Press, New Haven, CT.

Fraenkel, J. M. 1999, 'Why it Happened the Way it Did', *The Review*, June: 44–6.

2000, 'Fiddling with Democracy Fails', *The Sydney Morning Herald*, 8 June.

Furnivall, J. S. 1948, *Colonial Policy and Practice: A Comparative Study of Burma and Netherlands India*, Cambridge University Press, Cambridge.

Gallagher, M. 1986, 'The Political Consequences of the Electoral System in the Republic of Ireland', *Electoral Studies*, 5(3):253–75.

Geertz, C. 1963, 'The Integrative Revolution: Primordial Sentiments and Civil Politics in the New States', in C. Geertz (ed.), *Old Societies and New States: the Quest for Modernity in Asia and Africa*, Free Press, New York.

General Constitutional Commission 1983, *Final Report*, SPAFF Publications, Port Moresby.

Georghiou, M. 1993, 'Labour Responses to Plant', *Representation*, 31(116):81–3.

Gibbard, A. 1973, 'Manipulation of Voting Schemes: a General Result', *Econometrica*, 41:587–601.

Goodin, R. E. 1995, 'Political Ideals and Political Practice', *British Journal of Political Science*, 25:37–56.

1996, 'Institutions and Their Design', in Robert E. Goodin (ed.), *The Theory of Institutional Design*, Cambridge University Press, Cambridge.

Goot, M. 1985, 'Electoral Systems', in D. Aitkin (ed.), *Surveys of Australian Political Science*, George Allen and Unwin, North Sydney.

Gordon, R. and Meggitt, M. 1985, *Law and Order in the New Guinea*

Highlands: Encounters with Enga, University Press of New England, Hanover and London.

Gostin, O., Tomasetti, W. and Young, M. W. 1971, 'Personalities Versus Politics', in A. L. Epstein, R. S. Parker and M. Reay (eds.), *The Politics of Dependence: Papua New Guinea 1968*, Australian National University Press, Canberra.

Graham, B. D. 1962, 'The Choice of Voting Methods in Federal Politics, 1902–1918', *Australian Journal of Politics and History*, 8(2):164–81.

Green, D. P. and Shapiro, I. 1994, *Pathologies of Rational Choice Theory: A Critique of Applications in Political Science*, Yale University Press, New Haven, CT and London.

Griffin, J. 1974, 'Papua New Guinea', in R. Brissenden and J. Griffin (eds.), *Modern Asia: Problems and Politics*, Jacaranda Press, Milton.

1988, 'The Papua New Guinea Elections of 1987', *Journal of Pacific History*, 22:106–16.

Grofman, B. 1989, 'The Federalist Papers and the New Institutionalism: An Overview', in B. Grofman and D. Wittman (eds.), *The Federalist Papers and the New Institutionalism*, Agathon Press, New York.

Grofman, B. and Lijphart, A. (eds.) 1986, *Electoral Laws and their Political Consequences*, Agathon Press, New York.

Groves, M., Hamilton, R. M. S. and McArthur, M. 1971, 'A Town and its Hinterland', in A. L. Epstein, R. S. Parker and M. Reay (eds.), *The Politics of Dependence: Papua New Guinea 1968*, Australian National University Press, Canberra.

Gurr, T. R. (ed.) 1993, *Minorities at Risk: A Global View of Ethnopolitical Conflicts*, United States Institute of Peace Press, Washington, DC.

Hare, T. 1873, *The Election of Representatives, Parliamentary and Municipal*, Longmans, Green, Reader and Dyer, London.

Harris, P. and Reilly, B. (eds.) 1998, *Democracy and Deep-Rooted Conflict: Options for Negotiators*, International Institute for Democracy and Electoral Assistance, Stockholm.

Hart, J. 1995, *Proportional Representation: Critics of the British Electoral System 1820–1945*, Clarendon Press, Oxford.

Hegarty, D. 1979, 'The Political Parties', in A. Amarshi, K. Good and R. Mortimer (eds.), *Development and Dependency: the Political Economy of Papua New Guinea*, Oxford University Press, Melbourne.

Hegarty, D. (ed.) 1983, *Electoral Politics in Papua New Guinea: Studies in the 1977 National Election*, University of Papua New Guinea Press, Port Moresby.

1983a, 'The 1977 National Elections in Papua New Guinea – an Overview', in D. Hegarty (ed.), *Electoral Politics in Papua New Guinea: Studies in the 1977 National Elections*, University of Papua New Guinea Press, Port Moresby.

Hirczy, W. P. and Lane, J. C. 1997, 'STV in Malta: Some Surprises', *Representation*, 34(1):21–8.

Hogbin, I. 1973, 'Anthropological Definitions', in P. Ryan (ed.), *The Encyclopedia of Papua and New Guinea*, Melbourne University Press in association with the University of Papua New Guinea, Clayton.

Holzknecht, P. W. 1976, 'The Village Vote: The Lae Open Electorate', in D. Stone (ed.), *Prelude to Self-Government: Electoral Politics in Papua New Guinea 1972*, Research School of Pacific Studies, Australian National University and University of Papua New Guinea, Canberra and Port Moresby.

Holzknecht, H., Holzknecht, S. with Baing, A. U. 1976, 'Party Versus Personalities: The Markham Open Electorate', in D. Stone (ed.), *Prelude to Self-Government: Electoral Politics in Papua New Guinea 1972*, Research School of Pacific Studies, Australian National University and University of Papua New Guinea, Canberra and Port Moresby.

Horowitz, D. L. 1985, *Ethnic Groups in Conflict*, University of California Press, Berkeley, CA.

1991a, *A Democratic South Africa? Constitutional Engineering in a Divided Society*, University of California Press, Berkeley, CA.

1991b, 'Making Moderation Pay: the Comparative Politics of Ethnic Conflict Management', in J. V. Montville (ed.), *Conflict and Peacemaking in Multiethnic Societies*, Lexington Books, New York.

1991c, 'Ethnic Policy Management for Policymakers', in J. V. Montville (ed.), *Conflict and Peacemaking in Multiethnic Societies*, Lexington Books, New York.

1993, 'Democracy in Divided Societies', *Journal of Democracy*, 4(4):18–38.

1997, 'Encouraging Electoral Accommodation in Divided Societies', in B. V. Lal and P. Larmour (eds.), *Electoral Systems in Divided Societies: The Fiji Constitution Review*, National Centre for Development Studies, Canberra.

Howard, M. 1989, 'Ethnicity and the State in the Pacific', in M. Howard (ed.), *Ethnicity and Nation Building in the Pacific*, United Nations University, Tokyo.

Hughes, C. A. 1965, 'The Development of the Legislature: Preparing for the House of Assembly', in D. G. Bettison, C. A. Hughes and P. W. van der Veur (eds.), *The Papua-New Guinea Elections 1964*, Australian National University, Canberra.

1977, 'The Electorate Speaks – and After', in H. Penniman (ed.), *Australia at the Polls*, American Enterprise Institute, Washington DC.

1990, 'The Rules of the Game', in C. Bean, I. McAllister and J. Warhurst (eds.), *The Greening of Australian Politics: the 1990 Federal Election*, Longman Cheshire, Melbourne.

1997, 'Individual Electoral Districts', in C. Bean, S. Bennett, M. Simms and J. Warhurst (eds.), *The Politics of Retribution: the 1996 Australian Federal Election*, Allen & Unwin, Sydney.

Hughes, C. A and van der Veur, P. W. 1965, 'The Elections: An Overview', in

D. G. Bettison, C. A. Hughes and P. W. van der Veur (eds.), *The Papua-New Guinea Elections 1964*, Australian National University, Canberra.

Huntington, S. 1968, *Political Order in Changing Societies*, Yale University Press, New Haven, CT.

1989, 'The Modest Meaning of Democracy', in R. A. Pastor (ed.), *Democracy in the Americas: Stopping the Pendulum*, Holmes and Meier, New York.

1991, *The Third Wave: Democratization in the Late Twentieth Century*, University of Oklahoma Press, Norman, OK.

Iangalio, M. 1976, 'Wabag Open Electorate', in D. Stone (ed.), *Prelude to Self-Government: Electoral Politics in Papua New Guinea 1972*, Research School of Pacific Studies, Australian National University and University of Papua New Guinea, Canberra and Port Moresby.

Independent Commission on the Voting System. 1998, *The Report of the Independent Commission on the Voting System*, The Stationery Office, United Kingdom.

Ishiyama, J. 1994, 'Electoral Rules and Party Nomination Strategies in Ethnically Cleaved Societies: the Estonian Transitional Election of 1990', *Communist and Post-Communist Studies* 27(2):177–92.

2000, 'Institutions and Ethnopolitical Conflict in Post-Communist Politics', *Nationalism and Ethnic Politics*, 6(3):51–67.

Jackman, S. 1992, 'Split Parties Finish Last: Preferences, Pluralities and the 1957 Queensland Election', *Australian Journal of Political Science*, 27(3): 434–48.

Jaensch, D. 1995, *Election! How and Why Australia Votes*, Allen & Unwin, St Leonards.

Johnston, R. J. 1984, 'Seats, Votes, Redistricting, and the Allocation of Power in Electoral Systems', in A. Lijphart and B. Grofman (eds.), *Choosing an Electoral System: Issues and Alternatives*, Praeger, New York.

Jones, M. P. 1997, 'Racial Heterogeneity and the Effective Number of Candidates in Majority Run-off Elections: Evidence from Louisiana', *Electoral Studies*, 16(3):349–58.

Jupp, J. (ed.) 1984, *Ethnic Politics in Australia*, George Allen & Unwin, North Sydney.

1991, 'Managing Ethnic Diversity: How Does Australia Compare?', in F. G. Castles (ed.), *Australia Compared: People, Policies and Politics*, Allen & Unwin, North Sydney.

Katz, R. S. 1984, 'The Single Transferable Vote and Proportional Representation', in Arend Lijphart and Bernard Grofman (eds.), *Choosing an Electoral System: Issues and Alternatives*, Praeger, New York.

1986, 'Intraparty Preference Voting', in B. Grofman and A. Lijphart (eds.), *Electoral Laws and their Political Consequences*, Agathon Press, New York.

1997, *Democracy and Elections*, Oxford University Press, New York.

King, P. (ed.) 1989, *Pangu Returns to Power: the 1982 Elections in Papua New Guinea*, Political and Social Change Monograph 9, Department of Political and Social Change, Research School of Pacific Studies, Australian National University, Canberra.

King, G., Keohane, R. O. and Verba, S. 1994, *Designing Social Inquiry: Scientific Inference in Qualitative Research*, Princeton University Press, Princeton, NJ.

Kuabaal, L. 1976, 'Sinasina Open Electorate', in D. Stone (ed.), *Prelude to Self-Government: Electoral Politics in Papua New Guinea 1972*, Research School of Pacific Studies, Australian National University and University of Papua New Guinea, Canberra and Port Moresby.

Lakeman, E. 1974, *How Democracies Vote*, Faber and Faber, London.

Lal, B. V. 1988, *Power and Prejudice: the Making of the Fiji Crisis*, New Zealand Institute of International Affairs, Wellington.

1999, *A Time to Change: The Fiji General Elections of 1999*, Australian National University, Department of Political and Social Change Discussion Paper 23, Canberra.

Laponce, J. A. 1957, 'The Protection of Minorities by the Electoral System', *Western Political Quarterly*, 10(2):318–39.

Larmour, P. 1994, ' "A Foreign Flower?" Democracy in the South Pacific', *Pacific Studies*, 17(1):45–77.

Laver, M. 2000, 'STV and the Politics of Coalition', in S. Bowler and B. Grofman (eds), *Elections in Australia, Ireland and Malta Under the Single Transferable Vote: Reflections on an Embedded Institution*, University of Michigan Press, Ann Arbor, MI.

Laver, M. and Schofield, N. 1991, *Multiparty Government: the Politics of Coalition in Europe*, Oxford University Press, Oxford.

Lawson, S. 1988, 'Fiji's Communal Electoral System: A Study of Some Aspects of the Failure of Democratic Politics in Fiji', *Politics*, 23(2):35–47.

1991, *The Failure of Democratic Politics in Fiji*, Clarendon Press, Oxford.

Leach, J. W. 1976, 'The 1972 Elections in the Kula Open', in D. Stone (ed.), *Prelude to Self-Government: Electoral Politics in Papua New Guinea 1972*, Research School of Pacific Studies, Australian National University and University of Papua New Guinea, Canberra and Port Moresby.

LeDuc, L., Niemi, R. G. and Norris, P. (eds.) 1996, *Comparing Democracies: Elections and Voting in Global Perspective*, Sage, Thousand Oaks, CA.

Levine, S. 1997, 'Culture and Conflict in Fiji, Papua New Guinea, Vanuatu, and the Federated States of Micronesia', in M. E. Brown and S. Ganguly (eds.), *Government Policies and Ethnic Relations in the Asia-Pacific*, MIT Press, Cambridge, MA and London.

Lewis, W. A. 1965, *Politics in West Africa*, George Allen and Unwin, London.

Lieven, A. 1993, *The Baltic Revolution: Estonia, Latvia, Lithuania and the Path to Independence*, Yale University Press, New Haven, CT and London.

Lijphart, A. 1969, 'Consociational Democracy', *World Politics*, 21:207–25.

    1977, *Democracy in Plural Societies: A Comparative Exploration*, Yale University Press, New Haven, CT.

    1984, *Democracies: Patterns of Majoritarian and Consensus Government in Twenty-One Countries*, Yale University Press, New Haven, CT and London.

    1985, *Power Sharing in South Africa*, Policy Papers in International Affairs No. 24, Institute of International Studies, University of California, Berkeley, CA.

    1986, 'Degrees of Proportionality of Proportional Representation Formulas', in B. Grofman and A. Lijphart (eds.), *Electoral Laws and their Political Consequences*, Agathon Press, New York.

    1990, 'Electoral Systems, Party Systems and Conflict Management in Segmented Societies', in R. A. Schreirer (ed.), *Critical Choices for South Africa: An Agenda for the 1990s*, Oxford University Press, Cape Town.

    1991a, 'The Alternative Vote: A Realistic Alternative for South Africa?', *Politikon*, 18(2):91–101.

    1991b, 'Proportional Representation: Double Checking the Evidence', *Journal of Democracy*, 2:42–8.

    1991c, 'The Power-Sharing Approach', in J. V. Montville (ed.), *Conflict and Peacemaking in Multi-ethnic Societies*, Lexington Books, New York.

    1991d, 'Foreword: "Cameral Change", and Institutional Conservatism', in L. D. Longley and D. M. Olson (eds.), *Two Into One: The Politics and Processes of National Legislative Cameral Change*, Westview Press, Boulder, CO.

    1994a, *Electoral Systems and Party Systems: A Study of Twenty-Seven Democracies, 1945–1990*, Oxford University Press, New York.

    1994b, 'Prospects for Power-Sharing in the New South Africa', in Andrew Reynolds (ed.), *Election '94 South Africa: the Campaigns, Results and Future Prospects*, David Phillip Publishers, Claremont.

    1995a, 'Electoral Systems', in S. M. Lipset (ed.), *The Encyclopedia of Democracy*, Congressional Quarterly Press, Washington, DC.

    1995b, 'Multiethnic Democracy', in S. M. Lipset (ed.), *The Encyclopedia of Democracy*, Congressional Quarterly Press, Washington, DC.

    1996, 'Double Checking the Evidence', in L. Diamond and M. F. Plattner (eds.), *The Global Resurgence of Democracy*, Johns Hopkins University Press, Baltimore, MD and London.

    1997, 'Disproportionality Under Alternative Voting: The Crucial – and Puzzling – Case of the Australian Senate Elections, 1919–1946', *Acta Politica*, 32(1):9–24.

Lijphart, A. and Grofman, B. (eds.) 1984, *Choosing an Electoral System: Issues and Alternatives*, Praeger, New York.

Linz, J. 1990, 'The Perils of Presidentialism', *Journal of Democracy*, 1(1):51–69.

Linz, J. and Stepan, A. 1996, *Problems of Democratic Transition and Consolidation: Southern Europe, South America, and Post-Communist Europe*, Johns Hopkins University Press, Baltimore, MD and London.

Lipset, S. M. 1960, *Political Man: The Social Bases of Politics*, Doubleday, New York.

Loveday, P. 1987, 'The Poll and the Aboriginal Vote', in D. Jaensch and P. Loveday (eds.), *Challenge from the Nationals: The Territory Election 1987*, Australian National University North Australia Research Unit, Darwin.

Loveday, P. and May, R. J. 1981, 'Electoral Education', in D. Jaensch and P. Loveday (eds.), *Under One Flag: The 1980 Northern Territory Election*, George Allen and Unwin, Sydney.

Low, D. A. 1991, *Eclipse of Empire*, Cambridge University Press, Cambridge.

Lucas, J. 1976, 'Two Mile Settlement – Lae Open Electorate', in D. Stone (ed.), *Prelude to Self-Government: Electoral Politics in Papua New Guinea 1972*, Research School of Pacific Studies, Australian National University and University of Papua New Guinea, Canberra and Port Moresby.

Lucy, R. 1982, 'Wran Acts: the 1981 NSW State Election', *Politics*, 17(1): 100–10.

1985, *The Australian Form of Government*, Macmillan, South Melbourne.

Mackenzie, W. J. M. 1958, *Free Elections*, Allen and Unwin, London.

Mainwaring, S. 1993, 'Presidentialism, Multipartism, and Democracy: The Difficult Combination', *Comparative Political Studies*, 26(2):198–228.

March, J. and Olsen, J. 1984, 'The New Institutionalism: Organizational Factors in Political Life', *American Political Science Review*, 78(3):734–49.

May, R. J. 1982, 'Micronationalism: What, When and Why?', in R. J. May (ed.), *Micronationalist Movements in Papua New Guinea*, Political and Social Change Monograph 1, Department of Political and Social Change, Research School of Pacific Studies, Australian National University, Canberra.

1996, 'Managing the Ethnic/Religious/Cultural Challenge to National Security', paper presented at Tenth Asia-Pacific Roundtable, Kuala Lumpur.

McLean, I. 1987, *Public Choice: An Introduction*, Basil Blackwell, Oxford.

1996, 'E. J. Nanson, Social Choice and Electoral Reform', *Australian Journal of Political Science*, 31(3):369–85.

McLean, I. and Hewitt, F. (eds.) 1994, *Condorcet: Foundations of Social Choice and Political Theory*, Edward Elgar, Cheltenham.

McLean, I. and London, J. 1990, 'The Borda and Condorcet Principles: Three Medieval Applications', *Social Choice and Welfare*, 7:99–108.

McLean, I. and Urken, A. B. (eds.) 1995, *Classics of Social Choice*, University of Michigan Press, Ann Arbor, MI.

Mill, J. S. 1958 [1861], *Considerations on Representative Government*, Liberal Arts Press, New York.

1972 [1910], *Utilitarianism, On Liberty and Considerations on Representative Government*, J. M. Dent and Sons, London.

Milne, R. S. 1988, 'Bicommunal Systems: Guyana, Malaysia, Fiji', *Publius: The Journal of Federalism*, 18:101–13.

Minority Rights Group 1997, *World Directory of Minorities*, Minority Rights Group International, London.

Morauta, L. 1984, 'Social Stratification in Lowland Papua New Guinea: Issues and Questions', in R. J. May (ed.), *Social Stratification in Papua New Guinea*, Working Paper No. 5, Department of Political and Social Change, Research School of Pacific Studies, Australian National University, Canberra.

Nanson, E. J. 1900, *The Real Value of a Vote and How to Get it at the Coming Federal Elections*, J. T. Picken, Melbourne.

1995 [1882], 'Methods of Election, 1882', reprinted in I. McLean and A. B. Urken (eds.), *Classics of Social Choice*, University of Michigan Press, Ann Arbor, MI.

Nordlinger, E. A. 1972, *Conflict Regulation in Divided Societies*, Centre for International Affairs, Harvard University, Cambridge, MA.

Norris, P. 1995, 'The Politics of Electoral Reform in Britain', *International Political Science Review*, 16(1):65–78.

1999, 'Ballots not Bullets: Testing Consociational Theories of Ethnic Conflict, Electoral Systems and Democratization', paper presented to the Constitutional Design 2000 conference, University of Notre Dame, Indiana, December.

North, D. 1990, *Institutions, Institutional Change and Economic Performance*, Cambridge University Press, Cambridge.

O'Donnell, G. and Schmitter, P. 1986, *Transitions to Democracy: Tentative Conclusions About Uncertain Democracies*, Johns Hopkins University Press, Baltimore, MD.

O'Leary, B. 1999, 'The British–Irish Agreement of 1998: Results and Prospects', paper presented to the Constitutional Design 2000 conference, University of Notre Dame, Indiana, December.

Oliver, M. 1989, 'Kerema Open Constituency', in M. Oliver (ed.), *Eleksin: the 1987 National Election in Papua New Guinea*, University of Papua New Guinea, Port Moresby.

Oliver, M. (ed.) 1989. *Eleksin: the 1987 National Election in Papua New Guinea*, University of Papua New Guinea, Port Moresby.

Olson, M. 1971, *The Logic of Collective Action: Public Goods and the Theory of Groups*, Harvard University Press, Cambridge, MA.

Ordeshook, P. 1996, 'Engineering or Science: What is the Study of Politics?', in J. Friedman (ed.), *The Rational Choice Controversy: Economic Models of Politics Reconsidered*, Yale University Press, New Haven, CT and London.

Ordeshook, P. and Shvetsova, O. V. 1994, 'Ethnic Heterogeneity, District

Magnitude and the Number of Parties', *American Journal of Political Science*, 38(1):100–23.

Ostrom, E. 1990, *Governing the Commons: The Evolution of Institutions for Collective Action*, Cambridge University Press, Cambridge.

Papadakis, E. and Bean, C. 1995, 'Independents and Minor Parties: the Electoral System', *Australian Journal of Political Science*, 30 (special issue):97–110.

Papua New Guinea Electoral Commission 1982, 'Views from the Electoral Commission', paper presented at University of Papua New Guinea Seminar on the Parliamentary Elections, Waigani.

   1983, *Report: First National General Elections 1977*, Government Printer, Port Moresby.

   1995, *The Voter*, Issue No. 1, Government Printer, Boroko.

Parker, R. S. 1971, 'From Dependence to Autonomy?', in A. L. Epstein, R. S. Parker and M. Reay (eds.), *The Politics of Dependence: Papua New Guinea 1968*, Australian National University Press, Canberra.

Parker, R. S. and Wolfers, E. P. 1971, 'The Context of Political Change', in A. L. Epstein, R. S. Parker and M. Reay (eds.), *The Politics of Dependence: Papua New Guinea 1968*, Australian National University Press, Canberra.

Parliament of Fiji 1975, *Report of the Royal Commission Appointed for the Purpose of Considering and Making Recommendations as to the Most Appropriate Method of Electing Members to, and Representing the People of Fiji in, the House of Representatives*, Parliamentary Paper No. 24, Government Printer, Suva.

Paypool, P. 1976, 'Ialibu-Pangia Electorate', in D. Stone (ed.), *Prelude to Self-Government: Electoral Politics in Papua New Guinea 1972*, Research School of Pacific Studies, Australian National University and University of Papua New Guinea, Canberra and Port Moresby.

Permanent Election Law Working Group 1999, *Draft Election Law for Bosnia and Herzegovina*, OSCE Mission to Bosnia and Herzegovina, Sarajevo.

Plant Commission 1992, *Second Interim Report of the Working Party on Electoral Systems*, Labour Party, London.

   1993, *Report of the Working Party on Electoral Systems*, Labour Party, London.

Pokawin, S. 1976, 'The Elections in Manus', in D. Stone (ed.), *Prelude to Self-Government: Electoral Politics in Papua New Guinea 1972*, Research School of Pacific Studies, Australian National University and University of Papua New Guinea, Canberra and Port Moresby.

Posen, B. 1993, 'The Ethnic Security Dilemma and Ethnic Conflict', in Michael E. Brown (ed.), *Ethnic Conflict and International Security*, Princeton University Press, Princeton, NJ.

Powell, G. B. 1982, *Contemporary Democracies: Participation, Stability, and Violence*, Harvard University Press, Cambridge, MA.

Premdas, R. 1977, 'Secessionist Movements in Papua New Guinea', *Pacific Affairs*, 50(1):64–85.

1978, 'Papua New Guinea: the First General Elections after Independence', *The Journal of Pacific History*, 13(1):77–90.

1989, 'Ethnicity and Nation-building: The Papua New Guinea Case', in M. Howard (ed.), *Ethnicity and Nation Building in the Pacific*, United Nations University, Tokyo.

Premdas, R. and Steeves, J. S. 1983, 'National Elections in Papua New Guinea: the Return of Pangu to Power', *Asian Survey*, 23(8): 991–1006.

Przeworski, A. 1991, *Democracy and the Market: Political and Economic Reforms in Eastern Europe and Latin America*, Cambridge University Press, Cambridge.

Punnett, R. M. 1987, 'The Alternative Vote with the Optional Use of Preferences: Some Irish Lessons for Britain and Australia', *Journal of Commonwealth and Comparative Politics*, 35(1):26–43.

Putnam, R. 1993, *Making Democracy Work: Civic Traditions in Modern Italy*, Princeton University Press, Princeton, NJ.

Rabushka, A. and Shepsle, K. 1972, *Politics in Plural Societies: A Theory of Democratic Instability*, Merrill, Columbus, OH.

Rae, D. W. 1967, *The Political Consequences of Electoral Laws*, Yale University Press, New Haven, CT.

Rae, D. W. and Taylor, M. 1970, *The Analysis of Political Cleavages*, Yale University Press, New Haven, CT.

Raiffa, H. 1982, *The Art and Science of Negotiation*, Belknap Press, Cambridge, MA.

Reay, M. 1965, 'The Minj Open Electorate', in D. G. Bettison, C. A. Hughes and P. W. van der Veur (eds.), *The Papua-New Guinea Elections 1964*, Australian National University, Canberra.

1982, 'Lawlessness in the Papua New Guinea Highlands', in R. J. May and H. Nelson (eds.), *Melanesia: Beyond Diversity*, Research School of Pacific Studies, Australian National University, Canberra.

Regan, A. J. 1995, 'Limiting State Action: Comparative Perspectives on Constitutionalism, Participation and Civil Society in Papua New Guinea', paper presented to the 1995 Waigani Seminar, Port Moresby.

1998, 'Case Study: Bougainville', in P. Harris and B. Reilly (eds.), *Democracy and Deep-Rooted Conflict: Options for Negotiators*, International Institute for Democracy and Electoral Assistance, Stockholm.

Reid, G. S. and Forrest, M. 1989, *Australia's Commonwealth Parliament 1901–1988*, Melbourne University Press, Melbourne.

Reilly, B. 1996, 'The Effects of the Electoral System in Papua New Guinea', in Y. Saffu (ed.), *The 1992 PNG Election: Change and Continuity in Electoral Politics*, Department of Political and Social Change, Research

School of Pacific and Asian Studies, Australian National University, Canberra.

1997a, 'Preferential Voting and Political Engineering: A Comparative Study', *The Journal of Commonwealth and Comparative Politics*, 35(1):1–19.

1997b, 'The Alternative Vote and Ethnic Accommodation: New Evidence from Papua New Guinea', *Electoral Studies*, 16(1):1–11.

1997c, 'Constitutional Engineering and the Alternative Vote in Fiji: An Assessment', in B. V. Lal and P. Larmour (eds.), *Electoral Systems in Divided Societies: The Fiji Constitution Review*, National Centre for Development Studies, Canberra.

1997d, 'The Plant Report and the Contingent Vote: Not So Unique After All', *Representation*, 34(2):95–102.

1998, 'With No Melting Pot, a Recipe for Failure in Bosnia', *International Herald Tribune*, 12–13 September.

Reilly, B. and Maley, M. 2000, 'The Single Transferable Vote and the Alternative Vote Compared', in Shaun Bowler and Bernard Grofman (eds.), *Elections in Australia, Ireland and Malta Under the Single Transferable Vote: Reflections on an Embedded Institution*, University of Michigan Press, Ann Arbor, MI.

Reilly, B. and Reynolds, A. 1999, *Electoral Systems and Conflict in Divided Societies*, National Research Council, Washington, DC.

Reynolds, A. 1995, 'Constitutional Engineering in Southern Africa', *Journal of Democracy*, 6(2):86–100.

1999, *Electoral Systems and Democratization in Southern Africa*, Oxford University Press, New York.

Reynolds, A. and Reilly, B. *et al.* 1997, *The International IDEA Handbook of Electoral System Design*, International Institute for Democracy and Electoral Assistance, Stockholm.

Richardson, G. 1994, *Whatever it Takes*, Bantam Books, Sydney.

Riker, W. H. 1986, *The Art of Political Manipulation*, Yale University Press, New Haven, CT and London.

Roberts, N. 1999, 'Living Up To Expectations? The New Fijian Electoral System and the 1999 General Election', paper presented to Citizens Constitutional Forum, Suva, Fiji, 18 July.

Robertson, R. T. and Tamanisau, A. 1988, *Fiji: Shattered Coups*, Pluto Press, Leichhardt, NSW.

Rokkan, S. 1968, 'Electoral Systems', in D. L. Sills (ed.), *International Encyclopedia of the Social Sciences*, Macmillan and the Free Press, New York.

1970, *Citizens, Elections, Parties: Approaches to the Comparative Study of the Processes of Development*, Universitetsforlaget, Oslo.

Rose, R. 1976, *Northern Ireland: A Time of Choice*, American Enterprise Institute, Washington, DC.

1983, 'Elections and Electoral Systems: Choices and Alternatives', in V. Bogdanor and D. Butler (eds.), *Democracy and Elections*, Cambridge University Press, Cambridge.

Rothchild, D. 1997, *Managing Ethnic Conflict in Africa: Pressures and Incentives for Cooperation*, Brookings Institution Press, Washington, DC.

Rothschild, J. 1981, *Ethnopolitics: A Conceptual Framework*, Colombia University Press, New York.

Rothstein, B. 1996, 'Political Institutions: An Overview', in R. E. Goodin and H.-D. Klingemann (eds.), *A New Handbook of Political Science*, Oxford University Press, New York.

Rumsey, A. 1999, 'Social Segmentation, Voting, and Violence in Papua New Guinea', *The Contemporary Pacific*, 11(2):305–33.

Saffu, Y. 1989, 'Survey Evidence on Electoral Behaviour in Papua New Guinea', in M. Oliver (ed.), *Eleksin: The 1987 National Election in Papua New Guinea*, University of Papua New Guinea, Port Moresby.

1996, 'Change and Continuity in PNG Electoral Politics', in Y. Saffu (ed.), *The 1992 PNG Election: Change and Continuity in Electoral Politics*, Department of Political and Social Change, Research School of Pacific and Asian Studies, Australian National University, Canberra.

Sauu, Y. (ed.) 1996, *The 1992 PNG Election: Change and Continuity in Electoral Politics*, Department of Political and Social Change, Research School of Pacific and Asian Studies, Australian National University, Canberra.

Samarasinghe, S. W. R. de A. 1983, 'Sri Lanka in 1982: A Year of Elections', *Asian Survey*, 23(2):158–64.

Sartori, G. 1968, 'Political Development and Political Engineering', *Public Policy*, 17:261–98.

1976, *Parties and Party Systems*, Cambridge University Press, Cambridge.

1994, *Comparative Constitutional Engineering: An Inquiry Into Structures, Incentives and Outcomes*, Macmillan, London.

Satterthwaite, M. A. 1975, 'Strategy-proofness and Arrow's Conditions: Existence and Correspondence Theorems for Voting Procedures and Social Welfare Functions', *Journal of Economic Theory*, 10:187–217.

Scarr, D. 1988, *Fiji: The Politics of Illusion*, New South Wales University Press, Kensington.

Scarritt, J. R. 1993, 'Communal Conflict and Contention for Power in Africa South of the Sahara', in T. R. Gurr (ed.), *Minorities at Risk: A Global View of Ethnopolitical Conflicts*, United States Institute of Peace Press, Washington, DC.

Schaffer, H. B. 1995, 'The Sri Lankan Elections of 1994: the Chandrika Factor', *Asian Survey*, 35(5):409–25

Schumpeter, J. 1947, *Capitalism, Socialism and Democracy*, Harper, New York.

Second National State Assembly 1978, *Report of the Select Committee of the National State Assembly Appointed to Consider the Revision of the Constitution*, Government Printer, Colombo.

Sharman, C. and Miragliotta, N. 2000, 'Western Australia', in M. Simms and J. Warhurst (ed.), *Howard's Agenda: the 1998 Australian Election*, University of Queensland Press, St Lucia.

Sharp, S. 1994, 'A Statistical Study of Selective Candidate Withdrawal in a British General Election', *Electoral Studies*, 13(2):122–31.

Shastri, A. 1997, 'Government Policy and the Ethnic Crisis in Sri Lanka', in M. E. Brown and S. Ganguly (eds.), *Government Policies and Ethnic Relations in Asia and the Pacific*, MIT Press, Cambridge, MA and London.

Shugart, M. S. and Carey, J. 1992, *Presidents and Assemblies: Constitutional Design and Electoral Dynamics*, Cambridge University Press, Cambridge.

Sinnott, R. 1998, 'Centrist politics makes modest but significant progress: cross-community transfers were low', *Irish Times*, 29 June.

Sisk, T. 1993, 'Choosing an Electoral System: South Africa Seeks New Ground Rules', *Journal of Democracy*, 4(1):79–91.

1995, *Democratization in South Africa: The Elusive Social Contract*, Princeton University Press, Princeton.

1996, *Power Sharing and International Mediation in Ethnic Conflicts*, United States Institute of Peace Press, Washington, DC.

Smith, A. D. 1986, *The Ethnic Origin of Nations*, Blackwell, Oxford.

Smith, B. 1960, *European Vision and the South Pacific: A Study in the History of Art and Ideas 1768–1850*, Oxford University Press, Oxford.

Souter, G. 1963, *New Guinea: The Last Unknown*, Angus and Robertson, Sydney.

Stagg, M. 1976, 'The Kavieng Open Electorate', in D. Stone (ed.), *Prelude to Self-Government: Electoral Politics in Papua New Guinea 1972*, Research School of Pacific Studies, Australian National University and University of Papua New Guinea, Canberra and Port Moresby.

Standish, W. 1976, 'New Men for an Old Society: the Chimbu Regional Campaign', in D. Stone (ed.), *Prelude to Self-Government: Electoral Politics in Papua New Guinea 1972*, Research School of Pacific Studies, Australian National University and University of Papua New Guinea, Canberra and Port Moresby.

1994, 'Papua New Guinea: the Search for Security in a Weak State', in A. Thompson (ed.), *Papua New Guinea: Issues for Australian Security Planners*, Australian Defence Studies Centre, Australian Defence Force Academy, Canberra.

1996, 'Elections in Simbu: Towards Gunpoint Democracy?', in Y. Saffu (ed.), *The 1992 PNG Election: Change and Continuity in Electoral Politics*, Department of Political and Social Change, Research School of Pacific and Asian Studies, Australian National University, Canberra.

Steed, M. 1975, 'The Evolution of the British Electoral System', in S. Finer (ed.), *Adversary Politics and Electoral Reform*, Anthony Wigram, Great Britain.

Stone, D. 1976a, 'The Electoral Organisation', in D. Stone (ed.), *Prelude to Self-Government: Electoral Politics in Papua New Guinea 1972*, Research School of Pacific Studies, Australian National University and University of Papua New Guinea, Canberra and Port Moresby.

——— 1976b, 'The Political Turning Point: The Birth of the National Coalition Government', in D. Stone (ed.), *Prelude to Self-Government: Electoral Politics in Papua New Guinea 1972*, Research School of Pacific Studies, Australian National University and University of Papua New Guinea, Canberra and Port Moresby.

Stone, D. (ed.) 1976, *Prelude to Self-Government: Electoral Politics in Papua New Guinea 1972*, Research School of Pacific Studies, Australian National University and University of Papua New Guinea, Canberra and Port Moresby.

Strathern, A. 1976, 'Seven Good Men: The Dei Open Electorate', in D. Stone (ed.), *Prelude to Self-Government: Electoral Politics in Papua New Guinea 1972*, Research School of Pacific Studies, Australian National University and University of Papua New Guinea, Canberra and Port Moresby.

——— 1993, 'Violence and Political Change in Papua New Guinea', *Pacific Studies*, 16(4):41–60.

Strom, K. 1995, 'Political Parties', in S. M. Lipset (ed.), *The Encyclopedia of Democracy*, Congressional Quarterly Press, Washington, DC.

Taagepera, R. 1990, 'The Baltic States', *Electoral Studies*, 9(4):303–11.

——— 1996, 'STV in Transitional Estonia', *Representation*, 34(1):29–36.

——— 1998, 'How Electoral Systems Matter for Democratization', *Democratization*, 5(3):68–91.

Taagepera, R. and Shugart, M. S. 1989, *Seats and Votes: The Effects and Determinants of Electoral Systems*, Yale University Press, New Haven, CT and London.

Taylor, M. 1987, *The Possibility of Cooperation*, Cambridge University Press, Cambridge.

Tsebelis, G. 1990, *Nested Games: Rational Choice in Comparative Politics*, University of California Press, Berkeley, CA.

Turner, M. and Hegarty, D. 1987, *The 1987 National Elections in Papua New Guinea*, Institute of International Affairs, Occasional Paper No. 6, Canberra.

United Nations 1997, *World Urbanisation Prospects*, United Nations, New York.

United Nations Visiting Mission 1968, *Report of the United Nations Visiting*

Mission to the Trust Territories of Nauru and New Guinea: Report on New Guinea, United Nations, New York.

Valenzuela, A. 1993, 'Latin America: Presidentialism in Crisis', *Journal of Democracy*, 4(4):3–16.

Vermont Commission. 1999, *As Easy as 1–2–3: Final Report of the Vermont Commission to Study Instant Runoff Voting*, paper presented to Vermont House of Representatives pursuant to H.R. 37, January.

Voutas, A. C. 1970, 'Elections and Communications', in M. Ward (ed.), *The Politics of Melanesia: Papers Delivered at the Fourth Waigani Seminar*, The Australian National University and the University of Papua New Guinea, Canberra and Port Moresby.

Wallensteen, P. and Sollenberg, M. 2000, 'Armed Conflict, 1989–99', *Journal of Peace Research*, 37(5):635–49.

Warhurst, J. 1990, 'The National Campaign', in C. Bean, I. McAllister and J. Warhurst (eds.), *The Greening of Australian Politics: The 1990 Federal Election*. Longman Cheshire, Melbourne.

Watson, J. B. 1965, 'The Kainantu Open and South Markham Special Electorates', in D. G. Bettison, C. A. Hughes and P. W. van der Veur (eds.), *The Papua-New Guinea Elections 1964*, Australian National University, Canberra.

Wesley-Smith, T. 1994, *New Directions for Pacific Islands Studies*, Department of Political and Social Change, Research School of Pacific and Asian Studies, Australian National University, Canberra.

White, O. 1972, *Parliament of a Thousand Tribes*, Wren, Melbourne.

Whitlam, E. G. 1985, *The Whitlam Government 1972–1975*, Viking, Victoria.

Wilder, P. 1998, 'A Pluralist Parliament for a Pluralist People? The New Northern Ireland Assembly Elections, 25 June 1998', *Representation*, 35:97–105.

Wilson, A. J. 1980, *The Gaullist System in Asia: the Constitution of Sri Lanka 1978*, Macmillan, London.

Winnett, B. and May, R. J. 1983, 'Yangoru-Saussia Open: the Disappearance of an 83 Per Cent Majority', in D. Hegarty (ed.), *Electoral Politics in Papua New Guinea: Studies in the 1977 National Elections*, University of Papua New Guinea Press, Port Moresby.

Withey, L. 1987, *Voyages of Discovery: Captain Cook and the Exploration of the Pacific*, University of California Press, Berkeley and Los Angeles, CA.

Wolfers, E. P. 1966, 'The Elections' (book review), *New Guinea*, 1(6):77–80.
     1968a, 'The Elections – The Mixture as Before?', *New Guinea*, 2(4):67–70.
     1968b, 'The Elections – II', *New Guinea*, 3(4):8–31.

Wright, J. F. H. 1980, *Mirror of the Nation's Mind*, Hale and Iremonger, Sydney.

Young, C. 1976, *The Politics of Cultural Pluralism*, University of Wisconsin Press, Madison, WI.

Newspapers

The Economist, various issues.
The Guardian, various issues.
The National (PNG), various issues.
The Sydney Morning Herald, various issues.
The Washington Post, various issues.

Index